KU-502-044

CLARICE CLIFF

LYNN KNIGHT

BLOOMSBURY PUBLISHING

LONDON · OXFORD · NEW YORK · NEW DELHI · SYDNEY

BLOOMSBURY PUBLISHING
Bloomsbury Publishing Plc
50 Bedford Square, London, WC1B 3DP, UK
29 Earlsfort Terrace, Dublin 2, Ireland

BLOOMSBURY, BLOOMSBURY PUBLISHING and the Diana logo
are trademarks of Bloomsbury Publishing Plc

First published in Great Britain 2005
This edition published 2022

Copyright © Lynn Knight, 2005

Clarice Cliff © Bizarre © and Fantasque © are registered trademarks of Josiah
Wedgwood & Sons Ltd, Barlaston, Stoke-on-Trent. All images in this book are
reproduced with permission.

Lynn Knight has asserted her right under the Copyright,
Designs and Patents Act, 1988, to be identified as Author of this work

All rights reserved. No part of this publication may be reproduced or
transmitted in any form or by any means, electronic or mechanical,
including photocopying, recording, or any information storage or retrieval
system, without prior permission in writing from the publishers

Bloomsbury Publishing Plc does not have any control over, or responsibility for,
any third-party websites referred to or in this book. All internet addresses given
in this book were correct at the time of going to press. The author and publisher
regret any inconvenience caused if addresses have changed or sites have
ceased to exist, but can accept no responsibility for any such changes

A catalogue record for this book is available from the British Library

ISBN: PB: 978-1-5266-5474-8; EBOOK: 978-1-4088-0686-9

2 4 6 8 10 9 7 5 3 1

Typeset by Palimpsest Book Production Ltd, Polmont, Stirlingshire
Printed and bound in Great Britain by CPI Group (UK) Ltd, Croydon CR0 4YY

MIX
Paper from
responsible sources
FSC® C171272

To find out more about our authors and books visit
www.bloomsbury.com and sign up for our newsletters

In memory of A. Thompson and E. Nash

CONTENTS

'A Designer of Note: Miss Clarice Cliff, a distinguished figure in the Potteries, considers some of her work of modern decor and finds it (as others do) good.'

The Brilliant Young Girl Artist

'Come to Lawley's and Meet Miss Clarice Cliff,' the *Daily Mail* announced in June 1930. 'To enable our many friends to see this female pottery artist,' the advertisement continued, 'we have arranged a special Pottery Painting Demonstration.'[1]

A grainy black and white photograph shows Clarice Cliff examining the pattern on an 'Inspiration' vase. She is dressed in a white technician's coat, with a dark skull cap pulled low on to her forehead. This was the 'brilliant young girl artist'[2] who had come to the attention of the press two years earlier with a design of table-ware whose patterns and colouring were as startling as their name. Each piece of 'Bizarre' was stamped with Clarice Cliff's signature and found immediate favour with women who responded to the modern spirit of her work. Clarice Cliff's work was different, at a time when women hoped their lives would be different too. Early sales of 'Bizarre' coincided with the achievement of universal female suffrage; Clarice Cliff spoke to the possibilities of that moment. 'Colour combined with novel decorative designs made an instant appeal to the middle-class housewife,' the *Daily Sketch* reported;[3] *Woman's Life* was all the more insistent: 'Women simply clamoured for this new pottery.'[4]

Now, the London branch of Lawley's department store in Regent Street was opening its doors to a demonstration of the tableware responsible for Clarice Cliff's success. From Monday to Saturday,

ten-thirty am to five-thirty pm, members of the public watched
Clarice Cliff and her young paintresses demonstrate the various
stages of hand-decoration: saw enamel wisps of smoke rise from
cottage chimneys, watched everlasting flowers bloom in tangerine
and coral paint. Though not the first of Clarice Cliff's public demonstrations, the week at Lawley's was significant. By now, her name
was sufficiently well known that an invitation to meet her drew the
public, while the central location of the London store attracted the
national press. Noting that the event was 'visited by a number of
connoisseurs', the *Daily Telegraph* observed that 'its results certainly
go far in . . . enlivening the aspect of the modern table,'[5] but it was
the *Daily Mirror*'s more emotional response which captured a major
element of Clarice Cliff's press appeal when she was introduced as
'one of the romances of the pottery trade'.[6] Here was a woman who
'only a few years ago' had been 'a humble little gilder in a china
factory'.[7] Now she was a newsworthy designer. 'No movie star can
tell a more romantic story of "How I Was Discovered".'[8]

Clarice Cliff's beginnings were shared by thousands of girls and
women of the early 1900s. She was just another factory girl, with
a rolled-up pinny in her coat pocket and nothing much expected of
her future, but the development of her narrative runs counter to
theirs, confounding and disputing expectations. Within the strong-
hold of traditionalism and class that was the Staffordshire Potteries,
her success was without precedent. Although other women emerged
as designers during this period – most notably Susie Cooper[9] – it
was a working-class woman whose story captivated the press.

Clarice Cliff's work struck the latest note during a period in which
domestic design was becoming a matter of fashion, as well as a
significant force in debates about the role of the industrial designer.
The vibrancy of her patterns and audacity of her shapes enabled
her to capture and project modernity; commercial courage allowed
her to influence and interpret new trends. The 'exceptional versatility' for which Clarice Cliff was praised led to her becoming an
enormously prolific designer: some 270-plus 'Bizarre' patterns alone
and hundreds of shapes are attributed to her name.[10] The Newport
Pottery was recalled as producing 18,000 pieces of 'Bizarre' a week

at the height of her success, with a weekly turnover of £2,000 – almost double that of the average pottery.[11] Approximately 8.5 million pieces overall were sold.[12] Today, Clarice Cliff's work regularly commands thousands of pounds at auction. Even those with no especial knowledge of, or interest in, design can recognise a piece of 'Clarice Cliff'; for many she epitomises Art Deco. (For some, she represents everything dislikeable about the style.)

Although Clarice Cliff's professional life was widely documented, she did not leave behind – and, most likely, did not write – the letters and journals that generally furnish the private lives of public individuals. Factory hours afforded little time for leisure, and working-class young women were, in any case, not encouraged to write about themselves: their lives were hardly thought worthy of record. Clarice Cliff's silence is doubly insistent: by the time she had stories of her own, she had reason to withhold them. By the late 1920s, she was familiar with the snatched meetings and discreet hotels that characterise a relationship with a married lover.

Clarice Cliff's story belongs not to London or Paris – although both cities figure within it – but to industrial Stoke-on-Trent, a harsh creative backdrop, with far less scope for the unconventional. An environment of strong local flavours, it stamps its power upon the personalities it creates. Though the writer Vera Brittain knew Staffordshire only as a very young girl, she described herself as 'Staffordshire to the core'.[13] Clarice Cliff spent her life in the Potteries. Its social and cultural history is stitched into the fabric of her existence.

Although she worked within a community, Clarice Cliff was neither part of the establishment nor an adherent of provincial codes, yet despite her apparent bravado, she was an intensely private woman. Hers was a life of contradictions in a period rife with contradictions of its own. The inter-war years ushered in the modern: the advent of the wireless and talking films revolutionised communication and changed the cultural fabric; mass production and labour-saving devices overhauled domestic and industrial life. Art, literature and design thrilled with the new, old forms were overthrown and risks embraced, but this was only part of the picture. Those years were also characterised by economic uncertainty, the Depression and social flux – by retrenchment as well as possibility. For most women of the period, the 1920s and '30s were years of restricted employment opportunities and rigid social and sexual mores. The penalties for those who transgressed were great; in small provincial towns, like those comprising the Potteries, the risks were even greater.

Good design does not draw attention to itself, and nor should women, so say tenets of the period (and thereafter). Yet Clarice Cliff's exclamatory designs could take away the breath. Though her vocabulary was domestic tableware, she was nevertheless a radical, a modernist in spirit, if not in the capitalised letters of design terminology. Like many modernists, she was an outsider, reconfiguring the landscape, extending and reshaping the boundaries of professional life for women. There were too few women like her for Clarice Cliff to fit comfortably within her milieu. Most women leave to break the rules; Clarice Cliff stayed and broke them. Who was the woman in the black skull cap, to whom 'romance' so readily attached itself? Who was the 'brilliant young girl artist', Clarice Cliff?

ONE

Family, Childhood, Smoke and Flame

Clarice Cliff – the name has a certain ring to it and seems almost designed as a style label. The pairing of Clarice with Cliff suggests possibilities not envisaged for her older sisters, Sarah Ellen and Hannah. Their first names were family names, biblical and serviceable; their younger brother, Harry, was named for his father. With family obligations paid, their mother, Ann – for surely it was she? – was free to indulge herself with 'Clarice'. Although the name was much more common then than now, perhaps Ann Cliff was expressing some undefined hope for her newborn daughter. It was said within the family that Clarice was always regarded as 'the special one'.[1]

Indulgences were few for Clarice Cliff's mother, Ann, especially during the first years of her marriage, when she and her husband, Harry, seemed to be constantly on the move within the Staffordshire pottery town of Tunstall. Their married life began in Tunstall High Street, part of the extensive road which, in its different guises, fastens all the pottery towns together. When the Cliffs lived there in 1892, tram lines ran along its length and industrial traffic was constant; the sound of cart wheels and hawkers' cries provided the backdrop to their daily life. These were hardly ideal circumstances for a young couple with a baby, but 116 High Street was where their first child, Sarah, was born, possibly in rooms above a shop. At number 118, a Mr William Walley ran the Wheatsheaf public house; some doors

further down stood the Swan Inn. With beer plentiful and cheap –
a mere threepence a pint – and public houses open from six in the
morning until eleven pm, Ann and Harry Cliff must have faced
continual disturbances.

The young couple did not stay long. Within two years, they found
a terraced house in Madeley Street, a short walk further north, with
space for a growing family. Their daughter Hannah was born there
in 1894 and their first son, Harry, three years later. Although barely
any distance from their initial married home, it was nevertheless at
one remove from the cacophony of the High Street, and safer for
the children too, who could sit on the front step or venture into the
road without immediate fears for their wellbeing. There was little
time to put down roots, however. At some point during the next
two years, with three small children in tow, Ann and Harry crossed
the High Street yet again, to another terraced house, this time in
Meir Street. Although the date of their removal is not known, they
were living there on 20 January 1899, when their third daughter,
Clarice was born.

Like many workman's cottages in the area, the Meir Street house
is small – a two-up, two-down, plus back kitchen – and appears to
be no larger than the one the Cliffs vacated, but it was practically
next door to Fuller's iron foundry where Harry worked and was
probably rented from his employer. There were other advantages
too, if living near a foundry can be considered an advantage.[2] Meir
Street's red-brick terrace was built later than the one in Madeley
Street, and looks to be of sounder construction; the network of
streets of which the terrace forms a part is also wider. Today, Meir
Street is the more airy of the two, although in the years before the
Clean Air Act, with a foundry on the doorstep, any thoughts of
airiness belonged to the future.

With girls aged six and four, a boy of two and a new baby, Ann
Cliff certainly had her hands full, but she had learned mothering at
a very early age as a child of Ralph and Mary Machin, née Cope.
Mary had married at nineteen and by the age of thirty-five had nine
children. The oldest, her namesake, was aged sixteen; the youngest,
named for her husband, Ralph, was not yet one year old. At times,
she must have felt her maiden name was all too prescient. Her third

child and third daughter, Ann, was born in 1868 and, by the time she was thirteen, had six brothers and sisters younger than herself to look out for. Small wonder if Ann hoped for something better for her own children. Small wonder if she hoped for something better for herself, but expectations were few when Ann Machin was a girl and the pattern of her life was not unusual.

Ann's father, Ralph, was a child of the 1840s and must have known privation as a boy. In *When I Was a Child*, Charles Shaw's account of growing up in the Potteries during that decade, he recalled the dreadful winter of 1842 and the extreme hardship it caused throughout the country: 'Semi-starvation was the normal condition of thousands, pinched faces and shivering bodies were seen everywhere ... carts were followed for miles for any coal they might lose on their journeys ... Shord rucks* were searched by shivering women and children for cinders, as hens scratch and search for food ... Those were the good old days when the Corn Laws made rent high and living low, and made semi-famine the ordinary condition of the country for the toiling masses.'³ Those were the good old days in which Clarice Cliff's maternal grandparents were born.

Ralph Machin was the son of a collier, Samuel; his older brother, Charles, was also employed as a miner. Their mother, Hannah, and three sisters, Lydia, Thirza and Martha, completed the Machin family⁴ – a small family, by standards of the time, although other children may have been born, but not survived: rates of infant mortality were always high within the region. Ralph was already working by the age of ten, although there was nothing unusual in that in the days before compulsory education. He and his sister, Lydia, aged thirteen, were employed in the pottery industry. Perhaps brother and sister worked side by side at the Greenfield Pottery which was responsible for much of the development of Pitts Hill, Chell, the village to the immediate north-east of Tunstall where the family lived. The industrial expansion of the region was such that, between 1831 and 1851, Chell's population almost doubled.⁵ Even so, the village remained a 'pleasant and healthy place' when Ralph Machin was a boy, 'with green fields stretching far away'.⁶ One

* See Glossary.

building 'cast a blighting shadow',[7] however: the workhouse, known locally as the 'Bastille', threatened all who lived within its presence.

By the age of twenty-two, Ralph Machin had moved to Tunstall, where he married and settled in Amicable Street, which is the address recorded on the birth certificate of Clarice Cliff's mother, Ann. Like her father before her, Ann worked in the pottery industry and was employed as a potter's assistant by the age of thirteen; at twenty-four she married Harry Cliff. No occupation is given on her marriage certificate, although she was unlikely to have been without work. When Ann was eighteen her father died, making her own wage all the more crucial with so many mouths to feed. Perhaps she took in washing, as she was to do when her own children were young, although the taking in of washing was generally a married woman's trade. More likely, Ann's occupation was simply omitted from the certificate.

Not so for her future husband, Harry Cliff, who, by the time they married, was an ironmoulder, a trade to which he was probably apprenticed on leaving school. The wrought-iron gates that mark the entrance to Tunstall Park, together with the elaborate sign that swings outside Tunstall's Queen Victoria Jubilee Buildings, are testaments to the skills of Clarice Cliff's father and his fellow workers. As a moulder, his was a workshop job, one of the more skilled tasks in the foundry, and one of which he was evidently proud: it was Harry Cliff who told his children the wrought-iron work was his.

As the second of seven children born to Isaac James Cliff and Sarah Cliff (née Gater), Harry must have been grateful for the security of a trade. His father turned his hand to numerous jobs, starting out, at the age of twelve, as an errand boy. By 1869, when Harry Thomas was born, Isaac had become a colliery labourer. Some years later, he left the pit and started selling beer – a popular occupation in nineteenth-century Tunstall – and, later still, was established as an ironmonger, and a tinplate worker after that. The family lived in Sneyd Street, Harry's place of birth, where they occupied several addresses over the years. With his father's various jobs and the family's different homes, Harry's was an uncertain childhood, although perhaps no more uncertain than many at that time.

To add to the uncertainties of Harry Cliff's young life, his mother died when he was fourteen. Childbirth may have weakened Sarah

Cliff, who was only forty-one. She died from bronchitis, having lingered eleven days, a terrible end for her and her young family. Four of Harry's siblings were below the age of ten and his oldest sister, Minnie, only eleven. Although a servant, Sarah Sargeant, took on the role of housekeeper, Minnie would have had to grow up fast. Harry's own responsibilities were also on the increase at this time, as a lad setting out as an apprentice.

Harry Cliff was twenty-two when he and Ann Machin married; when they started courting is not known. Perhaps they met at St Mary the Virgin, where they later exchanged vows, and welcomed the chance to dawdle on the way home from Sunday service; they may have taken a shine to one another while walking out with mutual friends in the nearby fields that were a popular spot for 'Sunday wanderings' and the later scene of their courtship walks. Before a mass of industrial works 'choked . . . and disfigured' the valley, spring flowers were 'abundant'[8] and the meadows rich with saxifrage, fairy flax and eyebright. They could have met at any time: their homes were not too far apart but, then, no Tunstall street is any great distance from another.

Tunstall is the northernmost pottery town, 'the extremity of civilisation in those parts',[9] Arnold Bennett thought, when describing Tunstall of the late nineteenth century ('Turnhill'), in the novel *Hilda Lessways*, one of his many fictional portraits which have contributed to the area's renown. Although Bennett wrote of 'Five Towns', there are actually six, which nowadays form the city of Stoke-on-Trent. Tunstall, Burslem, Hanley, Stoke, Fenton and Longton comprise a straggling line, some eight miles in length, along the belt of coal and clay that gave rise to the industry for which the Potteries are named. No other area of Britain acquired the name of the industry responsible for its success. 'The Five Towns . . . are unique . . . you cannot drink tea out of a tea cup without the aid of the Five Towns . . . you cannot eat a meal in decency without the aid of the Five Towns.'[10]

Much of the towns' development stemmed from the Industrial Revolution, which saw the rapid expansion of the pottery trade. With the construction of new roads and the building of the Trent and Mersey Canal, begun in 1766 and opened eleven years later, the region was transformed. The first parliamentary census in 1801 recorded a district population of 24,000; by 1841, this figure had almost trebled.[11] Unlike the Lancashire textile industry, whose vast mills dwarfed its towns, the pottery industry gave rise to myriad small workshops which expanded over time. The towns and their satellite villages evolved alongside, creating an unusual degree of intimacy between the domestic and the industrial. In one street after another, smoke from family hearths and factory kilns entwined, thickening the bonds between them.

With success came the smoke for which the Potteries are famous and famously abused. One of their most vociferous complainants was Bernard Shaw who, on visiting Hanley in 1911 to lecture on socialism, was appalled by what he found there. Typically, Shaw did not mince his words: 'I have only been in the Potteries for a day – Hanley is a fearfully ugly place . . . How do you stand it? I suspect that the people of the Potteries are mad . . . I wanted to get into fresh air, but the more I went up the hill (to Hartshill) the worse the air got . . . I never used to believe what [Arnold Bennett] told me . . . I now understand why he lives most of his time in Paris.'[12]

The smoke that was so derided by outsiders was a symbol of prosperity within. 'Smoke . . . spells business,'[13] proclaimed the *Pottery Gazette and Glass Trade Review*, before the Clean Air Act put paid to such industrial disgorgings. When the kilns were firing, all was well. A population grew up fiercely protective of the industry that sustained it, loyal even to the smoke that soured its streets. 'This place soots me nicely,'[14] one picture-postcard read, in a succinct demonstration of local humour.

Self-reliance – and defiance, to a degree – was (and remains) an integral part of the Potteries' temperament. Writing in *Time and Tide* in 1939, as part of a series, 'Spotlight on the Provinces', Colonel Josiah Wedgwood of the pottery dynasty of that name, and MP for Newcastle-under-Lyme, concluded: 'There is no doubt that North Staffordshire is one provincial unit – even very provincial, with its own code, its own language, its own newspapers, and its own local pride . . . we know the rest of the world as aliens, towards whom we have a just and kindly toleration.'[15] This strong sense of identity

Stoke-on-Trent. "Always Merry and Bright."

was compounded by the geography of the region. Though Birmingham and Manchester are easily accessible, the pottery towns lie within the protection of a valley; moorland to the north and east defined their isolation. When the main railway was built, it went around the towns, not through them. There was relatively little interference from without. Despite the growth of an industry with a worldwide reputation, the pottery towns retained their 'moorland stoicism and more than their fair share of parochialism'.[16]

If the region thrived within its own frame of reference and the rest of the world be damned, the pottery towns themselves were fiercely individual. Each town had and held fast to its own identity.[17] Burslem was the first town to develop, emerging from a seventeenth-century community of potter-farmers who produced butter pots from local clay, fired with local coal, into a more substantial town during the late eighteenth century. As the 'mother town' of the Potteries, Burslem always held its head high. Tunstall's reputation as a pottery town devolved from the manufacture of earthenware, the Adams dynasty, Alfred Meakin, Booths and Enoch Wedgwood being among the potteries established there. Hanley owed its development to the sister industry of the Potteries, coal mining; Stoke-upon-Trent (the town, as distinguished from Stoke-on-Trent, the city) gained early status by virtue of its church

and went on to become an administrative centre, advantaged by
its valley setting and, later, the main railway station. Fenton, the
smallest of the towns, was the one Arnold Bennett overlooked,
while Longton, once known locally as 'Neck End' (and said to be
the roughest of all), was a major producer of bone china during
the nineteenth century and held the dubious distinction of being
the town with the greatest number of bottle ovens. On a good day
in Longton – so local legend had it – you could see beyond your
outstretched hand. Though the towns were pulled together for
administrative purposes to form the federated borough of Stoke-
on-Trent in 1910, and the title of 'city' was conferred upon the
county borough by George V in 1925, their individuality persisted.
They remained 'six towns in search of a city'.[18]

A visitor to Tunstall around the time of Clarice Cliff's birth would
have seen grey streets, grey sky, smoke-blackened buildings; shades
of black and grey relieved by random bursts of white: young girls
in their white pinafores, whose presence vivifies contemporary
photographs. A relatively late developer among the pottery towns,
Tunstall was regarded as 'the pleasantest village in the Potteries' in
1795.[19] The laying out of the market square in 1816 marked the
beginning of its expansion, and by the mid-nineteenth century the
majority of Tunstall's streets were in place. During the early years
of the town's development its population rose rapidly, increasing
almost ninefold between 1811 and 1851.[20] In 1901, two years after
Clarice Cliff was born, the population of the urban district of
Tunstall (following some boundary changes) had reached 19,492.
   The heart of this small town was, and still remains, its market
square (now Tower Square). Standing there today, little seems to
have changed. A great deal has changed, of course, including several
street names, but many buildings survive as reminders of the town
Clarice Cliff knew. Not just the majestic public buildings, such as
the old town hall (Tunstall's second), with its Renaissance-style
façade of brick and rusticated stone, and exhortation to 'Peace
Happiness Truth Justice' scrolled across its upper storey, but
reminders of domestic life as well: numerous terraced houses,
including some of those on Paradise and Piccadilly Streets at Tower

Square's west end, and the Wolstanton School Board building at the head of Forster Street, whose windows are a reminder of the fearsome gothic architecture of late nineteenth-century schooling, or the dark, narrow entry through to the back of 116 High Street, which is surely as grim now as when the newly married Ann Cliff carried her first child along its passageway.

Ann Machin was already pregnant when she married Harry Cliff, although pregnancy may have been the occasion rather than the reason for their marriage.[21] By the time they married, they had both known years of hard work and responsibility and may have longed to establish a life of their own. They had only four months of married life before the birth of their first child, and then a second, third and fourth child, and three homes in swift succession. In all, there would be seven children: Sarah Ellen, sometimes known as Nellie (born 1892), Hannah (1894), Harry (1897), Clarice (1899), Dorothy, or Dolly (1901), Frank (1903) and Ethel (1906).

Some time after Ethel's birth, the family moved to Edwards Street,[22] where they remained. At least their removal involved minimal fuss: Edwards Street (now Fuller Street) is literally around the corner from Meir Street. Clarice Cliff may even have carried her own belongings down the road. 1 Edwards Street is an end-of-terrace house, with a small yard to the rear which backs on to an alley that intersects a further row of houses and back yards. With three, perhaps four bedrooms, the house was an improvement on Meir Street and Clarice's father barely had to stretch his legs to reach the foundry.

Recollections of the Cliff family home belong to the Edwards Street house which, aside from the conversion of a bedroom into a bathroom during the 1930s, seems to have remained the same for many years. A house like many others of the period, with kitchen, living-room and parlour, its décor paid no heed to changing fashions. Remembering her visits to Edwards Street as a young child, Hannah's daughter recalls 'an old-fashioned, sturdy house',[23] with a large table in the living-room, where the family congregated and, standing proud against the wall, a dresser piled with crocks which – even at the height of Clarice Cliff's success – were cream with a slim green border. Ann Cliff's tastes remained traditional. A black-

Harry Thomas Cliff, 1928

leaded range and a mangle met you as you opened the back door
– the only door in use, the front door being 'for best' (and funerals).
A wooden clothes rail hung suspended from the ceiling, while a
large pendulum clock, its face yellowing with the years, counted out
the Cliff family history. 'It was like a time capsule,' Sarah's grand-
daughter recalled, picturing the house years later. 'It was like walking
back in time.'[24]

With three rooms downstairs, plus a cellar, the family was now
better off for space. Outside, however, there was still only a small
yard, with room for a narrow flower bed and a flush lavatory, and
despite the extra room upstairs, bedrooms – and beds, most likely –
were still shared. Five girls and two boys. Perhaps they marked their
heights on a door to see how far they had grown, as Clarice later
measured a young employee. If so, their kitchen door would have
been scarred like a ruler, a monument to seven different childhoods.

Clarice Cliff's older sisters, Sarah and Hannah, were unlikely to
have been willing playmates for her when she was a child. They
were far too old: girls of thirteen and eleven, when she was only
seven. Sarah would be starting work, and Hannah setting her sights
on doing the same. Clarice's nearest sister in age was Dorothy, but

Dorothy was younger by two and a half years, which, although an acceptable gap on some occasions – someone to be pupil to her teacher – would not have suited Clarice every day. Frank and Ethel were younger still: a toddler and a baby. Her brother Harry was nearest in age and would have been Clarice's ally, surely, if she had one as a small child. In years to come, when Harry had a daughter, she was christened Clarice, perhaps as a mark of their early closeness as much as a recognition of his sister's later success.

On fine days, brother and sister could walk to the nearby Greengates Works, Tunstall's oldest pottery, to search for buried treasure, and there discover sapphires, emeralds and sharp-edged slivers of gold: remnants of the broken plates and breakfast cups that formed the rubble of the shord ruck. There would be other games to play, games that stretched whole streets without any fear of traffic: skipping ropes to swing, hopscotch markings scratched on pavements, lions stalked through rough ground with long sticks. Cousins came to call: Sidney Machin, who later became head modeller at the pottery firm Midwinter, visited Clarice and her family as a child.[25] And if they did not live too far away, the cousins could play in and out of one another's houses. In summer they could stay outside until theirs were the only voices cutting through the evening, and watch the setting sun, 'a huge empyreal reflection of the furnaces, like an angry ball of flame descending upon a smouldering world'.[26]

Ann Cliff c.1932

Descriptions of Clarice Cliff's mother belong to the Edwards Street years. A Victorian by temperament as well as birth, Ann Cliff is recalled as being old-fashioned. In a long dark dress concealed beneath a long white apron, with her hair scraped into a bun, she was a woman who would not stand any nonsense and was described by her children as somewhat strict. With a large family round her skirts, who would blame her? For almost the first fifteen years of her married life, Ann Cliff was either pregnant or nursing a child, and was no doubt exhausted much of the time. Though taking in washing was an easier occupation to fit around small children than factory hours, she must have found it difficult to manage, with a house 'messed up wi' babies and wet clothes'.[27] These were the days when the family wash was hard enough:

> Wash day was a whole day's work. First of all you sorted out your whites from your coloureds and put them all in to soak. Then you gave everything a good scrub with a brush on a washboard, especially the collars and cuffs. Then you boiled up the whites in the copper, poking them down all the time with a wooden stick and plenty of soap – pieces cut off a big block. After that you rinsed and blued them – you put a 'bluebag' into the water to bring the whites up white. Then the coloureds had to be done, everything rinsed and put through the mangle . . . Then you had to clean out the copper and scrub it ready for next time.[28]

Such practical difficulties were compounded by the clothes themselves: layers of woollen underclothes and outer garments which were heavy and held water when wet, plus all the whites that needed starching. There were no man-made fibres to ease the housewife's load. And what of napkins for the baby, and, later, sanitary wear for the girls? Everything had to be hung out to dry on as many lines as could criss-cross the yard, or else hoisted skywards on the rail, and left to chill the kitchen on damp mornings. This rigmarole accounted for the family wash, never mind the washing for which Ann Cliff was paid – eighteenpence for the weekly wash of two adults and two children was the going rate in the early 1900s – and which would be returned to her customers 'rough dry'.[29] Then came the family ironing, with the small, heavy flat irons that were heated on the range. Clarice's mother must have prayed the clothes were not too dry by the time she brought them in, especially the girls' white pinafores, essential wear for school, whose pin-tucks were the very devil to iron.

Clean washing on a line was as much a measure of a working-class housewife's respectability as the front step whitened weekly with donkey-stone and the door knob polished to a shine, jobs made all the harder when soot from the local potbanks* and the foundry settled on pegged shirts as readily as it soiled front steps and crept through windows. Though every day was wash-day as far as Ann Cliff was concerned, there were other jobs to tackle: saucepans to be scoured and put back on the range, which had to be black-leaded, and carpets to be beaten or brushed outside. Dust was every woman's nightmare. 'You couldn't get rid of the dust – you just moved it from one place to the next – as you swept it off the floor you watched it settling on the mantelpiece.'[30] Jobs allocated to particular days imposed order on tasks that otherwise seemed insurmountable, given the volume of dirt to be overcome, and, with each day's chores complete, there was still the mending to be tackled. Clarice would often have watched her worn-out mother sink into a chair, only to see her peer into the gaslight and take up her darning needle, with fingers raw with soda and carbolic. Girls discover life's possibilities through their mothers. These were some of the lessons Clarice was absorbing as a child.

With three younger siblings by the time she was seven, and a mother with much to occupy her time, Clarice learned to look out for herself. Being the middle child of a large family had distinct advantages. Neither the oldest, bearing the heaviest responsibilities, nor the youngest, to be watched, it was relatively easy for her to slip away. Perhaps she soon discovered how to amuse herself, and how to make herself invisible, if need be. In later years, she liked to read. The art of fading into the background with a book was probably acquired early; one tucked beside the newspapers in the privy, another slipped on to a chair beneath the living-room table, ready to be retrieved at the right moment.

Nevertheless, Clarice could not avoid all household chores. Responsibility came early to working-class children, especially girls. Minding the younger ones would be high on the list for Sarah and

Hannah, along with turning the mangle, a heavy job passed down the line as their younger sisters gained in strength. Their mother would have done the same as a girl herself, and may have been kept from school to help with the weekly wash if, like many nineteenth-century parents, her own mother felt that the best education for a young girl was that acquired at home (Clarice Cliff's maternal grandmother could not write, and would have had little opportunity for learning). There would be further household tasks, divided along gender lines, and probably more numerous for the Cliff girls. Oral testimony suggests mothers could be harder on their daughters than their sons, mindful of what lay ahead of them.[31]

There would be errands to run, of course, which also meant shop windows to explore. The usual establishments on Tunstall's High Street: a butcher, draper, tailor, hatter and confectioner, among others, not forgetting Naylor's Bon Marché, with its display of bombazine coats and frocks in chiffon-finished velveteen, or the pawnbroker further down, his weekday windows crammed with Sunday suits and their white tickets. Saturdays and Mondays were market days in Tunstall. Pausing to shift the weight of heavy shopping bags from one hand to another, Clarice would often have stood in Market Square and considered the inscription on the clock tower, erected by public subscription in 1893, in honour of Sir Smith Child, Bart, Philanthropist, who 'by generous gifts and wise counsel sought to brighten the lives of the WORKING CLASSES'.

Religion played its part in the Cliff household, where dates of birth were recorded in the family bible and regular church attendance was a must. Christ Church, Tunstall's parish church, was their place of worship. An austere-looking building, which has lost its spire in the intervening years, it stands on the corner of Furlong Street, with a vantage point of the High Street, a landmark and a reproach for members of its flock tempted to stray. One incumbent celebrated a Sung Mass, his need to assert a High Anglican creed perhaps sharpened by the fact that Christ Church towered above chapel rooftops.

As Anglicans, the Cliffs were in a minority. Protestant Nonconformity, Methodism, in particular, shaped the pottery towns,

High Street, Tunstall c.1910

dating back to 1760 when John Wesley visited Burslem for the first time. Over the next twenty-odd years, Wesley and his associates preached regularly throughout the towns, his message appealing to a community under industrialisation's thumb; the first Wesleyan chapel in Tunstall, described by Wesley as 'the most elegant I have seen since I left Bath',[34] was completed in 1788. The spirit of revivalism kept pace with the expanding population, and chapels were established throughout the district. By 1851, the Potteries housed some sixty-four Nonconformist meeting places; by contrast, Anglican churches numbered only seventeen.

Tunstall has its own place within the history of Methodism. At the turn of the eighteenth century, following schisms within the movement, two new sects emerged. Tunstall and the isolated moorland to the north and east became the seat of Primitive Methodism, whose evangelical tendencies Arnold Bennett outlined: 'Go northwards out of [Tunstall's] Market Square, and you would soon find yourself amid the wild and hilly moorlands, sprinkled with iron-and-coal villages whose red-flaming furnaces illustrated the eternal damnation which was the chief article of their devout religious belief.'[35] The Mount Tabor Chapel, built in 1824 by the opposing sect, the Methodist New Connexion, stood behind Market Square, overlooking shoppers, standing as their conscience, just as Christ Church loomed above the High Street further up. Congregationalists, Unitarians, Baptists and Christian Brethren also established places of worship in the area; by the late nineteenth century, the Salvation Army had gained a foothold too. By 1900, one year after Clarice Cliff was born, Protestant Nonconformist meeting places within the Potteries exceeded 100. Methodism remained the dominant voice, its values dictating the moral tone of the district as surely as the pottery industry shaped its skyline.

Despite their minority status – or, perhaps, in part, because of it – the Cliffs' religious observance was staunch. For Clarice and her siblings this meant Sunday school as well as Sunday service, with a wagonette trip to Trentham Gardens – where the Duke of Sutherland opened his park gates once a year – as a reward for good attendance. Ann Cliff must have felt a strong sense of relief as well as a clear conscience when the children disappeared for afternoon instruction, enabling her to glance at the *Sunday Companion* or the next chapter of *East Lynne*, if she were a reader[36] (and if the pile of mending were under control). Hannah was confirmed at St Mary the Virgin, which suggests that Clarice and her younger siblings were confirmed at Christ Church in their turn. Community feeling ran high, with fêtes and bazaars the order of the day, in aid of the Christ Church Mission Fund or the new church organ. Church and Sunday school, Church Parade and Empire Day – Clarice in her Sunday best, saluting the Union Jack, her parents looking on, all smiles. Family, church and school: the three pillars of a working-class childhood.

TWO

How Pleased I Was to Miss Some Lessons

The pressures of large families and paid work encouraged working-class parents to send their children to school at the earliest opportunity. Although class registers for the period have not survived, a schoolfriend, Lilian Taylor, recalled meeting Clarice Cliff at elementary school at the age of three,[1] the earliest age at which pupils could be accepted.

The High Street School was a ten-minute walk from both Meir and Edwards Streets. Built in 1894, it was one of the 'monuments to government intervention, civic pride and high Victorian values',[2] built by the local School Boards following the 1870 Education Act which introduced compulsory schooling. The architecture of such 'monuments' tended towards the severe and the High Street School was no exception: an imposing brick façade and high windows overlooked an enclosed yard. With layers of factory grime coating its brickwork, the school must have looked particularly forbidding. It also faced particular difficulties.

Standing at the edge of Tunstall's main thoroughfare, the school had to contend with constant interruptions from heavy traffic. Year after year, His Majesty's Inspectors commented upon the problems they experienced because of the volume of street noise, which they describe as a 'serious disadvantage'[3] and 'a permanent hindrance to work'.[4] Their rebukes not only indict the conditions in which Clarice Cliff was taught, but are a reminder of the disruption her parents encountered as a young, married couple in their first home. Other problems experienced by the school were common to the time, such as the epidemics of measles and scarlet fever which closed the building for a fortnight during the autumn of 1904. In his reports on the district's elementary schools in 1909, the Medical Officer of Health recorded 'numerous instances of poor nutrition . . . indifferent clothing or poor footgear' and 'defective teeth'. A quarter of all the children he examined (a representative sample of the whole) were found to be below average height and weight.[5]

The role of public elementary schools was outlined in the Elementary School Code. 'Practically as well as intellectually', schools were required to fit their young charges for 'the work of life'.[6] Taught the 'habits of industry, self-control and courageous perseverance in the face of difficulties', children were to learn 'self-sacrifice and . . . a strong respect for duty'.[7] This ethos was to guide Clarice Cliff's schooling.

The High Street School contained eight partitioned classrooms, enabling the headmistress to oversee the whole school and its teachers, should she wish, but requiring each teacher to compete with the sound of adjacent classes as well as noises from the street. In 1902, the school employed six teachers – all women; within a few years their number had risen to nine. Large class sizes – sixty-three pupils in one instance – encouraged formal teaching, while the constant presence of the cane ensured that discipline prevailed. 'You were terrified,' one elementary schoolgirl recalled. 'No, not terrified, but the respect was there, you were held in awe. Everything they told us to do must be done.'[8] Each day began with inspection. Cleanliness was next to godliness and, for the elementary schoolchild, was something to be measured. Clean pinafores for girls, clean handkerchiefs and polished boots all round; these were inspected daily, the morning line-up in the yard a trial in which hands were held out flat and straight – palms up, then down – with a sharp retort from a ruler for anyone whose clothes and personal hygiene did not satisfy requirements.

The lessons that followed were determined by the Elementary Code and comprised the teaching of the English language – including writing, oral and written composition, and grammar – Arithmetic, Knowledge of the common phenomena of the external world, Geography, History,

Drawing, Singing, Physical Exercises and, for the girls, Plain Needlework. By the time Clarice Cliff completed her education, in addition to the knowledge of fractions, averages and percentages she amassed, she had graduated from reading a short passage from an elementary school book to the works of Milton or Shakespeare, or to reading from a history of England describing 'the great persons and events in English history' and 'the growth of the British Empire'.[9]

Just as Clarice must have learned to ignore the competing voices of two brothers and four sisters, reading in class offered a chance to disappear into another world and shut out the sound of heavy drays outside. This was an aspect of schooling Clarice Cliff enjoyed – she kept her copy of *Lamb's Tales*, which she later passed to a great-niece, advising her that Shakespeare would prove useful at grammar school.[10] Sunday school prizes – a copy of *The Wide, Wide World* or *The Daisy Chain*, perhaps – further nurtured reading, as did the public library, where her father's wrought-iron sign served as a constant demonstration of endeavour.

As the log book for Tunstall's High Street School makes plain, elementary schooling was regimented. Though younger pupils were allowed to write on slates, by Standard III only paper was permitted; pupils were expected to write in a style both 'upright' and 'rounded'[11] – a lesson Clarice Cliff took to heart, judging by her later handwriting – and individual writing exercises were to be transcribed without mistakes. The teaching of arithmetic was equally severe: 'Absolutely prohibit finger work,'[12] a teacher noted in her Scheme of Work for the youngest pupils. The note is underlined, either to remind the schoolmistress herself, or to impress His Majesty's Inspector. One inspector commented on the need for instruction to be less formal; others complimented the school on its 'signs of earnest work' and good order, and observed that 'the children are kindly treated and are happy',[13] a not insignificant achievement, given educational methods of the time.

During the late nineteenth and early twentieth centuries, the teaching of girls was the subject of intense debate, with concerns raised that they were leaving school without the domestic skills that would equip them to be good wives and mothers, an anxiety heightened by the undernourished condition of many of the soldiers who presented themselves for military service during the Boer War (and again in the First World War, and during the Second). Classes in laundry work and domestic hygiene joined the curriculum; needlework also formed part of the debate and acquired a '*symbolic* importance': 'Proficiency with a needle implied femininity [and] thrift.'[14] Sewing exercises were introduced – a High Street Scheme of Work lists thimble, hemming and knitting drills – which, in the case of thimble drill, required pupils to put on and remove thimbles repeatedly, in unison. How this benefited their needlecraft is unclear, although dextrous fingerwork and a willingness to perform repetitive tasks would prove useful to many girls in their future employment. The importance of needlework was such that it was subject to its own inspection and criticism: 'Improved work will be expected in this important subject,'[15] the teachers of the High Street School were warned. Contemporary primers emphasised this priority: 'Elder sisters, you may work,/Work and help your mothers,/Darn the stockings, mend the shirts,/Father's things, and brothers.'[16]

The teaching of drawing for girls was in its infancy when Clarice Cliff attended school. Prior to the publication of the 1904 Code, drawing was not part of their curriculum. While the High Street boys learned 'to form various patterns from the first and second stroke of the brush',[17] girls sewed strips of calico in blue cotton. By 1906, however, when Clarice was seven, the district art director was able to commend the 'good work in all classes' at the school.[18] With the pottery industry reliant upon decorating skills, art classes were subject to regular inspection by masters from the local art schools as well as district education officials. The art master of the Tunstall School of Art checked the High Street pupils' brushwork and free-arm drawing, while the art director of the Burslem School of Art, Stanley Thorogood, whose books *Free Brush Drawing Applied to Pattern in Seven Stages* and *Manipulation of the Brush as Applied to Design* were used in the local schools, asserted: 'Children should be taught to fill in spaces with colour, make lines of various thicknesses . . . and, generally speaking, learn to draw and sketch with the brush from the Infant School upwards in the same manner as they would with a pencil.'[19] Drawing classes laid the foundations of their industrial future.

Even as a schoolgirl, Clarice Cliff's artistic skills were evident –. 'She would pick up a pencil and do anything with it,' Lilian Taylor recalled[20] – but Clarice herself was not enamoured of the teaching she received: 'I remember when drawing classes in school were of only half an hour a week's duration,' she complained years later. 'How pleased I was to miss some lessons and to be entrusted to make large papier-mâché maps built up on nails of varying heights and coloured, for use in geography.'[21] One teacher, at least, seems to have discovered how to occupy a pupil whose energy and inventiveness were not satisfied by the curriculum. Despite the hope expressed in the Elementary Code that schools would develop their pupils' 'special gifts',[22] turn-of-the-century schools were rarely able to meet particular enthusiasms. In later years, Clarice Cliff set great store by education, perhaps because she felt her own was so inadequate.

Clarice Cliff attended a different school from her siblings because she was required to deliver a lunch box to a friend of her father's en route, an errand which underlines the frequency with which family responsibilities took precedence over learning. That her errand sometimes resulted in a caning for arriving late in class cannot have improved her liking for the institution. Although family members recalled Clarice attending the High Street School, another local elementary school, Summerbank, was mentioned on one occasion.[23] The Summerbank School opened in July 1909, and was built to replace Tunstall's King Street schools, not to take pupils from the High Street. Although it would not have been impossible for Clarice to transfer there at the age of ten, the move would have been unusual at such a late stage in her schooling. Whichever school or schools she attended is of less significance than the kind of instruction she received: hers was an elementary education, with a curriculum laid down by the Elementary Code. What matters most are the lessons she was taught, not just the reading, writing and arithmetic, but the lessons in conformity, in doing as she was told, and in understanding and accepting her place in the scheme of things – as a working-class girl, wife and mother. Clarice Cliff absorbed the three Rs; the rest she chose to disregard.

Twelve miles away, in Buxton, Vera Brittain, who was five years older than Clarice Cliff, was also frustrated by the education she

Sarah Cliff as a young child

received, albeit of a different calibre. As the daughter of a director of one of the paper mills which supplied the Potteries with printed transfer patterns, hers was a middle-class household that ran to three maids and a garden boy. Vera Brittain was taught by a governess until the age of eleven, when she transferred to 'a school for the daughters of gentlemen'[24] and at thirteen – the age at which Clarice Cliff completed her schooling – was sent to a Surrey boarding school; thereafter she began her struggle to enter Oxford University. Though Vera Brittain's education was far superior, it was nevertheless inferior to her own brother's. Raised to become 'an entirely ornamental young lady',[25] Vera Brittain received the lessons of her class, as Clarice Cliff was taught the very different lessons of her own.

Sarah Cliff

No portraits of Clarice Cliff as a very young girl have survived, although photographs of her eldest sister, Sarah, provide clues to those which surely existed at some point. In the first of these, a studio portrait, Sarah stands in front of a faded pastoral scene, with the look of a child instructed to keep still. She is wearing her best clothes, a white dress with a lace collar and long gloves; her fringe looks freshly cut, while her crinkled hair suggests she has spent the previous night with it bound tight in rags. Not used to being photographed, she looks uncomfortable. This may be the first occasion on which her picture has been taken. It is difficult to judge her age: she might be as young as six or as old as nine. Consider Clarice Cliff herself, some years later, experiencing a similar discomfort, gazing at the camera, with her mother's frown before her as a warning to stand still, and her own white gloves prickling her fingers.

In a later studio portrait, Sarah looks self-possessed, quite the calm young girl, in a suit of some stiff, dark stuff and a blouse with the conventional high neckline of the day. Her clothing is far less formal in another photograph, which captures Sarah standing in the Cliffs' back yard. She is looking at the photographer – her brother, Harry, most likely; it was he who took other family snaps. Perhaps Clarice is just out of sight, beyond the frame, sitting astride the wall, watching her older brother and sister.

Even in the larger house at Edwards Street, with nine in the family space must have been at a premium. This may have been one of the considerations that prompted Clarice's sister, Hannah, to find work away from home. At some point in her youth, Hannah Cliff entered domestic service, and must have done so with her mother's blessing. Fifteen was typically the age at which young girls became servants and, if Hannah followed this pattern, she took up her post around 1909. Until well into the twentieth century, domestic service was the chief employment for women, although it is perhaps surprising that Hannah entered service from the Potteries: most domestic servants came from rural communities where work was more difficult to find. Perhaps the prospect of five girls in the pottery industry seemed unwieldy, perhaps Hannah wanted to get away from home; the economic uncertainties of the early 1900s may have played a part in the decision. The position she obtained was in Scotland, a long journey for a girl leaving her family for the first time, and an especially long journey for one who had rarely ventured far from Tunstall.

Watching her sister pack her bag, ten-year-old Clarice must have considered her own future. Although Hannah was leaving home, she was not going to seek her fortune, but to rake out grates and carry coal up several flights of stairs; and her bag contained no finery, but pairs of lisle stockings and clean aprons. Domestic service was a hard life and, as house- or kitchen-maids, the majority of girls occupied its lowliest positions; few attained the elevated rank of lady's maid. Wherever Hannah worked, below-stairs life was onerous, its hours long, its free time circumscribed. If Clarice put herself in Hannah's shoes, she saw not the adventure of story-book imaginings, but the endless duties of a life at someone else's bidding. Anything Hannah told her sister of her time in service would have reflected two distinct Edwardian worlds and their own place within them, and given Clarice a further glimpse of the scant opportunities life offered young women of her class.

THREE

A Humble Little Gilder

Although the statutory school-leaving age was fourteen when Clarice Cliff was young, the Factory Acts provided exemptions enabling students who attained appropriate levels of literacy and numeracy or a sufficient number of attendances to leave school early. For children whose earnings were destined for the family purse and who rarely acquired a voice within their household until they earned a wage, the prospect of leaving school was appealing; it was all the more appealing for bright pupils: 'The bright child was the one who demonstrated his academic prowess by leaving as early as legally possible.'[1] Clarice Cliff left school at the age of thirteen, in 1912.

There was little choice as to the nature of her employment. 'I was born in Stoke-on-Trent,' she told an interviewer in 1931, 'and there, if one must earn one's living, there is little to do on leaving school except to work in a factory.'[2] Women have always worked in potbanks*, although the proportion of women employed has changed with time. During the nineteenth century, about half of the women of North Staffordshire were engaged in paid work and the pottery industry was their largest employer. Prior to the introduction of the Factory Acts, conditions in the industry were harsh: contemporary accounts describe brutalised child labour and intolerable hours. Women were thought to face particular burdens with regard to industrial life: 'It has invaded the sanctuary of the home and broken up family and social ties,' Samuel Smiles wrote in 1843. 'It has taken the wife from the husband, and the children from the parents. Especially has its tendency been to lower the character of woman. The performance of domestic duties is her proper office.'[3] Despite the concerns of commentators such as Smiles, the number of women employed in the industry continued to rise: in 1901, 24,477 women worked in potbanks; by 1911 – the year before Clarice Cliff started work – that figure had risen to 29,439, an increase of 20.3 per cent.[4]

Although women were engaged in every stage of pottery manufacture, the division of labour within the industry was generally along gender lines, with women's work attracting lower status and lower pay.[5] When Sylvia Pankhurst visited the Potteries in 1907 as part of her investigation into the industrial conditions in which women were employed, she observed that 'women turned the wheels for men throwers, and trod the lathe for men turners. In each case the woman was employed by the man for whom she toiled – she was the slave of a slave.'[6] She also noted the extent to which arrangements between employers and craft unions served to keep women from skilled employment. One exception was the female pottery decorator, or paintress, as she was known. Even within decorating departments, however, the most prestigious work was frequently reserved for men. At Royal Doulton, for example, until the Second World War, only men were thought capable of painting the faces of figurines.[7]

Pottery production involves two main processes – the forming of clay and its decoration. Work at the 'clay end' was dirty and often heavy. Here women fettled, towed and scoured newly formed tableware – the vocabulary itself an indication of the brute force of their labour. This was rough work and so considered unwomanly, despite the fact that women had always done it. The clay end was regarded as a male enclave and its female workers tainted by association with it; accounts of their bad language are rife.[8] Decorating, on the other hand, was a ladylike occupation, a view supported by the assumption that, by their very nature, women possessed the necessary skills. Practical considerations compounded this division. Workers at the clay end wore old clothes and old shoes (known as trashers); they were often drenched in slip (liquid clay) and the amount of dust in which they worked was appalling. Paintresses, by contrast, wore

The thrower and his attendant

pinafores over their ordinary clothes and, however dusty their workshop, the work itself was dainty (leaving aside the implications of working with lead paint). They wouldn't touch the clay end, they insisted, while women at the clay end said paintresses always thought themselves to be 'a cut above'.

A series of photographs taken at the Wedgwood factory in 1913 illustrates some aspects of women's employment and the attitudes accompanying them.[9] One photograph shows the 'thrower' at the potter's wheel: 'His attendant is generally a woman or girl (the baller), she weighs out the clay and knocks it into the right-sized "balls" and takes the made piece off the wheel.' Some pages further on, cup-making is demonstrated: 'The "Jolley" machine bring[s] the profile into the mould. Cups and small bowls and other "open" ware are made by women and girls. (The worker in this case is called a "Jolley woman", and nearly always is)' the writer notes. The caption accompanying the photograph of a freehand paintress asserts her status within the hierarchy of women's work with the briefest explanation: 'This gives opportunity to the cleverest girls.'

Woman at the 'jolley' machine

Mothers generally 'spoke for' their daughters, as Clarice Cliff's sister Ethel recalled: 'In those days we didn't get our own jobs – no – Mother went and asked if I could learn painting, as she called it. And that's how I came to work at William Adams, because it was quite near to the house.'[10] Their mother may have found work for Clarice, too, on the recommendation of a relative or neighbour; alternatively Clarice may have heard of a vacancy herself through a

schoolfriend. Sometimes schools were formally involved: 'With a view
to improve the class of people which Messrs Alfred Meakin Limited
have on their factories,' the headmaster of the Boys' Department of
Summerbank School wrote in his log on 15 October 1910, 'I have
received an invitation . . . to go round the Royal Albert factory . . .
I am also asked to send Messrs Meakin as many intelligent boys as
possible.'[11] Whoever was responsible for finding Clarice Cliff her first
job, convenience to home and availability of work were larger considerations than the choice of a particular factory, although the kind of
work on offer was undoubtedly a factor. Clarice's oldest sister, Sarah,
and – later – Hannah, were both employed as gilders. Having worked
as a potter's assistant herself, Ann Cliff had experience of the clay
end. She wanted her daughters to be decorators.

The hand-decoration of pottery involves a variety of techniques,
including gilding, enamelling and freehand painting, all of which
Clarice Cliff acquired during the formative years of her early employment. 'I went through all the decorating processes, both practical
and theoretical,' she explained.[12] The exact history of her early
employment is not known. Although in interviews she described the
breadth of skills she learned during her early years, she did not name
the factories where she was taught them. Details are based on information from her sister Ethel and the conflicting recollection of a
schoolfriend, Lilian Taylor. Ethel Cliff recalled that her sister started
work as an enameller at a local factory, Lingard Webster & Co.
Ltd, where she stayed for some three years before switching to lithography at Hollinshead & Kirkham, and then at A.J. Wilkinson.[13] In
interviews, however, Clarice Cliff herself spoke of starting as a gilder,
an account supported by Lilian Taylor, who worked alongside her
at W.H. Grindley, where Taylor's older sister was already employed;
she may have been responsible for finding the younger girls work.[14]
Lilian Taylor remembered working with Clarice Cliff until they
separated at the age of sixteen.

Ethel Cliff was only six years old when her sister started work
in 1912 and, looking back on events years later, may have forgotten
W.H. Grindley, especially if Clarice was there only for a short time.
Lilian Taylor spoke of Clarice Cliff on the occasion of her hundredth
birthday and could have forgotten how long they worked together.

Tunstall is such a small town their paths would have continued to cross, regardless of their places of employment (and Lilian Taylor lived on nearby Station Road, which Clarice would have walked almost daily). As the relevant factory records no longer exist, these details cannot be verified but it is likely that she spent some time at all three factories.

The issue of who employed her, and when, is less significant than the fact that she amassed a variety of skills within a short period and moved from one factory to another in order to do so. The range of her early knowledge and mobility suggests a degree of independence unusual for the time. Most pottery workers stayed put, if possible. Loyalty was prized and indeed anticipated of employees with apprenticeships to serve. Moreover, those who did change factories tended to move within the same field – Lilian Taylor, for example, worked for several manufacturers, but always as a gilder. Those who sought new skills had ambition.

With houses and potbanks cheek by jowl, and the flaring mouths of bottle ovens a familiar sight, the pottery industry was already known to Clarice Cliff when she started work. Tunstall boasted some fifteen potbanks within easy reach of the High Street, and sometimes during school holidays Clarice visited her sister Sarah at Johnson's Alexandra Pottery, down the road, and a Machin aunt who was in charge of the decorating shop at Alfred Meakin, higher up. Clarice Cliff's Machin grandfather had worked as a potter, as had her great-grandfather Cope; and her mother had surely told her children tales of her own experiences and those of her sister, Mary, who was also a potter's assistant as a girl.

Nevertheless, the world of work itself was new to Clarice and potbanks could be daunting environments. There was the tyranny of the kilns, which fired for up to seventy-two hours and could not be left unattended, and whose heat could knock a strong man off his feet; the hiss and slam of pistons from within the engine room; the din of the saggar makers,* with their scratched and bleeding hands, battering the hell out of the marl,* and the placers* gradually disappearing beneath quantities of dust. Dust smothered everything, insinuating itself into every nook and cranny of the potbank.

Buildings were often ramshackle and haphazard;[15] additions and extensions were piecemeal, with new workshops tacked on to old, and original buildings left to stand until they fell. In his *Enquiry into Industrial Art in England*, published in 1937, Nikolaus Pevsner remarked on the tendency of factories to keep the 'same blackened sheds and the same kilns . . . for more than a hundred years',[16] a fact he noted as indicating the strength of tradition within the industry. (Though perhaps it equally demonstrates parsimony and a curmudgeonly attitude to change.) The different industrial processes – engine room, slip house, dipping shop and kilns; decorating departments, offices and warehouses – were separate from one another, self-contained. The result was a warren of workshops, often built around a yard, which were reached by narrow passageways, outside staircases and numerous closed doors, all of which could be confusing for the newcomer. The transformation from Friday afternoon schoolgirl into Monday-morning factory worker involved a swift initiation into adulthood.

Like the majority of pottery workers, Clarice Cliff started work in her home town. W.H. Grindley was only a short walk from Edwards Street. Here Clarice began her apprenticeship as a gilder, learning how to decorate tableware with gold. 'I started . . . at the bottom of the ladder,' she recalled. 'When a girl takes up decorating, she has to sign on for an apprenticeship lasting seven years. Usually, she starts at the age of fourteen, earning five shillings and fourpence per week pocket money, and this goes on for six months. At the end of that time she proceeds to piecework. But her efforts are usually still very immature and she usually wastes a good deal of her employer's material. To make up for this she is paid only half the amount she earns in piece rates until she is sixteen. Then, for another five years, she forfeits fourpence in the shilling. At the age of twenty-one, when her apprenticeship comes to an end, she is considered a fully qualified worker and takes all she earns.'[17] This explanation presupposes an employee staying with the same employer throughout her training, which Clarice Cliff's own experience contradicts, but however formal the arrangement, and whatever length of apprenticeship was served, all trainee decorators were required to forfeit a portion of their wages.

As a gilder in a decorating shop, Clarice Cliff's days were directed by the 'missus' who oversaw its work; she also learned from the more accomplished women who shared her workshop bench. During lunchbreaks, she would be expected to run errands for them: 'learners' were required to do their 'kale'. Ethel Cliff again: 'We got a tin saucepan. We went round to the bottle ovens and hotted [*sic*] the water in one of the feeding mouths for the coal to heat the ovens ... and perhaps boil an egg for someone as well as make the tea. There wasn't a canteen or anything.'[18]

W.H. Grindley specialised in dinner and tea ware which was said to be of such quality that 'it would almost deceive one into the belief that it was china'. Assessing the factory's output in June 1915 at the first British Industries Fair, the *Pottery Gazette* reported that 'there is practically no limit to the number and styles of their decorations'[19] and remarked upon the factory's extensive trade in royal-blue banded and gilt tableware. Gold was considered to be 'one of the most important forms of decoration'[20] at the time, with the majority of superior patterns introducing it in some form or other. The most expensive form of gilding, 'best gold', an alloy of gold and mercury, transferred the highest percentage of pure metal to the ware and was generally used in the production of bone china. On emerging from the kiln, best gold was dull and needed burnishing. Burnishing was 'always women and girls' work', the Wedgwood photograph album confirms.[21] A cheaper form of gilding, liquid gold – bright gold – was a species of gold lustre, which was thinner and more easily erased. This was probably the gold Clarice Cliff applied to Grindley's tableware. Even so, she would have done so sparingly. 'We ... had a special rag to wipe it off,' one gilder recalled. 'This had to be handed in every night for the gold to be burned off and extracted because it was too expensive to be lost.'[22]

Clarice Cliff earned one shilling a week as a gilder, in return for which she learned to paint a series of gold lines with fine brushes. She may also have learned to produce the occasional sprigs and flourishes that gave the finishing touch to floral tableware. Gilding was careful work and required a steady hand, but it was dull work nevertheless, particularly given the limited number of ways in which gold was applied as decoration. It taught Clarice Cliff patience and precision and an early, important lesson in the cost of materials, but is unlikely to have satisfied her for long.

In January 1912, the *Pottery Gazette* reported that, during the previous year, the borough of Stoke-on-Trent '[had sent] more pots out into the world than . . . ever before'.[23] An auspicious introduction to Clarice Cliff's working life, but the industry's pride was short-lived. Britain was experiencing a period of profound political and industrial unrest; Irish nationalism was gaining ground and the Liberal government's failure to address female suffrage was attracting an increasing number of women to the militancy of the Women's Social and Political Union (WSPU), the suffragette body led by the Pankhursts. A railway strike in 1911 had jeopardised national industry; there were threats of industrial action all round.

A miners' strike in February 1912 put paid to all confidence. Soon the *Pottery Gazette* was describing the 'deplorable state of affairs' in the Staffordshire Potteries. 'From all directions . . . comes the sad tale of a complete cessation of work, or of operations being conducted on a limited scale, with the prospect of a total stoppage in the near future,'[24] it noted the following month. The average consumption of coal within each potbank was in the region of 200 tons per week: without coal there was no pottery industry. 'As far as I could find,' the *Gazette*'s journalist reported, 'there were only about five firms in the whole district who were able to keep their factories fully at work.'[25] Approximately 50,000 people connected with the pottery trade were unemployed. In no time at all, the industry was 'completely paralysed'.[26] The coal strike followed within weeks of Clarice Cliff's thirteenth birthday. No sooner was she introduced to the world of work than she found herself with little work to do.

Even as a young apprentice, Clarice Cliff could not fail to be aware of the extreme hardship experienced by the district during the coal strike. Only about 2,000 of those working in the pottery industry were entitled to employment benefit. Funds were quickly organised to alleviate distress and arrangements made to assist local children. Headmaster William H. Calkin recorded events: 'Coal Strike. Since 12th inst. Free dinners have been daily supplied to scholars.' Seven boys received free dinners on 12 March;

seventy-seven received them six days later. By the time Calkin wrote his log on 1 April, that number had almost doubled.[27] As the strike wore on, breakfast and tea were also supplied from the Mayor's Distress Fund, as were fifty pairs of children's boots and clogs. Contemporary photographs show men, women and children scratching for coal, or standing in a long queue, awaiting handouts from their local chapel.

The Cliffs could not have escaped the impact of the strike. As a foundry man, Clarice's father would have been affected and, like her sister Clarice, Sarah must have found herself on short time. The strike would also have caused difficulties for their mother – how could she take in washing, with coal so hard to find, and, even if she did, who could pay her? This was not the first time the people of the Potteries experienced hardship, nor the last, but for Clarice Cliff it was a dramatic introduction to working life.

By April, the miners' strike was over and, by June, the *Pottery Gazette* was commenting on the industry's 'surprisingly rapid recovery'.[28] This was not the end of industrial action, however. Some 'lively scenes'[29] were witnessed at Tunstall the following year during a strike by tile workers, one of four local strikes at the time.[30] The Royal Visit to the Potteries in April 1913 provided a distraction from these tensions. The King and Queen spent three days touring the district, whose towns responded with patriotic enthusiasm. As befit her status as the mother town, Burslem was 'beautifully decorated', while 'plucky little Tunstall did itself proud as always',[31] with a series of electric lamps in the shape of crowns providing 'one of the most beautiful illuminated schemes in the Potteries'. The High Street and streets nearby were decked with 'streamers, flags and artificial flowers',[32] red drapes fringed with gold dressed window sills. Schoolchildren packed Market Square; large numbers lined the streets, among them the pottery workers – including Clarice Cliff, no doubt – who had been expected to remain at their benches demonstrating industrial enterprise.

Despite concern that suffragettes would disrupt the occasion, the Royal Visit passed without incident. It is a measure of the anxiety their activity generated at this time that even the *Pottery Gazette* felt compelled to comment. 'Having done so much for the glass trade,' its columnist joked nervously when suffragettes set fire to several crates of ornamental tiles, 'the militants apparently wanted to give the potters a turn.'[33] Numerous suffrage meetings were held in the Potteries, as in other industrial towns,[34] and women pottery workers in their aprons formed part of the Pageant of Women's Trades and Professions that took place in April 1909. The Wedgwood archive contains two suffragette crests, the first proclaiming 'Votes for Women', the second featuring the initials of the Women's Freedom League.[35] A tea service bearing the WFL crest, with its fervent motto, 'Dare to be Free', was produced around 1910, while a tea set designed by Sylvia Pankhurst herself, displaying the trumpeting angel of the WSPU, was manufactured by the Staffordshire company Williamson. It is to be hoped the young lithographers heard her clarion call as they stamped the printed angel on to the ware. Although Clarice Cliff was only a girl at the time, she must have been aware of the issues. Already she was learning that the world of work did not offer equal opportunities.

Short-time work at W.H. Grindley, following on from the coal strike, may have provided the impetus for Clarice Cliff to seek work as an enameller at Lingard Webster & Co. Ltd. Just as likely, restless ambition led the way. She soon tired of the predictability of gilding and wanted something different for herself. Based at the Swan Bank Pottery, on the corner of Tunstall's Hunt Street, Lingard Webster was even closer to the Cliff family home. Known for its extensive range of tea services, the company was making 'wonderful strides' in the decoration of the Rockingham body of its teapots.[36] Typically, their patterns were finished off with lustre, with which the firm was said to be 'thoroughly at home'. In 1913, a trade reporter praised their 'green and silver decorations' and 'a really charming combination' of cream and gold,[37] while a 'green ground with "a dash of Art Nouveau"' was one of the patterns produced the following year. Two of their best-selling teapots – the 'Eclipse' and the 'Unique', the latter a 'safety pot' designed to secure the teapot lid while pouring – were 'graciously accepted' by the Queen during the Royal Visit, Lingard Webster being one of the firms which donated tableware for the occasion.

The girls and women engaged in hand-decorating transferred colour directly on to blank ware with their brushes. Colour could be used to fill in a printed outline or to construct a pattern freehand, with the decorator herself copying a design in paint on to the ceramic surface. Although both kinds of decorator were defined as paintresses, the ones who filled in outlines were also called enamellers. The most famous description of the enameller is provided by Arnold Bennett in *Anna of the Five Towns*:

> Contiguous with the printing-shop was the painting-shop, in which the labours of the former were taken to a finish by the brush of the paintress, who filled in outlines with flat colour, and thus converted mechanical printing into handiwork. The paintresses form the *noblesse* of the banks. Their task is a light one, demanding deftness first of all; they have delicate fingers, and enjoy a general reputation for beauty: the wages they earn may be estimated from their finery on Sundays. They come to business in cloth jackets, carry dinner in little satchels; in the shop they wear white aprons, and look startlingly neat and tidy. Across the benches over which they bend their coquettish heads gossip flies and returns like a shuttle; they are the source of a thousand intrigues . . . On the bank they constitute 'the sex'.[38]

'You were posh if you . . . went learning enamelling, or painting, or something like that – you'd got a posh job, see,' a pottery worker recalled.[39] With a 'posh job' as an enameller, a working-class young woman had every reason to feel pleased, and Clarice Cliff's mother must have felt her middle daughter was now set on a good path. Although it required less skill than that of the freehand paintress, patience and precision were essential to an enameller's craft. 'It was intricate work and a delicate sort of job which required a good eye and a steady hand.'[40] Paintresses mixed fat oil and turpentine with powdered enamel paint to produce a paste 'a bit thicker than double cream',[41] which they then applied to tableware. Paint coated their hands and fingers and lodged beneath their nails, while the smell of turpentine seeped into their clothes. Its pungency became so familiar that they barely noticed the extent to which it was a

Paintresses, Wedgwood, 1913

marker of their craft: you could always identify a paintress by
that smell.

Pottery decorating skills were often acquired at night school.
Clarice Cliff recalled receiving a scholarship to attend evening classes
at the Tunstall School of Art.[42] Although the dates of her attendance
are not known, pupils with artistic flair generally started classes on
leaving elementary school, with scholarships awarded in open
competition. The relationship between the Potteries' art schools and
local industry was a close and sometimes vexed one. While some
maintained that industrial skills were best learned on the factory
floor, others recognised the benefits of an art education, whether
from an aesthetic or a purely commercial point of view. Apprentices

themselves were keen; parents – like Clarice Cliff's – with ambitions for their daughters to be paintresses were also enthusiastic, as were some employers. Royal Doulton expected its paintresses to take art classes and the manufacturer A.E. Richardson paid for his to attend.

In 1912, two years after the federation of the pottery towns, a new curriculum was established within the local art schools with the intention of strengthening their links with industry. Nine courses were available, each offering preliminary, advanced and honour grades, and catering for a wide range of pottery workers as well as architects, elementary school teachers and general art students. Preliminary-grade instruction was to consist 'almost entirely . . . of plant drawing, common object drawing, geometrical drawing and the study of the history and styles of ornament'.[43] The preliminary and advanced grades were each designed to occupy two years of part-time study, with the honour grade taking up a further three.

Clarice Cliff was probably one of the first students to benefit from the new curriculum. Nevertheless, just as elementary schooling had failed to satisfy her appetite for learning, her local art-school training left her unimpressed. Years later, she recalled that 'drawing from plaster casts and vases of honesty were the sum total of tuition'.[44] Hanley and Burslem held the principal art schools of the district at this time; Tunstall's Victoria Institute fared less well, although all the Potteries' art establishments were hampered, to some extent, by inadequate facilities. A report by the local Education Committee into the Victoria Institute some years earlier commended its teaching, but described a building in need of better ventilation, redecoration and electric light.[45] Plants housed in the poorly heated conservatory struggled to thrive from week to week, which doubtless accounts for the vases of honesty Clarice Cliff was required to paint.

Whether at an art school or in a potbank, paintresses were taught a variety of brushstrokes, which 'learners' practised repeatedly – often for weeks on end – by decorating damaged ware, intially using one colour. They learned to paint lines that matched on pots of different shapes and sizes, lines that swept the rims of tea cups and chased the lips of plates, forming their brushstrokes over and over, until they were proficient at their craft. As soon as Clarice Cliff convinced Lingard Webster's decorating manager that she was adept at brushwork, she graduated to enamelling printed patterns intended for sale – perhaps the 'pencilled red, blue and gold'[46] design that was one of the firm's principal decorations, or the gold and floral pattern overlaying wide blue bands that was produced around this time.[47] Holding her brush as lightly as she could, Clarice applied colour to a line of rosebuds and made their petals blush.

Although the work was skilled, wages were not high. A young girl's wages were, in any case, not her own. Girls gave their earnings to their mothers, who returned pocket money to them with which to buy the palette knife and assorted brushes – liners, banders, tracers, stripers – that were the tools of a paintress's trade, and which they themselves were expected to provide. Brushes – known as pencils in North Staffordshire, where the eighteenth-century meaning of the word is retained – were guarded jealously. New ones had to be schooled to produce light sweeping strokes; reliable, elderly brushes were hard to part with.

Despite the skill required, and the touch of glamour attaching to the role, the work itself was repetitive. In his description of the paintress, Arnold Bennett goes on to describe 'the stupendous phenomenon of absolute sameness'[48] an enameller's work entailed. The ceramic designer Alfred Powell echoed this view: 'We put little girls . . . to sit in factories day after day placing little dabs of green and red on printed patterns until they turn into automatons. Their little minds stiffen up to the dull work and do it professionally, but it is a real tragedy and a loss that pottery cannot afford.'[49] Too few within the industry agreed. Monotonous work was thought to be appropriate for women.

Though Clarice Cliff spent her days painting repetitive patterns, she was also looking about her, and acquiring a knowledge that exceeded the paintress's role. Two of the teapots produced by Lingard Webster at this time were dependent upon one another, the second shape evolving from the inverse of the first[50] – a valuable lesson in design economy and inventiveness, and one which Clarice Cliff remembered when creating her own shapes in years to come. Even as a young enameller in her teens, she was beginning to think like a designer.

FOUR

Women Workers in the Firing Line

The Potteries reacted to the outbreak of the First World War in much the same way as other provincial towns and cities – its first few weeks were characterised by anxiety and recruitment drives, with notices pinned to the doors of town halls. In the absence of hard information, the rumour mill worked overtime. In the Derbyshire town of Buxton, the Russians were said to have landed in England and passed through Stoke;[1] no doubt the inhabitants of Stoke heard that a similar contingent had recently marched through Buxton. The arrival of Belgian refugees in the area in October 1914, and news of the 'bombardment of Scarborough'[2] two months later, brought the reality of war close to home. By January 1915, 20,000 recruits from Staffordshire alone had joined the armed forces.[3] As a mere schoolboy aged eleven, Clarice Cliff's brother Frank was too young to take the King's shilling. Not so her brother Harry, who joined the Royal Artillery Force as a gunner.

The First World War offered the astute pottery manufacturer new business. Shelley, for example, combined patriotism with commerce by producing ceramic models of aeroplanes and battleships, together with a miniature fireplace scene to remind the armchair patriot to 'Keep the Home Fires Burning'. Within the industry in general, the stoppage of German, Austrian and some French exports to the colonies, America and the UK increased the demand for all cheaper grades of English pottery, although richly decorated and higher-priced tableware experienced something of a slump. In a notable exception to the general trade picture at the beginning of the war, the pottery industry suffered from a lack of unskilled (rather than skilled) operatives, who quickly found more remunerative work elsewhere. Men left for the collieries, women for munitions factories or silk weaving, some of them never to return, but as increasing numbers of men volunteered for the front line, the war opened up employment opportunities for women.

An intriguing photograph has come to light, which may show Clarice Cliff around this time. The young woman said to be Clarice is wearing a fashionable bow in her hair and, although part of a group, has asserted her presence. The white-haired woman seated at the centre is also believed to be a Cliff and her wedding band and age, given the photograph's likely date, fits with her being Ann Cliff, Clarice's mother. The general style of dress is consistent with this period if allowances are made for the fact that 'best' clothes were not always in the latest styles; a taffeta bow was one thing, a whole new outfit was a different matter.[6]

Group photograph, c.1914, with the young woman thought to be Clarice Cliff, back row, fourth from the left

In or around 1915, Clarice Cliff gave up her job as an enameller and found work at Hollinshead & Kirkham's Unicorn Pottery, just off Tunstall High Street. Here she was taken on as an apprentice lithographer, 'much to the disgust of her parents',[4] who were concerned that their daughter's painting skills would now be neglected. Years later, Ethel Cliff agreed that lithography 'was not in keeping' with her sister's 'artistic talent',[5] but Clarice was evidently making her own decisions by this time and, as a contributor to the family income, felt entitled to change direction if she wished. Even so, she must have marshalled a convincing argument. At sixteen years of age, or thereabouts, Clarice Cliff remained very much within her parents' jurisdiction. Perhaps her continuing attendance at evening classes helped win them round.

Ethel Cliff recalled that her sister moved to Hollinshead & Kirkham because she 'decided to try a change',[7] yet lithography attracted less prestige than paintressing, as their parents' disapproval makes clear. In an industry which valued craftsmanship, and in which work as a freehand paintress was the most skilled occupation to which a working-class young woman could aspire, they wanted the best for their daughter. They may also have felt that Clarice's restlessness did not bode well: she was secure in her job as an enameller and should not be changing factories once again. Clarice Cliff thought otherwise.

Lithography had been making inroads for some time. Introduced to England during the mid- to late-nineteenth century, the lithograph was recognised as an efficient and economical form of decoration. Manufacturers needing to produce elaborate patterns in quantity while keeping costs low could do so much more readily with lithographs. Though the designs on offer were limited and of little artistic merit, lithographic transfers were provided by print houses and so dispensed with the need to employ designers, a factor that increasingly appealed to manufacturers.[8]

At the British Industries Fair in 1915, Hollinshead & Kirkham displayed 'all the regular run of everyday kitchen goods, from fluted white teas upwards, as well as hospital and institution goods', together with a range of ornamental wares 'much on the lines of the Bonn specialists'[9] in vogue at that time. The firm's 'Tudor Rose' design, a rose on a marbled surround, and a border pattern in Canton blue were currently proving popular with the 'medium-class' trade. Clarice spent her days applying transfer patterns such as these to quantities of dinner ware and tea sets. She brushed each cup with size* and applied the transfer print to its wet surface, sliding the printed paper into place, starting at the back of the tea cup, near its handle, and working round to the front, from left to right. She slid and smoothed and eased each transfer into position, and when two dozen cups stood ready and felt tacky to the touch, a damp rag lifted the paper and left the pattern behind.

By looking to lithography, Clarice Cliff was observing current trends; she may even have felt that she would need experience in this field in order to secure employment in the future.[10] But there is another way of interpreting her decision. Lithography helped complete the decorating jigsaw. The more skills she acquired, the better placed she would be. '[E]ver since she left school, Clarice Cliff has had only one idea, and has concentrated every atom of her brains, energy and talent on achieving success in it,' the *Sunday Express* reported in 1935.[11] An easy assessment to make with hindsight, and yet one which corresponds with Clarice Cliff's early progress. She wanted something from her life, despite being taught to ask for and expect little. From the very beginning, she had ideas.

Between 1916 and 1918,[12] in a move that was to have an extraordinary impact on her future, Clarice Cliff changed factories for the last time when she transferred to A.J. Wilkinson as a lithographer. A.J. Wilkinson's Royal Staffordshire Pottery was based in Middleport, Burslem, which meant a longer journey each day. An earlier start each morning, when jobs could be had locally – especially with the war creating vacancies all the time – suggests this was a factory that particularly appealed. She already had a job as a lithographer; she did not need another further away.

By 1916, the First World War was transforming the lives of women as well as men. The introduction of Universal Male Conscription in May that year, and the realisation that women were now required to provide the backbone of the workforce, led to comprehensive changes on the domestic front. As middle-class women threw off their ornamental roles and found employment – most for the first time – working-class women continued to find new outlets for their skills. As well as the higher wages, greater independence (and greater risks) of the munitions factories, further vacancies appeared within existing industrial environments.

The *Pottery Gazette* was confident about the increased role of women in the industry: 'The Potteries have always been well to the fore in finding suitable outlets for female labour,' it boasted in June 1916, without pausing to define the word 'suitable'. 'Few industries can show such a large proportion of female operatives working under such favourable conditions.'[13] (Women in the dipping house who drank half a pint of milk each day to stave off lead poisoning may have begged to differ.) Others greeted the expanding female workforce with less enthusiasm. In the light-hearted 'Fragments' column of the same issue, a different voice spoke up: 'It was a bumptious junior who, when he heard of the suggestion that more women should be employed in the pottery trade, remarked, "By Jove! There are too many old women in it now."'[14]

Nevertheless, needs must. With the industry finding it increasingly difficult to function, women began to be accepted into areas hitherto defined as male. The ways in which their lives changed is perhaps demonstrated most graphically by two examples which span the industrial spectrum. Audrey Wedgwood, the daughter of Major Cecil Wedgwood, became the first female company secretary of that firm and took over the running of the factory, single-handed, while further down the industrial scale the expanding role of women was such that, towards the end of the war, the manufacturer L.L. Grimwade was able to advertise tableware 'Made by the Girls. Fired by the Girls. Decorated by the Girls. Packed by the Girls.'[15] An illustrated article picked up this theme, showing the Grimwade women at work and offering retailers a photograph of this novelty for their windows. 'That girls can stand this hard work at the kilns is most remarkable,' the article explained. 'They endure it for ten and eleven hours a day; and the work is so arduous that an untrained man could not undertake to do it for an hour at a time.'[15] Women were achieving the unexpected.

The developments taking place in the Potteries were not confined to industry, but were visible within the wider world as well – women took the fares on the trams in Tunstall High Street and steered the heavy carts that delivered coal, milk and vegetables to the door. Everywhere Clarice Cliff looked, the world was changing. This was surely in her thoughts when she responded to the vacancy at A.J. Wilkinson. For someone who longed for a future less predictable than the one envisaged for her, the First World War crystallised possibilities: it demonstrated that the improbable could happen.

A.J. Wilkinson was regarded as 'a go-ahead' concern[17], and a company 'ear-marked for its inventiveness'.[18] Significantly, the firm employed designers, and, by 1916, had gained a considerable reputation for art ware, particularly with the design 'Oriflamme', which was shown at international exhibitions and received Diplomas of Honour at Turin (1911) and Ghent (1913), and a Gold Medal in San Francisco (1915), shortly before the war interrupted its production. A 'splashed, veined and marbled' effect,[19] 'Oriflamme' consisted of a series of striated colours with a lustrous finish. As the appearance of any one piece was determined by the impact of the kiln upon a particular combination of colourings, 'Oriflamme' gained a further cachet as prestige ware: no two pieces were alike. From 1912, a department was devoted to its production; trade reports continually refer to its success. Looking back some years later, the *Pottery Gazette* was of the impression that 'this firm's modellers and decorators were being given a free hand in the production of artistic wares that were to be regarded as real departures from customary styles'.[20] This was a firm in which a young woman might discover new ways to use and develop her skills.

In addition to award-winning art ware, A.J. Wilkinson was responsible for more prosaic creations directed at the general market: dinner, tea and toilet ware, together with an extensive range of ornaments or 'fancies'. An extract from the *Pottery Gazette* in April 1917 gives some sense of its style during this period: 'Their rose-and-trellis decorations have always been pre-eminent . . . the latest version . . . has a symmetrical black quadrilateral trellis, well-covered with roses and foliage in natural clusters. Three styles of

Inset is the noted "ORIFLAMME WARE" of which
we are the sole manufacturers.

A. J. WILKINSON, Ltd., Royal Staffordshire Pottery, BURSLEM.

A.J. Wilkinson advertisement, with examples of
'Oriflamme', centre

colouring are available . . . pink flowers with green leaves, heliotrope
flowers with smoke-grey leaves and pink flowers with smoke-grey.'[21]
The lithography department was also singled out for praise:
'A.J. Wilkinson Ltd have been successful in securing some superior
specimens of litho work for their dinner ware, a department which
is moving vigorously just now, one very attractive type having a ring

of dainty rose sprays on two narrow black lines.[22] Whatever her
hopes for the future, for the time being, at least, Clarice Cliff
exchanged one rose pattern for another.

Not long into the First World War, Harry Cliff was wounded: a
shrapnel injury to his jaw brought his military service to an end and
he spent the rest of the war in hospital blues. He was hospitalised
in London, where he was visited by Clarice. She also visited their
New Zealand cousin, Arthur Cliff, accompanied on that occasion
by one of her sisters – perhaps Hannah, who had already ventured
away from home and who probably returned to the Potteries at the
outbreak of war, or her younger sister Dorothy, who would certainly
have enjoyed the adventure. A sister may have been Clarice Cliff's
companion during her visit to Harry too. Although the war gave
young women greater freedom of movement, London was a different
world from Stoke-on-Trent and her parents were unlikely to have
permitted her to travel there alone. Some would have balked at their
daughters going to London at all, but if Harry was wounded,
someone from the family needed to visit him, and a hospital visit
helped to sanitise the capital city's reputation. Clarice was probably
prime mover in this scheme.

   With so many of the wounded transported from French field
hospitals to London, the sisters may have travelled as part of a
larger party from Stoke-on-Trent. A darkened city met them: 'The
searchlight, a faint, detached glimmer, quivered at the edges of the
clouds, or slowly crawled, a luminous pencil, across the deep indigo
spaces between.'[23] A strange way to greet the capital, but Clarice
Cliff's thoughts would doubtless have been elsewhere, caught up
with the practicalities of locating her brother in the military hospital
to which he had been taken. 'The traditional imagination of a
hospital . . . is really hardly correct at all,' Vera Brittain told her
fiancé Roland Leighton in 1915, writing from the 1st London
General Hospital, where she was nursing as a VAD. Her account
gives some indication of the kind of scene that greeted the Cliff
sisters on Visitors' Day:

Certainly my ward is so long and narrow that the vista of beds . . . makes one quite dizzy. But in a surgical ward the nurses hardly occupy the silent-footed, gliding role which they always do in story-books & on the stage. For one thing there is too much work to be done in a great hurry. For another, the mixture of gramophones and people shouting or groaning after an operation relieves you of the necessity of being quiet . . . One does not often have to play the bedside Angel of Mercy.[24]

The 1st London General, which was 'run on strictly military lines'[25] and had over 1,000 beds, was one of the many London hospitals set aside for the war wounded, any one of which might have nursed Harry Cliff: seven out of every ten hospital trains from the front lines were dispatched to the UK capital. In the aftermath of the Somme, for example, trains came into Charing Cross and Paddington stations almost every hour, with the 1st London General increasing its bed spaces to nearly 3,000.[26] Even if Clarice hoped that Harry's injury would keep him safe from further harm, it must have been disturbing to see her brother in these circumstances.

The visit to her cousin, Arthur, was more of an adventure. Clarice was meeting him for the first time. Arthur James Cliff was the son of George Kidwell Cliff, her father's second cousin, whose own father had left Hanley with his father in 1862, on their emigration to New Zealand. In 1917, at the age of twenty-one, Arthur enlisted in the New Zealand Artillery Regiment. The following September, while serving in France, he was gassed and sent to the General Hospital, Brockenhurst, where Clarice's father managed to locate him in response to his cousin's request for assistance.[27]

During Arthur's recovery, Clarice took him into London and introduced him to the sights, and when he was discharged in December 1918, Arthur travelled to Stoke-on-Trent to spend Christmas with his English relatives. Tunstall must have come as something of a shock after the open spaces of New Zealand, but, perhaps, if he appreciated the Potteries' sense of humour, Arthur sent a postcard home – a drawing of a thatched cottage surrounded by trees, with happy children playing hoop and ball – a rural idyll, inscribed: 'With all kind thoughts from Tunstall.'[28]

*

By 1918, the contribution women had made to the First World War was the subject of congratulations all round. The gratitude of the pottery manufacturer Grimwade was such that he proposed that the women whose work had sustained the industry throughout should be thanked in a 'lasting and tangible way'. Money should be raised, he said, without a trace of irony, for 'a Women's Wing at the North Stafford Infirmary, or half a dozen cots'.[29] So much for the changing perception of women workers. Others took a more encouraging – if optimistic – view. In May 1919, an article entitled 'Female Labour in the Pottery Industry' concluded: 'The part which women have played in keeping the works going has entitled them to be fully considered in every future development of the industry.'[30]

FIVE

A Talented Lady Modeller

'The past year has been one of continued progress for women,' the *Daily Mail* reported on 1 January 1920.[1] Some now had the vote, a partial franchise granted in 1918;[2] women were now entitled to sit on juries; and the Sex Disqualification (Removal) Act of 1919 admitted them to professions, such as the Bar, from which they had formerly been excluded. What is more, with the appointment of Nancy Astor, who took her husband's seat in parliament when he was elevated to the House of Lords, a woman MP sat in the House of Commons for the first time. The decade promised new possibilities and new freedoms.

For Clarice Cliff and her family, the decade began with a marriage. In the spring of 1920, at the age of twenty-five, Hannah married William Crutchley. Like her brother Harry, he had served as a gunner in the First World War; he now worked as a secretary for a local bus company. Clarice's oldest sister, Sarah, was not far behind. The following year she married William Craddock, a colliery worker from the nearby village of Fegg Hayes, with whom she moved to Salisbury Street, a mere hundred yards from her mother. Sarah was now aged twenty-eight; like many of her generation, she married late, the war delaying as many courtships as it hastened others. The sisters married at Christ Church: a short walk to the service, a scattering of confetti, and then home.

By now, the family was well established within Tunstall's parish church. With her long experience of taking charge, Sarah became a

Sunday school superintendent. Clarice taught classes at Sunday
school, a useful early lesson in authority, with Dorothy and Ethel
following in turn. Their brother Frank sang in the Christ Church
choir, while Dorothy, a keen seamstress, made the costumes for
the Christmas pantomime as well as her own clothes. Sundays
were an opportunity for 'the Cliff girls' to look their best – collars
straightened, hats just so – in advance of morning service.

By 1920, all the Cliff children were working. Ethel, the youngest,
turned fourteen that year and began work as an enameller in the
job her mother found for her nearby, at William Adams. Frank's
journey to work was even shorter – he accompanied his father to
the foundry across the road – while Dorothy followed in Clarice's
footsteps and was taken on as a decorator at A.J. Wilkinson. Along
with her gift for sewing, Dorothy's love was dancing. She caught
the bug which raged throughout society after the First World War.
'There is no doubt that dancing is first, foremost and pre-eminently
It,' the *Ladies' Field* reported,[3] while, further down the social scale,
My Weekly informed its readers, 'No foxtrot is complete without
that alluring little "twinkle" now and again.'[4] Dorothy danced
whenever she could – three or four nights a week, if possible –
demonstrating the latest steps at the Hippodrome in Stoke and
performing in revues, dressed in costumes of her own creation. She
painted patterns along the edge of her skirts and later, as hems
rose, dyed her underwear, ensuring a uniform colour for the high
kicks of the Charleston. She was slim, 'just like a doll',[5] and must
have looked the part when she shimmied across the dance floor or
strutted to the Soft-Shoe Rag. All the sisters liked to dance, with
one exception: Clarice. 'She was never interested ... Her work
always came first.'[6]

When Clarice Cliff joined A.J. Wilkinson, she already had at least
four years' decorating experience behind her, as well as the accumulated knowledge of three potbanks, which greatly increased her
self-confidence. By starting work at an early age, young women
anyway acquired a professional sophistication in excess of their
actual years. Though at home they were mere young lasses, at their
parents' beck and call, at work they were skilled employees.

The journey to A.J. Wilkinson involved a fifteen-minute tram ride. Down Scotia Road and into Burslem, along Wedgwood Street and through Swan Square, out through Brown Hills into Longport, heading for Canal Street, rising and dipping all the while, following the uneven contours of the landscape, jolted by the progress of the tram. Past tall, dark chimneys, cigarette-thin, and the stumpy ones of bottle ovens, some with cones standing proud, others poking dirty snouts out from factory rooftops. Pressed up hard against them, terraced houses, row upon row, completed the band of slate and coughing chimneys. At Middleport Park, a walk of similar duration took Clarice Cliff to the factory that commanded the bottom of Prospect Street and overlooked the Trent and Mersey Canal.

A.J. Wilkinson

Years later, in a recollection that is tantalisingly brief, and incomplete, she looked back to her early days at A.J. Wilkinson, 'when people took a pride in their craft, and generations of families worked for the same firm, and in spite of little squabbles, the whole factory was more or less one big family. Of course I could go on and on,' she wrote. 'Polly Green (Durber) with a jam jar full of lobby [stew] and every time the tram car bounced, the gravy would trickle down; and old Sam Durber, boss of the steam kettle . . .'[7] Her days were punctuated by the shouts and whistles of the bargees who loaded coal and the flint and clays with which the slip* was made, and stacked and loaded crates of finished ware. Their children worked alongside, sitting astride the carthorses that pulled the narrow boats. On fine days, young lads skimmed stones across the water and, in summer, dived into its depths. You could swim 'as far as Shelton Bar in one direction or Westport Lake in the other, diving off all the bridges along the way'.[8] Clarice Cliff knew that stretch of murky water well, and the shord rucks in the distance – those sharp, false hills of rubble and broken crockery, grassed over with the years. Grey sky, grey mounds, grey water. Grey undernourished children playing on the bank. A young girl who later worked for A.J. Wilkinson and lived in one of the houses the company owned on Prospect Street was among those who stood at the factory lodge and begged for bread each morning. She always asked the decorators because they were better paid, and always promised cake the following day.[9]

The A.J. Wilkinson Royal Staffordshire Pottery was a family concern, owned by Arthur Shorter and thereafter his two sons, Arthur Colley Austin and John Guy.[10] Like many who made their mark upon the district, Arthur Shorter's origins were humble. The son of a Staffordshire railwayman, he began work as a clerk, but was soon apprenticed to the pottery trade and was employed by a number of potteries as a landscape painter, among them the prestigious company Minton, before setting up Shorter & Son in Copeland Street, Stoke-upon-Trent, in 1878. By then, he had married Henrietta Elizabeth Wilkinson, the daughter of a Burslem school teacher, with whom he was to have six children.

Arthur Shorter's interests extended far beyond his factory gates. A leading Liberal of the district, he was chairman of his local Liberal club for several years, a member of the Education Committee and a one-time vice-chairman of his local School Board. He was also a prominent Wesleyan and, by the time of his death, was said to have held every Church position available to a layman. As a lifelong teetotaller, Shorter's pleas for abstinence rang out from public platforms, but, despite this proselytising image, he is recalled as a kind and gentle man. (His wife Henrietta seems to have been the sharper of the two, with something of the reputation of a tartar.) His pastimes were quiet ones. He liked to paint – his portrait of their house at Maerfield Gate, Wolstanton, still decorates a family home – and was a keen gardener, but his passion was photography; he was president of the Hanley Photographic Society. Social gatherings, holidays and family groups – all were recorded by Arthur Shorter's lens.

Shorter's involvement with A.J. Wilkinson followed the death of his brother-in-law, Arthur Wilkinson, who had himself set up as a manufacturer of earthenware during the 1880s, but was killed while mountaineering shortly thereafter. Shorter acquired an interest in the firm and thus established a long association between the two factories, which were run as separate operations but were nevertheless connected. By the early 1900s, in addition to gaining a reputation for decorative and ornamental ware, A.J. Wilkinson had extended its markets both at home and overseas. By now, Arthur Shorter had been joined by his two sons: Colley was involved in the commercial side of the business; Guy was responsible for production.

Production and commerce. Two different sides of the manufacturing process; two very different temperaments. Guy was always the gentleman; Colley was a man with whom it was wise to tread carefully. Guy was a team player; he played hockey for his county and was a keen cricketer. Colley liked to hunt; it was his commerical instincts that continually extended the firm's reach. During the First World War, Guy took a commission in the North Staffordshire Regiment; Colley stayed behind to manage the factories with his father. In 1916, both were appointed company directors and, on their father's semi-retirement two years later, responsibility for the business and more than 700 employees passed pretty much into their hands. During the war years, Colley Shorter appointed new staff and may have interviewed Clarice Cliff for the post of lithographer.

The lithography and painting departments shared one large room at A.J. Wilkinson, enabling her to observe a range of decorating techniques and practise them herself during spare moments. Skilled

paintresses could graduate the colour of a petal with one brush-
stroke, and make their brushes halt at the fine point of a leaf. Passing
through the decorating shop one day, the works manager, Jack
Walker, saw Clarice 'showing one of the paintresses how to sketch
and colour a butterfly',[11] and was so impressed he brought her work
to the attention of Colley Shorter. A skilled craftsman himself, who
drew delicate pen-and-ink drawings in his spare time, Walker was
married to Shorter's sister Mabel, and his word carried weight.
Colley Shorter was equally impressed. He recognised that Clarice
Cliff's skills exceeded those of the decorating shop and moved her
to work alongside the company's two designers.

John Butler and Fred Ridgway were responsible for the
ornamental ware that brought the company such prestige. Butler,
art director and a talented designer well known within the industry,
was responsible for the award-winning 'Oriflamme' and the equally
colourful 'Tibetan' and 'Rubaiyat' designs. Ridgway favoured lustre
and Oriental-style ware, which he decorated with exquisite
precision. The chance to work with two designers of such long
standing gave Clarice Cliff vital insight into their technical expertise.
'I . . . had many opportunities for studying art as applied to pottery
design which the average girl does not always have,'[12] she later
commented, in words that do not begin to convey the excitement
she must have felt at the time.

'In the early 1920s,' Clarice Cliff explained, 'I had progressed as
far as modelling in clay, keeping pattern and shape books up to
date, very fine filigree gilding with a pen, tracing spiders' webs,
butterflies etc. to hide small imperfections on expensive ware.'[13]
Decorative spiders' webs and butterflies feature in trade reports of
A.J. Wilkinson as early as 1920 and may have been the work to
which she alluded. Among the firm's exhibits at the British Industries
Fair that year were translucent bowls and vases whose 'delicacy of
colouring' was described as 'a cascade of tones, shades, and effects
of bright light . . . with spider-web effects in gold',[14] while 'a drop
butterfly in gold and black' added the finishing touch to a 'Rubaiyat'
vase that autumn.[15]

The shape and pattern books which Clarice Cliff maintained were
every factory's bible and similarly revered. Each shape the manu-

facturer produced was allocated a number and photographed, with measurements or salient features detailed below. Pattern books fulfilled the same descriptive function, but it surely gave her greater pleasure to draw patterns in black ink and describe each outlined colour: 'cadmium yellow', 'powder blue'. She could roll their sounds around her tongue and hear poetry in the methods described: 'Blown in Chrome Green, Coral Red', 'waterfalls . . . in greens and browns. Yellow lustre all over.'[16]

On 1 September 1922, Clarice Cliff was indentured as a modeller. Her Certificate of Indenture, signed by Colley Shorter and witnessed by John Butler, is the only surviving document relating to the terms of her employment that predates the creation of 'Bizarre'.[17] The indenture brought with it a weekly salary of two pounds and two shillings, an amount which was a considerable improvement on her previous wage,[18] and would have paid for quantities of drawing paper for sketching new ideas, or a felt hat in the latest style from Bon Marché. Most likely, Clarice's earnings went straight to her mother, as before.

If it was unusual for an employee to change from one field of pottery work to another, it was all the more unusual for a young woman to be apprenticed as a modeller. Modelling involves the building up of a shape from lumps of clay and is an essential skill for anyone wishing to be comprehensively involved in ceramic design. The acquisition of modelling skills in addition to those of decorating signalled Clarice Cliff's intention to become a designer. In the early 1920s, this was unusual indeed. Openings for designers of either sex were few; women faced particular limitations.

Opportunities for women designers had become available during the nineteenth century with the establishment of design schools bolstered by the Aesthetic Movement, with its belief in women's innate decorating skills. When increasing numbers of middle-class women found themselves in need of employment during the latter half of that century, pottery decoration was work they could pursue without undermining their femininity. However, assumptions about women's natural capabilities, coupled with the indelicate business of shaping wet clay, restricted them to the creation of surface patterns. Although women working in studio potteries were able to establish fuller roles for themselves, on the (relatively few) occasions they were employed as commercial designers, they were generally excluded from designing shapes.[19]

This situation persisted well into the twentieth century. By signing modelling indentures, Clarice Cliff breached tradition. She crossed a class divide as well: working-class women did not become pottery designers, irrespective of distinctions between shape and pattern. Clarice Cliff was twenty-three in 1922; her flair and self-assurance were considerable. There were no blueprints to guide her; determination and skill pushed her on. The Shorters were equally forward-thinking in encouraging her ambition; the impact on the factory of having younger men at the helm, with 'keen up-to-date ideas',[20] was remarked upon by the trade press. The decision to train Clarice Cliff further was a vital step towards her attaining success on terms more usually reserved for men. That her new status corresponded with changing perceptions of women within society as a whole was no coincidence.

This was an extraordinary time for Clarice Cliff – plucked from the obscurity of the decorating shop and introduced to a wealth of new techniques and materials; no longer one of the workshop girls, but an assistant to the company's designers. She used her time productively, eager to absorb as much as possible. During this period she 'gained very useful knowledge of the making and firing of pottery',[21] and acquired an understanding of the different industrial processes. There was the Colour Room to explore, with its walls of glass-fronted cabinets and heavy, stoppered jars, each one beautifully labelled in careful copperplate: the powdered metal oxides – Antimony . . . Chromium . . . Cobalt . . . Copper . . . Gold . . . Tin – and the smaller jars containing the extenders: Anis Turpens, Eucalyptus, Lavender, Oil of Cloves. A pottery designer's alphabet, capable of conjuring rust-red out of iron or an ardent splash of purple from manganese.

Unmoved by the traditional antipathy displayed towards the clay end, Clarice Cliff befriended a young man there, Reg Lamb, who was able to purloin the scraps of modelling clay with which she practised her new craft at home. On more than one occasion, her sister

Clarice Cliff (right), with fellow workers at A.J. Wilkinson

Ethel sat while Clarice modelled her head and shoulders. Ethel was surely delighted to be captured in clay, if reluctant to sit still for so long. No doubt Clarice was able to persuade her, the art of persuasion being a skill she had already acquired: when her parents gave Clarice a violin as a young girl, she made Ethel learn the instrument instead. If there was no clay to model, anything would do – scraps of bread or orange peel, any form that could be moulded with her fingers; she was constantly busy with her hands. And if she wasn't modelling at home, Clarice was probably painting: a series of painted butterflies flew across the living-room blind – in celebration, perhaps, of the motif that had brought her so far.

The first pattern book in which Clarice Cliff's name appears dates from October 1921–5. A drawing of a seventeen-inch plaque which describes a fantastical bird and dragon is accompanied by the words 'Painted by Mr Ridgway, Gilt by CC', and has been attributed to February 1923.[22] This was a period of firsts. In October of that year, the *Pottery Gazette* commended 'the wonderfully good models in figures that are continually being brought out by A.J. Wilkinson Ltd. The person who is chiefly responsible . . . is an artist first of all and a modeller as the outcome of being artistically minded.'[23] Illustrating the report with a photograph of two Dutch figures which are known to be the work of Clarice Cliff,[24] the journal remarked, 'There is an unspoilt directness about some of these figures that is distinctly refreshing.'[25] An 'unspoilt directness' would be a feature of her figure work for years to come.

The following year, two further figures created by Clarice Cliff were shown at the British Empire Exhibition. These 'rugged but lifelike' models in 'the old Staffordshire style' drew on a series of decorative plaques known as 'London Cries', originated by Fred Ridgway, and show 'a woman crying "Seville Oranges" and a pedlar selling pins'; each bears Clarice Cliff's embossed signature.[26] Also exhibited, and praised by the press, was a large ginger jar in 'Tibetan'. This is likely to be the jar created by John Butler and signed and gilded by Clarice Cliff that was one of the few pieces of her work that she kept until her death, and was probably created as a show-piece for the exhibition.[64]

The British Empire Exhibition was opened by George V on 23 April 1924. Among the specially constructed pavilions, designed to showcase the 'architecture, art and industry of all the races . . . under the British flag'[28] and representing seventy-eight different governments, were Palaces of Industry and Engineering, a replica of a fortress from West Africa's Gold Coast and a copy of the Taj Mahal. Wembley was transformed for the occasion. The public responded enthusiastically to this elaborate hymn to Empire: attendance on Whit Monday, one month after the exhibition opened, exceeded all records – 321,232 visited that day, representing 75,000 more visitors than those who saw the Great Exhibition during the whole of its first week in 1851. There were queues for everything, from the replica of Tutankhamun's tomb, complete with imitation treasure, to the diamond-washing plant from South Africa, for which thousands of tons of diamond-bearing soil were transported to London. In keeping with an exhibition designed to reveal 'the whole of the Empire in little',[29] Clarice Cliff also produced her own miniature: a replica model of A.J. Wilkinson, which was described as the work of 'a talented lady modeller' and caused 'considerable interest' on the company's stand.[30]

That autumn, Clarice Cliff's name appeared in print for the first time. 'We mentioned some little time ago that this firm has a clever lady modeller in Miss Cliff,' the *Pottery Gazette* noted, referring to the earlier report which had praised Clarice Cliff's work without naming her, 'and at the hands of this lady there has just been produced an . . . attractive novelty in the form of a puff-box, to be known as "Milady". Instead of a knob, the cover has a graceful figure of an English lady, reminiscent of the Victorian age. This is a production which we think should specially appeal to the trade.'[31] Did Clarice Cliff see this article? Did she tell her mother? She probably had no idea her name was now in print.

While Clarice Cliff's professional life was beginning to take shape, changes were taking place in the Cliff household. In 1924, Sarah's husband, William, died of pleurisy and degenerative heart failure, a cruel death for a man of thirty-one. A combination of circumstances is likely to have weakened him: his colliery work, his war experience, a weak constitution and poor diet. This cannot have been the future Sarah Cliff envisaged on marrying William Craddock three years earlier. She was left with their two-year-old daughter, Nancy, to support.

A mother now and widowed, though scarcely a wife, Sarah returned to Edwards Street where she picked up her gilding brushes, took a job at the Tunstall factory Johnsons, and reacquired the role of eldest daughter. It was a full house – never fuller with young Nancy round their feet – although it would not remain so for long. That year, Harry Cliff, who at twenty-seven was working as a fitter, married a publican's daughter, Annie Hulse, and left to set up a home of his own. Harry later became a publican himself, running Tunstall's Cottage Hotel and then the Pack Horse Hotel at Longport.

Though Clarice Cliff's modelling skills were being praised by the *Pottery Gazette*, she was described as a pottery decorator when she signed up for evening classes at the Burslem School of Art in the autumn of 1924. Perhaps the definition was not her own. Years later, she recalled attending Burslem as a scholarship pupil, although the register indicates that she paid one pound and one shilling to attend classes during the academic year 1924–5. The range of students that year was broad and included a teacher, tube liner, builder, accountant, pottery decorator, hand paintress and wagon repairer, in addition to a mould maker, gilder, lithographic artist and tile draughtsman. Though some students list no occupation within the register, the designation 'none' is rare: the ethos of the school was vocational. One of that year's students was Susan Vera Cooper, aged twenty-one, who was then in her third year of a senior scholarship. Later known as the ceramic designer Susie Cooper, she was currently employed by the manufacturer A.E. Gray and is described in the register as a designer. Although the Burslem School of Art register lists a number of courses taught there – Design, Etching, Embroidery, General Art, Hand Painting, Elementary, Life and Teaching, among them – the course notation is frequently left blank – and was in the case of Clarice Cliff.[32] Established workers within the industry frequently continued with their studies after their initial training. Clarice Cliff was probably fine-tuning a variety of skills now that she was working on prestige ware.

While Clarice Cliff was studying at the Burslem School of Art, the Exposition Internationale des Arts Décoratifs et Industriels Modernes was staged in Paris. Between the end of April and the end of October 1925, this 'Cubist dream city'[33] brought together the latest architecture, ceramics, fashion, furnishings, metal work, textiles and jewellery. 'The note of the Exposition is set from the moment one enters the wrought-iron gateway of the Porte d'Honneur,' a commentator observed. 'From this point of vantage the Exposition can be seen at a glance, its Cubist shapes and Futurist colours stretching away from the Alexander Bridge to the Great Dôme of Les Invalides, looking like nothing so much as a Picasso abstraction.'[34] The Exposition marked 'the coming of age of a new décor'[35] and affirmed the existence of a modern style, cognisant of the extraordinary innovations that had been taking place in the visual arts since before the First World War. Effusive ornamentation gave way to the dynamism of the straight line.

With the exception of Germany, most European countries participated in the Exposition, although the only country whose designers were comprehensively represented was France. The British presence was muted, with only a small number of pottery manufacturers taking part; A.J. Wilkinson is not among those listed in the official report.[36] For many British manufacturers, the Exposition was seen as a decorative rather than a business proposition and France was not regarded as a significant export market. The absence of America was also a consideration for those with strong transatlantic links, and probably influenced A.J. Wilkinson's decision. With the British Empire Exhibition opening for a further season that summer, and the Shorters exhibiting at Philadelphia the following year, they may have felt they already had sufficient demands upon their time.

Few plaudits were offered the pottery manufacturers who did show their work. In his official report on behalf of the British delegation, Hubert Llewellyn Smith commented that many observers, 'while impressed by the excellence of [British] craftsmanship and finish, were also struck by their comparative dullness and aloofness, and the absence of the spirit of adventure'.[37] Pottery manufacturers had been slow to respond to the transformations taking place in the visual arts, preferring reproductions of the old to the development of the new. Defending this tendency some years earlier, the *Pottery Gazette* asked 'whether good reproduction is not better than bad originality; an argument which gains in force from a contemplation of the eccentricities of the Art Nouveau, the Cubists and the Futurists'.[38]

Gordon Forsyth

Some within the Potteries were keen to overcome such resistance. Chief among them was Gordon Forsyth, superintendent of art instruction since 1920, based at the Burslem School of Art, and art adviser to the British Pottery Manufacturers' Foundation. A former pupil of W.R. Lethaby, a key figure in the Design and Industries Association, and a member of the DIA himself, Forsyth was determined to instil the 'spirit of adventure'[39] into pottery design. 'It was only by art that the pottery industry would gain fresh ground and find new fields to conquer,' he reassured the National Pottery Council.[40] His audience was less easily convinced. The designs the public favoured, one manufacturer insisted, were 'borders with naturalistic rose sprays tastily displayed [and] scattered flowers connected by choice bits of ornament',[41] while another asserted the impossibility of satisfying Forsyth's demand. 'No man can appreciate and produce things of beauty whose colour sense is outraged every day by the grime and soot that cover everything . . . and which offend the eye at every turn.'[42] In the Potteries, at least, the art renaissance had some way to go.

Just as art and architecture were rejecting ornament in favour of straight lines, similar developments were taking place in fashion. The tubular frocks and flattened breasts that now became the vogue and gave women much more freedom spoke to the energetic spirit of the age and to the need to represent the modern. Reports from the Paris fashion shows in the autumn of 1925 paid homage to this mood and to the new ways in which art and fashion were merging. A fabric design of colourful diagonals and geometrics was 'like a modern painting in tissue',[43] while a 'slip of a gown' was stitched with 'Cubist embroidery'.[44] '*Si la peinture est entrée dans la vie, c'est que les femmes la portaient sur elles!*' Sonia Delaunay explained. ('If painting has become part of our lives, it is because women have been wearing it!')[45] She made no distinction between her paintings and her fabric designs. The boundaries between art and daily life were slipping. 'In small things as well as great,' *The Studio Yearbook* observed, 'mankind is beginning to feel the need of the service of art in the common life.'[46]

Colour overflowed into interiors. 'How like Jennifer was her room!' Rosamond Lehmann wrote in her novel *Dusty Answer*. 'Yellow painted chairs, a red and blue rug on the hearth, cowslips in coloured bowls and jars, one branch of white lilac in a tall blue vase . . . a silken Italian shawl, embroidered with great rose and blue and yellow flowers flung over the screen: wherever you looked colour leapt up at you.'[47] For those unable to adopt the latest trends in such a wholesale manner, *Homes and Gardens* advised the use of black paint to disguise the ornate tiles of Victorian fireplaces.[48] The past was to be erased or rejected.

The 'naturalistic rose sprays' of which pottery manufacturers were so fond could not hope to speak to this changing mood. The sense of fracture that followed in the wake of the First World War offered a challenge to ceramic design as surely as it challenged other forms of expression. 'The war seems to have marked the end of a definite period in art, and we now appear to be at the beginning of the development of a new style,' Gordon Forsyth told a meeting of the Ceramic Society in December 1925. 'The universality of this striving for new artistic expression leads one to believe that it has the quality of permanency; it is something much bigger than a mere change of fashion.'[49]

The Burslem School of Art had its part to play in these developments. Forsyth was an early advocate of freehand painting: the future of ceramic decoration lay in this direction, he believed. Some forward-thinking manufacturers agreed. The freshness and simplicity of freehand brushstrokes, and the expression of individuality they allowed, appealed to those within the industry who wanted to shake off uniformity and restore craft and invention to pottery manufacture. 'If we got a girl to paint a pattern,' A.E. Gray explained, 'she would not do so many pieces, but each piece would be a treasure.'[50]

By the time Clarice Cliff attended the Burslem School of Art, Forsyth was well established and was stamping his personality upon the district. His was the vision that shaped the relationship between design and the pottery industry between the two world wars.[51] '[A] compelling influence upon the artistic life of the Potteries',[52] Forsyth worked to forge closer links between the art schools, local industry and the community, and was a mentor to many, writing letters of introduction on behalf of promising pupils and directing them to the manufacturers he felt would make best use of their talents. Within an industry that produced characters as colourful as its tableware, it was a measure of his success that Forsyth's 'dominating person-ality' was sometimes resented, but those he supported spoke of him with enormous respect. When Clarice Cliff studied at Burslem, she was already established as a modeller, and so less in need of formal encouragement. Though Forsyth later spoke of her achievements, his response to her work as a student is not recorded.

The Burslem School of Art fostered ambition. 'For two years I worked as a gilder . . . But I was restless,' tube liner Rose Cumberbatch explained. 'I had started at Burslem School of Art and wanted something better.'[53] By day, the school was a quiet place; at night it crackled with anticipation: the release from the punching of the factory clock into the watercolour hush of the painting room upstairs.

SIX

A Strange New Creature Called Woman

'[I]f a future chronicler were to study the files of our newspapers,' the novelist Rose Macaulay wrote in 1925, 'he would get the impression that there had appeared at this time a strange new creature called woman.'[1] Clarice Cliff may have felt she fitted this description. These were extremely productive years and considerably varied in their productivity. By day she modelled and decorated fine ware; at night she perfected her skills at art school. It was as if the 1920s were the years in which Clarice Cliff became herself.

By 1925, she had modelled further traditional figures, among them the elegant 'Girl Figure Early Victorian'.[2] Other ceramic models produced during this period were less formal in concept: a honeypot shaped like a beehive, with a striped bee in place of a handle buzzing at its lid; chunky cottage-scene book ends and squat Arab figures are among them. While the models Clarice Cliff showed at the British Empire Exhibition responded to existing A.J. Wilkinson productions, these more quirky figures suggest she was already being allowed to develop her own style. Although she was capable of producing fine traditional ware, as the 'Early Victorian' figure demonstrates, she was nevertheless drawn to more idiosyncratic pieces, sometimes with a humorous slant, which were themselves a departure from tradition.

Touring the A.J. Wilkinson showroom in March 1925, a reporter from the *Pottery and Glass Record* congratulated the firm on a group of figures 'cleverly conceived and skilfully modelled . . . They doubtless feel proud of having in their employ the staff capable of making such really good-quality articles.' Although Clarice Cliff was not alone in modelling for the company during this period, a model of hers was singled out for attention: 'A classic has been success-fully produced in a figure fancy . . . the Greek Girl candelabra . . . The poise of the figure, the features and expression, the hang of the drapery, coupled with the pleasing point of view one gets at any angle of the object, makes us feel disposed to describe it as the pièce de résistance of the group.'[3] This continuing praise from a respected commercial source no doubt focused Colley Shorter's thoughts on how to develop further the skills of his 'talented lady modeller'.[4]

Colley Shorter thought it vital that manufacturers, especially the commercial principal of the firm, spend time with their designers: half an hour each day was his ideal. The experience of someone understanding and valuing her work was enormously flattering for Clarice Cliff. Shorter was perhaps the first person to ask her opinion and listen to her ideas. She recalled being 'eventually' allowed to experiment around 1924–5,[5] which suggests she had been longing for the chance to do so. Around this time, she was given her own studio in the Newport Pottery, a factory on an adjacent site to A.J. Wilkinson, which the Shorters had purchased in 1920 as part of the company's expansion.

The novelty of her role drew attention to Clarice Cliff, particu-larly as she was so much younger than the firm's established designers. Her youth and vitality ensured that, even as a relatively inexperienced designer, she fast became a presence in the factory. In a world that was visibly changing and at such speed, and with women at the forefront of many of those changes, Shorter clearly welcomed her perspective. He was more than seventeen years her senior. In commercial terms, Clarice Cliff represented the future.

If you could work with Colley Shorter, you could work with anyone, it was said. He was a tireless worker, but an edgy, difficult man. Paintresses were in awe of him; only two of his employees dared to answer back. He was used to getting his own way, not only within the factory, but beyond its walls as well. Shorter's answer, when crossed, on more than one occasion, was swift and simple: 'Go to hell.' Those who recollect Colley's brother, Guy, speak immediately of his charm, his kindness, his consideration – their words pointing up the contrast between his behaviour and that of his older brother. It was easier to get Colley to agree to something after he had lunched at the Leopard. Frequently, he argued with Guy and his other siblings; there were constant battles about the way the factory should be run. In descriptions such as these, Colley Shorter comes across as an archetypal factory owner, a character out of Arnold Bennett or Charles Dickens, whose underlings doffed their caps and were frightened of his commands. And so they were, but this was only one side of his personality. An employee who grew close to him in later years speaks of him with real and lasting affection, and confirms the sentimentality of this otherwise irascible man. Shorter was devoted to his factory and a salesman through and through; if you shared his ideals and his love of manufacturing, you joined a small, exclusive club; his respect and good opinion were worth having.

Photographs of Shorter's childhood tell a very different story from that of Clarice Cliff. Here are small boys riding dog carts; family groups at Christmas – compositions of velvet, fur, brocade. A formal portrait, the kind of which the Victorians were so fond, shows Colley as a young boy with his dog, pictured with a group of family and friends, among them Harold Hales, who described himself as Arnold Bennett's source for *The Card*.[6] In a later photograph, taken during a holiday in Ullswater, Colley poses with his brother Guy, two sisters and their friends: Tissot-like young ladies, all frills and lace and flowers, gaze patiently at Arthur Shorter's lens. Other pictures capture tennis parties at the family home, Colley dressed in flannels and a blazer, the well-heeled young Victorian at ease.

Born in Stoke-upon-Trent in 1882, Colley held the privileged position of first son, with three older sisters, Lucy, Mabel and Nora, to cosset him. Guy was the younger of the brothers by two years, though not the youngest of the family; that position was reserved for their sister Jessie. Life for Colley Shorter was not all tennis parties, however. He was sixteen when he left the High School, Newcastle-under-Lyme, to join his father's company as a salesman and within a few years

Nora, Mabel and Colley Shorter (far right), with
their parents, Henrietta and Arthur Shorter,
Christmas Day, 1901

was travelling far afield – South America, Canada, Australia and
South Africa were among the markets eventually won – in his quest
to expand the business of the Royal Staffordshire Pottery. At twenty,
Shorter vowed he would personally visit and know every customer
on his books, a not inconsiderable ambition, and one which, by the
time of his retirement, he had more or less achieved. 'There is still
a lot of sentiment in Business,' he said.[7] Shorter's letters home convey
a young man's determination to succeed and please his father; they
also reveal the isolation of a salesman's life at a time when journeys

Tennis at the Shorter family home; Colley Shorter is seated, right

took several weeks by ship and train. 'I have just been sitting out on one of these plazas feeling very lonely,' he wrote to his sister Jessie from Buenos Aires, during Easter 1910, thanking her for letters posted shortly after he left Staffordshire five weeks earlier. 'I was just starving for some news . . . What I wanted was just a sight of some handwriting I recognised and had some interest in.'[8]

These were toughening years for Colley Shorter, a young man early thrown on to his own resources, carrying family expectations thousands of miles. His father had established the business; as oldest son, it was his responsibility to extend it. He made a point of attending church on Sunday mornings when far away from home and described his pleasure at an organ recital heard there. Though business was his 'first thought in the morning and last at night', his dreams took him elsewhere: 'If I dream of England, so much the better.'[9]

In 1911, at the age of twenty-nine, Colley Shorter married Annie Rogers, with whom he had two daughters: Margaret, born in 1912, and Joan, born in 1920. Having a young family did not diminish Shorter's professional commitments; if anything, they intensified: the

year of his youngest daughter's birth coincided with the acquisition
of the Newport Pottery. In less than two years, Shorter was in New
York. 'By this time next year I think the results of my wandering
will have satisfied everybody,' he told his mother in January 1922,[10]
having evidently spent Christmas overseas. Though he described
orders secured in Chicago and dinners with business associates, he
also revealed his longing to be home. 'It seems an awful time since
I saw my girl and babies,' he confided,[11] a remark with an especial
poignancy, considering developments to come.

A photograph from 1926, or thereabouts, offers a glimpse of
Shorter family life. Arthur Shorter and his wife Henrietta, some of
their children, their spouses and offspring plus other family
members, are ranged across the porch of 'Chetwynd', the house
where Colley Shorter lived with his young family. Arthur Shorter
– no longer the photographer, but one of the photographed – and
his wife were visiting Staffordshire from Llandudno, where they
had settled on retirement. Colley purchased 'Chetwynd' in 1926;
perhaps this photograph records his family visiting his new home
for the first time. Though an informal grouping, it nevertheless
marks an occasion of some sort. If only the subjects of the
photograph could speak: gentle, charming Guy Shorter, frequently
railroaded by his older, tougher brother; their brother-in-law, Jack
Walker, whose relationship with Colley was soon to sour. Most of
all, Annie Shorter, Colley's wife, whose face is turned away from
the camera, just as she turns away from this narrative. Perhaps this
was the last time the Shorters posed together in this way: 1926 was
the year of Arthur Shorter's death. Perhaps this would, in any case,
have been the last portrait of its kind: Clarice Cliff was about to
enter the picture.

With her own 'studio-cum-workshop'[12] in a showroom at the edge
of the Newport site, where she was later joined by a young paintress,
Gladys Scarlett, Clarice Cliff was able to spend more time exploring
her own work. Opportunities for developing and refining new ideas
were likely to have been slim during 1926, however. The General
Strike and prolonged coal strike thereafter did little to encourage
thoughts of innovation. The coal strike, in particular, had a debili-

tating effect on the Potteries: by July of that year, its impact was described as 'disastrous',[13] with few potbanks working at all. At least 25,000 pottery operatives were inactive; the autumn was well advanced before normal factory production resumed.

The purchase of the Newport Pottery had included an extensive stock of whiteware. This had 'always interested' Clarice Cliff and now presented her with 'a challenge'.[14] Much of the whiteware was substandard, with tiny accretions spoiling the clean line of a handle or the belly of a vase. She needed to produce patterns that would disguise these imperfections and countermand the Newport shapes, which were mostly Art Nouveau and so belonged to the past there was such a strong desire to erase.

As a relatively new designer, Clarice Cliff needed to tread carefully. These were years of autocratic management, after all, and Shorter a supreme autocrat. Having gained her employer's support, she must have been at pains to maintain it. That she was able to propose new ideas suggests their professional relationship was already on a relatively comfortable footing. There was much to attract Colley Shorter in any experiment that made use of damaged ware. If the idea worked, the venture would be deemed a success; if not, there would be few losses, a prospect likely to appeal with costs a particular consideration in the aftermath of the coal strike.

At some point during this period, at Colley Shorter's request, Clarice Cliff modelled a bust of his father.[15] Perhaps Arthur Shorter sat for her on one of his occasional visits to the factory shortly before his death. Whether the bust was created from life or a photograph, its modelling called for further conversations between this ambitious young designer and her employer. 'It became evident [to Shorter] that here was a girl of rare talents, brimful of ideas, whose progress could not be kept in check, but could profitably be guided in the right channels.'[16] He now directed Clarice Cliff to the Royal College of Art.

SEVEN

A New World at Every Turn

'It was my first big opportunity,' Clarice Cliff told an interviewer in 1931. 'It *was* rather unusual,' she supposed, for an employer to allow time off for study in that way.[1] The decision may have been unusual within Stoke-on-Trent, but Clarice Cliff is likely to have attended one of the short courses specifically designed for those who worked in industry which were established at the Royal College of Art during the early 1920s. A preliminary report of the Industrial Art Committee of the Federation of British Industries in 1921 concluded: 'It would be of great value to manufacturers if arrangements could be made for their designers to take short refresher courses.'[2] The first 'refresher' students – two textile designers and a designer from a bedstead factory – attended the Royal College during that academic year, each paying a fee of ten guineas.[3] When everyone involved with the experiment declared themselves satisfied, the future of similar courses was secure.

Courses were designed to run for not less than one month in a college term, with employers paying the salaries of employees during their studies. Colley Shorter is said to have made the arrangements for Clarice Cliff to attend the Royal College; A.J. Wilkinson was required to pay her college fees, which now stood at twelve guineas per term. Unless exempt by the principal, applicants were required to submit drawings and sit an examination based upon the work submitted. In contemporary press reports, the story of Clarice Cliff's admission merges with that of her earlier 'discovery': '[O]ne day a designer passing by noticed that she had drawn a butterfly on the white paper covering the workbench. He was so impressed that he called attention to it, with the result that Miss Cliff was asked to model a bunch of violets for submission to the Royal College of Art. Having no tools of her own, she modelled the clay with a penknife and was admitted to the College without hesitation.'[4]

Records in the registry of the Royal College of Art show that Clarice Cliff attended from 14 March to 12 April 1927, and again from 27 April to 26 May, the intervening period corresponding with the college Easter holidays. She is noted as having 'left and rejoined',[5] which suggests she registered for one month and extended her studies thereafter. On arrival at the college, she gave her date of birth as 1900,[6] an alteration of one year which cannot have changed anyone's perception of her, but suggests a preference of her own: perhaps she had a fancy for being the same age as the year, part of the twentieth century, not the nineteenth.

The short-course programme consisted 'largely of Museum Study' at the Victoria and Albert Museum, with 'subsidiary instruction and workshop practice' offered in accordance with students' individual needs.[7] Clarice Cliff enrolled in the School of Sculpture, where she studied 'modelling the head and figure from live models, figure composition and life-drawing' under Professor Gilbert Ledward,[8] head of the sculpture school from 1926 to 1929. His assistant at the time was Henry Moore, himself a former student of the college, who was already making his name as a sculptor. The Victorian huts on Queen's Gate, where the sculpture school was housed, were somewhat shabby in appearance, having originally been built for casualties of the Crimean War, but they can have been as nothing compared to the grimy corners of a potbank; if anything, their tired paintwork would have made Clarice feel at home. Here she learned to adapt her provincial training to the rigours of the Royal College – not without some difficulty, it seems, for Ledward reported that, although she had 'a natural facility as a modeller', she was 'inclined to give a superficial finish to her work owing to her lack of knowledge of the construction of the human figure'.[9]

Life classes were held in the Painting School which occupied the studios behind the V&A. On his arrival at the school a year earlier, the painter John Piper was disappointed to discover that life-drawing could be 'made so boring'.[10] The sculptor Edna Ginesi, who, with Barbara Hepworth, Moore and Raymond Coxon, formed the Leeds Group at the Royal College during the early 1920s, offered a different perspective: 'We all worked like stink. We really did. We never wasted any time or played about ... The Life Room was a sacred sort of place and you talked in a lower voice once you got inside the doors ... if you talked at all.'[11] Though some of Clarice Cliff's fellow students were, perhaps, larger than life and too enamoured of themselves for someone schooled on factory hours to take seriously, most, like herself, were driven by their work and what it meant to them. To be in such an environment, to be free to study purposefully from morning until evening, was a new and valuable experience for Clarice. For the first time in her life, she was working alongside those for whom work was a vocation and not merely a means to earn a wage.

However, under Ledward's professorship (and that of his predecessor and immediate successor), the School of Sculpture eschewed the avant-garde. Not for them experiments with the modern. Modelling, enlarging and academic sculpture were prioritised, a nineteenth-century emphasis fitting students for the design of the public monuments that proliferated after the First World War. Ledward's own war memorial, designed in association with H. Charlton Bradshaw, had been unveiled on Horse Guard's Parade the year before. Earlier students of the sculpture school – Moore and Hepworth among them – had looked to museums to supplement the conservative curriculum. Museums provided fertile ground for industrial designers too, as the textile designer Marion Dorn told *The Studio*: 'You can learn much more in the museums than in any art school.'[12]

Clarice Cliff later described museums as 'sources of inspiration' for her own work,[13] and with museum study an essential part of the short-course curriculum, there was much to inform her in London. Most significant was the exhibition 'Modern French and Russian Designs for Costume and Scenery', which took place at the V&A between March and June 1927.[14] Nothing could better embody the spirit of adventure than the demonstrative colours of the Ballets

Russes, whose 'every new effect evoked a chorus of exclamations'.[15] Its influence had been everywhere apparent in the clothes and furnishings seen in Paris before the First World War; elements of London had been similarly wooed. 'Before one could say Nijinsky, the pale pastel shades which had reigned supreme on the walls of Mayfair for almost two decades were replaced by a riot of barbaric hues – jade green, purple, every variety of crimson and scarlet, and, above all, orange.'[16] To see a selection of these designs was to appreciate the possibilities of colour.

The exhibition comprised theatrical prints and drawings, mostly from the ballet, and included costumes by Léon Bakst for the 1910 production of *Cléopatre*, and for Victor Barthe's *Le Triomphe de Cubisme*, including his *Costume Picasso*; designs by Georges Braque; Natalia Gonchorova's stage set for Act One of *Le Coq d'Or*, together with some of her costume designs, and Picasso's backcloth and costumes for *Le Tricorne*, whose reproduction by pochoir* print must have lent a particular clarity to their vivid stripes. Recalling the first production of *Le Coq d'Or* in June 1914, C.W. Beaumont described it as 'the sensation of the season'[17] and Natalia Gonchorova's stage set as 'startling in the fantasy and assumed artlessness of its conception, design and colouring . . . Behind the singers rose a fantastic background of pointed towers, enormous houses and giant trees with enormous blossoms, an arrangement of simple bright tones of yellow, brown, rose, white and green, which, while crude, when considered in detail, collectively produced a richly decorative effect.'[18] This might almost be a description of one of Clarice Cliff's later designs. Also featured was Vladimir Polunin's drop curtain for *George and the Dragon*, a colourful print whose jewel-like intensity glows on the page. Rich colour and simple, stylised forms: these were valuable lessons for a young designer drinking in the spirit of the age.

There were other exhibitions and galleries for Clarice Cliff to explore: the V&A's pre-Renaissance collection; the Greek, Egyptian, Assyrian, African and Pacific art in the British Museum, whose corridors were empty of the public much of the time. The painter Nina Hamnett was repeatedly drawn to the museum's Greek vases; 'primitive art' was a source of inspiration to Henry Moore. In later life,

Clarice Cliff owned some Mexican pieces;[19] perhaps her interest stemmed from this period. By 1927, the Modern Foreign Gallery at the Tate had been open for a year, and featured work by Bonnard, Braque and Cézanne as part of its permanent collection. During his own provincial education, Henry Moore's secondary-school teacher had shown the class pictures of paintings by European artists[20] and, by the time he ventured to London and the Royal College of Art, he was also aware of Brancusi, Gaudier-Brzeska, Modigliani and Epstein. Moore was doubly lucky: Professor Sir Michael Sadler, vice-chancellor of Leeds University – the man who Roger Fry said had 'civilised a whole population'[21] – was his mentor during his studies at Leeds. How much Clarice Cliff knew of contemporary art before 1927 is impossible to know, but the likelihood is it was little. 'The kaleidoscopic exhibitions of modern art in London and Paris' had a 'comparatively small effect' on North Staffordshire.[22]

The smaller London galleries were also worth discovering: the Leicester Galleries, where Frank Dobson was showing his sculpture *Tallulah Bankhead*; the Lefèvre in St James's (which showed work by Modigliani in 1929 and Barbara Hepworth during the 1930s), while the design-conscious furnishing store Waring & Gillow – which would soon display and sell Clarice Cliff's own work – was hosting a home-making exhibition, a must for any ceramic designer. A young woman's work was receiving critical acclaim that spring. Dod Proctor's sculptural painting *Morning*, described as 'perhaps the most significant picture of the year',[23] was making waves at the Royal Academy. Its reception – 'by fairly general consent, considered to be the finest work in the RA'; 'in some ways the outstanding picture of the year'[24] – was such that Clarice Cliff surely attempted to view it; her later connection with Dod Proctor's work perhaps dated from this event. 'It is rather exciting to see that one of the best pictures in the Academy this year is by a woman,' the *Illustrated London News* reported, 'and a youngish woman at that, with her career before her.' Clarice Cliff would have liked the sound of those words.

While studying in London, Clarice Cliff stayed at a hostel run by the Young Women's Christian Association (YWCA).[25] Her parents must have been relieved to know she was in safe hands: a hospital visit was one thing; two months in the capital city quite another.

When Ethel Cliff travelled to London with her sister some years later, she recalled their parents being 'very particular'[26] about where they stayed; and a Staffordshire designer who came after Clarice Cliff, Mabel Leigh, was prevented by her father from studying in London at all.[27] Moral peril aside, there was a further, and equally pressing, consideration: 'How *can* you send your daughter to college?' an acquaintance enquired of Vera Brittain's mother. 'Don't you want her *ever* to get married?'[28]

The YWCA ran a number of hostels on a not-for-profit basis, designed to provide 'suitable' accommodation at affordable prices for girls and women up to the age of thirty, of the kind later immortalised by Muriel Spark in *The Girls of Slender Means*. There were nearly 1,000 YWCA beds in London during this period,[29] which suggests that Clarice was probably able to stay at the hostel of her choice. Of the three in Kensington, the one nearest the Royal College was Princess House in Brompton Square.

Applications for all hostels were made directly to individual wardens and references were required, most likely from a Church connection; the vicar of Christ Church probably wrote on Clarice Cliff's behalf. Princess House held beds for twenty-six women, a mixture of 'business girls' and clerks, whose stay might be anything from a matter of days or weeks up to three years, the hostels catering for the growing number of women who took up clerical and administrative work between the wars. Two kinds of accommodation were available: cubicles in small dormitories, which ranged in price from twenty-two shillings a week to twenty-six shillings and sixpence, or individual rooms, which were themselves small – YWCA hostels were converted family homes, not purpose-built – and cost between thirty-one and thirty-five shillings. These prices included morning and evening meals, plus full board on Sundays. (Saturdays, it was assumed, were taken up with work.) Rules and regulations varied with each hostel and depended, to an extent, on the temperament of the warden. At Princess House, keys could be obtained at the warden's discretion, although advance notice was required if residents wished to return late. Some hostels set aside quiet rooms for prayer; some, though not all, had sitting-rooms where visitors could be entertained within reasonable hours. Opportunities for

socialising arose through choir and drama groups, church and prayer
meetings, and hostels were the occasional recipients of free or
reduced-price tickets for concerts and exhibitions.

Moral welfare was important to the YWCA. Noticeboards over-
lapping with suggestions and advice were testaments to community
spirit and communal living; meals were taken at trestle tables astride
long wooden benches; curtains separated each bed, chest of drawers
and mirror from the beds, drawers and mirrors in adjoining cubicles; queues formed for the washroom down the hall. At the age of
twenty-eight, Clarice Cliff was one of the hostel's oldest residents;
she was further separated by her years of factory work. With so
much to absorb her, she was unlikely to have sought companionship within the hostel itself, but instead found excuses for solitude.
Why make conversation, when she could be upstairs alone, enjoying
a hot bath in a bathroom with a door that she could lock, instead
of crouching in a tin tub by the fire, or reading one of the books
she borrowed from the college library, jotting down ideas? The
experience of London was more than sufficient; simply being there
was enough.

The journey itself was a revelation, Stoke-on-Trent diminishing
with every inch of track, and Clarice Cliff's anticipation growing by
the mile. Yet anticipation counted for little when set against the
actual experience of the city. Henry Moore described his early forays
into London as 'a dream of excitement. When I rode on the open
top of a bus, I felt that I was travelling in Heaven almost.'[30] Each
day was a new discovery: 'a new world at every turn'.[31] 'Life is
marvellously free,' Barbara Hepworth wrote, shortly after her own
arrival.[32] Clarice Cliff surely shared their enthusiasm and sense of
release. Wartime and sick-visiting had shaped her first responses to
London. Now she was no longer a visitor in her teens, but a woman
poised on the verge of new discoveries, alone in the capital for the
first time.

Each street was an adventure. 'It was not beauty pure and simple
– Bedford Place leading into Russell Square. It was straightness and
emptiness of course; the symmetry of a corridor; but it was also
windows lit up, a piano, a gramophone sounding; a sense of pleasure-
making hidden, but now and again emerging when, through the

uncurtained window, the window left open, one saw parties sitting over tables, young people slowly circling, conversations between men and women, maids idly looking out . . . stockings drying on top ledges, a parrot, a few plants. Absorbing, mysterious, of infinite richness, this life.'[33]

Everything about the experience was different. There was no factory whistle six mornings a week, but the civilised hours of college life to follow: nine-thirty am to three-thirty pm, with an hour for lunch, and from four pm to six pm thereafter. Wednesday afternoons were free. How strange to finish classes at lunchtime, with a whole afternoon to spare before she was expected back for tea which, Clarice now discovered, was called 'supper'. Saturdays were her own,[34] and there was much to fill them: a bus ride to Trafalgar Square, 'one of the sights that no visitor to London can miss',[35] along with Buckingham Palace, Westminster Abbey, the Changing of the Guard and other tourist markers to be visited. She could take a bus with no idea of where the ride would lead her – a journey to St Paul's and into the City, past the Royal Exchange, or out to Crystal Palace, with its prehistoric monsters grouped about the lake. There was the Underground system to negotiate and fathom – the station at Piccadilly Circus was under construction that spring – and when Clarice tired of sightseeing, there were cheap seats at a cinema, or the 'music, inexpensive food and a taste of luxury'[36] provided by a Lyons Corner House.

'Every person and every scene tells me something,'[37] Clarice Cliff later said, having early acquired the habits of an observer, and London offered a great deal to observe. Its distinctive rhythm was nothing like the surge towards the factory gates, with its crowd of similar faces, intent on similar lives. This regiment of footsteps marched to a different tune. Ladies in fox furs and gloves rubbed shoulders with shop girls wearing neither, and men in pinstripe suits. Signs of individuality emerged among the shingled heads and office uniforms: a hat tilted just so, an outfit designed to say, 'Look at me, I'm different.' Such glimpses of bravado were Clarice Cliff's to enjoy. Among these unknown faces, where no one gave her half a glance or questioned her ideas, she could be at ease, part of the larger rhythm that embraced the city streets. 'I did what I expect

Clarice Cliff, 1930

all other young people who are interested in their trade or profession do,' she said of her time there. 'I utilised every opportunity to study the products of other people who were more advanced in their work than I was.'[38]

While in London, Clarice Cliff went 'shop-gazing'.[39] The fashion pages of the *London Illustrated News* that spring described 'knitted suits . . . in every colour of the rainbow'.[40] Colour was no longer the preserve of the exclusive or the bold, but was beginning to make an appearance in the more fashionable department stores. No doubt Clarice Cliff was drawn to them, seduced by shop windows unlike any she had seen, and by carpeted interiors, the likes of which would never come to Staffordshire. Millinery departments displayed the latest hats – serrated brims of green felt leaves, or feather trims descending to the jaw line – together with the very latest handbags: pochettes in crocodile, lizard, snake, whose tight chrome clasps snapped shut on careless fingers.

As soon as she could afford them, Clarice Cliff bought smart clothes; the Cliff sisters were said to dress well, anyway, thanks to Dorothy's dressmaking skills. In London, Clarice could discover fashions her sister could adapt with cheaper cuts of fabric than the crêpe de chine and printed chiffons which drew the eye to the rapidly advancing 'vogue for colour'.[41] A photograph taken some years later shows her wearing a Liberty scarf. Liberty had 'a multitude' of scarves on show that spring, whose 'gay colourings and designs [were] the epitome of youth and sunshine'.[42] This may have been when Clarice Cliff first saw those strips of crêpe, and the Spanish and Oriental shawls she wore on dress occasions, whose embroidery made bright statements in luminous silks. Even a shopping expedition was an invitation to gaze upon the modern.

That this was a time of new discoveries all round was underlined almost daily. Newspaper headlines announced further Egyptian excavations and celebrated Charles Lindbergh's solo Atlantic flight. The year 1927 had a particular piquancy for young women. By now, the agitation for universal female suffrage was reaching a crescendo. The so-called flapper vote would be granted the following year and, during 1927, was endlessly debated, as Clarice Cliff could not fail to be aware. Even breakfast cereals asserted female independence:

'Molly is a real Miss 1927,' an advertisement for Grape Nuts declared. 'She's . . . a bachelor-girl who depends entirely on herself for her "keep".[43]

Clarice Cliff's stay in London may have been brief, but the timing of her trip was crucial: by 1927, the city was asserting modernity. While her formal studies confirmed the importance of ambition and dedication in ways essential to her self-esteem, the broader experience of London also offered a vital education. As she grew in confidence, she may have approached the Potteries-born designer, Reco Capey, then an assistant at the Royal College School of Design. His advice would have appealed to her: 'Never be afraid to experiment.'[44]

That Clarice Cliff made real progress at the Royal College of Art is evident from the letter Gilbert Ledward wrote to Colley Shorter on 26 May 1927, the last day of her studies. 'There is little doubt she has native ability. I consider that the figure she has just modelled shows a surprising advance on her work of two months ago, and if financial circumstances had not to be taken into account, but only the development of her talent considered, I should say, go on studying for two or three years.'[45] There was no question of Clarice becoming a full-time student – her skills were required, and paid for, by A.J. Wilkinson – but if she made such surprising advances in modelling, she is likely to have made considerable gains in other areas too. For someone with her keen eye and intense thirst for knowledge, London offered a kaleidoscope of the new.

Clarice Cliff may not have left London immediately. A newspaper article from 1935 reported that, following her studies at the Royal College, she spent two or three months at the Central School of Art.[46] This was generosity indeed on the part of A.J. Wilkinson, which must have paid her college fees again; Shorter evidently felt she was gaining valuable experience. Even so, an absence from the factory totalling some five months – if her studies were consecutive – seems a considerable indulgence on the part of an employer with a reputation for being 'cute' about time and money, whatever his investment in his employee. Perhaps the length of time was exaggerated. Having studied at the Royal College until the end of May, Clarice may have transferred to the Central School for the last weeks of the summer term; alternatively, she may have attended later. All timing is conjecture: beyond the article written in 1935, and a further reference in 1949, nothing is known of her Central School studies. At the time, however, the school's artistic standard was judged 'perhaps higher than in any other English school'.[47] Clarice Cliff was aware of this: she sought the Central School because it was considered the most advanced.

Though students enrolled for both day and evening classes, evening students comprised by far the greater number and, during this period, men exceeded women by more than a third.[48] The classes in life-drawing, modelling and composition which, together with stone and ivory carving and pottery, formed part of the curriculum of the School of Painted and Sculptured Architectural Decoration would have offered Clarice Cliff the chance to develop her skills still further; she may have chosen classes from several disciplines. If she was allowed the flexibility to continue with her studies, she probably had the freedom to choose her subjects. Whatever she studied, the experience was likely to have been beneficial. In spirit, the Central School of Art was 'very much alive'.[49]

Buoyed up by the revelations of the city, Clarice Cliff was discovering a new world and, with it, a new willingness to dare. Not all the risks she took would be professional. A.J. Wilkinson had a London showroom to which Colley Shorter was a frequent visitor. His continuing fascination with his young designer's progress makes it likely that the two of them met. And Clarice Cliff herself was shining with new faith in her abilities; the one person she could share that with was Colley Shorter. The factory was their common ground; their mutual ambition tinder. Already, their relationship was changing.

London was a starting point for something, surely. Here, they could meet on neutral territory, with the differences between them less apparent. Shorter was no longer the factory owner, but a relaxed and engaging individual, who might confess his weakness for Chinese porcelain, ask Clarice's opinion of the V&A, and make her feel, once again, that he was someone she could talk to. The details of the personal relationship that developed between Clarice Cliff and

Colley Shorter were known only to themselves; its clandestine nature demanded silence, or an attempt, at least, to disguise the truth. But London offered discretion as well as adventure, new ground as well as distance, and what happened there seemed subject to a different set of rules and judgments. How Colley explained his personal circumstances can only be guessed, as can Clarice's decision to embark on a relationship which would cast her as 'the other woman' for years to come. His decision was the easier of the two; a man in Shorter's position had little to lose. For Clarice Cliff, the situation was more complicated.

For some, it seems straightforward: she was a gold-digger. 'Money'll do 'owt' is a phrase in Stoke-on-Trent. She knew what she wanted; she set her cap at him – these and other pejorative phrases applied to ambitious women are sometimes said of her. A personal relationship with Colley Shorter would undoubtedly bring immense benefits, but for Clarice Cliff it was also fraught with risks. She was already making her own way, and succeeding remarkably well on her own terms. Though Shorter had the power to advance her position, he also had the means to destroy it. Why risk all that she was achieving when talent alone was taking her there?

Power and influence are glib but inadequate answers, although both undoubtedly had their appeal. More important, surely, was the energy and dedication that fuelled Shorter's power. Just as he recognised in Clarice Cliff a young woman as driven and determined as himself, she responded to those qualities in Colley Shorter. He was described as good-looking – tall and fair-haired, with the looks of a matinee idol, it was said. Shorter was debonair, a man of distinguished appearance, whose enthusiasms rendered him younger than his years. That he was prone to displays of eccentricity – he wore his daughter's hat to work one day and occasionally came to the factory dressed in hunting pink – can only have made him all the more intriguing and wholly unlike anyone Clarice knew. He talked to her, encouraged her, flattered her, no doubt, and was immensely impressed by her resolution and achievements. To have captured the attention of this idiosyncratic man was exhilarating.

EIGHT

Bizarre

London was the catalyst – the culmination of her ideas – for the tableware with which Clarice Cliff made her name. 'It was, I think, during the dark winter days, when I went shop-gazing in London, that I first thought of my new idea,' she told a reporter,[1] adjusting the season for effect. 'I used to take a busman's holiday viewing all the china shops in London,' she informed the *Daily Mirror*. 'I thought how drab the old china was, and how ugly the few examples of modern work were.'[2] 'Why don't we use bright colours? I asked myself.'[3] Her return to the Potteries underlined her determination. 'It struck her forcibly how women, living the ordinary life of the housewife – perhaps in rather drab surroundings – must long for colour in the home – something inexpensive, yet artistic, to brighten their lives.'[4]

Returning to her studio in the Newport Pottery, Clarice Cliff stepped back into a different world: so much had changed for her in such a short time. Seeing her earlier work was like greeting her former self: her designs leaned towards but did not grasp the risks she now felt capable of taking. Yet, seeing them again, perhaps she did not mind their faults, nor even the compositions she now judged to be failures. In describing the past to Clarice Cliff, they pointed to the direction she would take. First, she had to convince Colley Shorter. Accounts of Shorter's response differ from one press report to another. One describes him as wholly positive – 'Let us see your ideas in concrete form'[5] – more often, though, he is said to have expressed reservations: 'The manufacturer showered cold water liberally on her suggestions. Her designs were too original – too out of the ordinary.'[6] Perhaps even Shorter was taken aback by her ideas; alternatively, his initial resistance makes for a better story. Clarice Cliff persisted, she 'knew she was right . . . She continued to bombard the manufacturer until at last he capitulated.'[7] This seems entirely characteristic.

Clarice Cliff's earliest experiments with geometric colour were perhaps those she made at home, where she transformed the bedroom she shared with her sister Ethel into a Cubist dream: 'The walls and woodwork were painted orange and yellow, the ceiling metallic gold, the wardrobes and chest of drawers orange with black relief, and the wrought-iron bedsteads with brass knobs were encased in orange-coloured leatherette.'[8] Their mother was shocked, but 'very nice about it. If we were going to sleep with it, it would do for her.'[9] Clarice was 'the arty one',[10] after all. Ethel thought the room would be 'a nightmare to most people'. Her sister disagreed. Clarice liked the bold effect and described it as 'bizarre'.[11]

Ethel Cliff recalled this transformation taking place when her sister was a teenager, which would date it before or during the First World War, a wonderful possibility, aligning Clarice Cliff with Diaghilev's gales of colour. However, Clarice's niece, Nancy Craddock, recalled pasting gold stars on to her aunt's bedroom ceiling as part of the redecoration, which, given Nancy's likely age at the time, ties the experiment more closely to the creation of 'Bizarre'. Whenever the transformation of Edwards Street took place, its impact was dramatic. Outside, the terraced houses all looked pretty much the same, but within one small back bedroom, the furniture dazzled with blocks of solid colour.

A trade review of A.J. Wilkinson's productions in September 1927 features three ornamental flower holders: a 'Viking' boat, modelled by Clarice Cliff, and two ceramic baskets. One of the baskets, 'Elegant', is decorated in strong horizontal bands of yellow and black. Commenting upon the 'many alternative styles of decoration' A.J. Wilkinson offered in this line of tableware, the *Pottery Gazette* noted, 'All seem to be new in their type and feeling.'[12] These are the work of Clarice Cliff, shortly before 'Bizarre' came to fruition.[13]

Clarice Cliff and Gladys Scarlett were joined in the Newport showroom by a small group of paintresses, aged fourteen and fifteen, who were plucked from a decorating shop run by Clarice's sister Dorothy, who was by then producing underglaze* patterns for A.J. Wilkinson. Her workshop was being wound down because its patterns were not selling. The girls' removal apparently caused some friction between the sisters; if Dorothy spoke to Clarice about her paintresses, she surely had cause to regret it.[14]

Due to the tendency for pottery manufacturers to copy one another's designs, the first 'Bizarre' patterns were developed in an atmosphere of secrecy. Situated at the edge of the A.J. Wilkinson site, with its own complicated warren of workshops, the Newport potbank was 'an enclosed world'.[15] Few within the adjacent factory were aware of the developments taking shape in the distant show-room, behind locked doors. The experimental tableware, once fired, was not deposited in the warehouse, as usual, but brought to Clarice Cliff in her office/studio.

Everything that mattered to her now required concealment. She must have wondered how she lived before daily life appeared to lay so many traps before her. Yet the need to be secretive about her new designs afforded a curious protection to Clarice's relationship with Colley; her work became their alibi, and the language of the factory, perhaps, a kind of private code, as she strove to put her new ideas into practice. Although the showroom was draughty and dingy and needed a lick of paint itself, within one corner of the room, blue enamels and sunshine yellows created seasons of their own.

Gradually, and almost without reference to herself, Clarice Cliff's designs pronounced themselves ready. 'Round shapes were covered from top to bottom with coloured bands,' she explained. 'Between guide lines [the girls] drew simple diamonds which in turn were filled in with bright colours . . . Then the article was passed on to be banded.'[16] The effect was far less prosaic. Triangles leaped and dived on vases and made radiant stars on plates in yellow, coral, orange, green, cobalt blue and purple; bands of colour circled candle-sticks and enveloped ginger jars. That these startling patterns emerged as the days darkened into autumn no doubt heightened the drama of their first appearance.

Such extravagance of colour and patterning was a shock to those who saw them. The designs were 'a source of much merriment and derision to travellers',[17] Clarice Cliff recalled. 'It is always difficult to make other people see with one's *own* eyes,' she told *Home Chat*. 'It meant . . . the breaking down of prejudices against anything so modern.'[18] Ewart Oakes, the salesman charged with securing the first orders of the experimental ware, acknowledged his misgivings. 'Mr Shorter asked me to go out for a few days and get a few clients' reactions. To be candid, I didn't feel too happy about it. It was so extreme.'[19] As Shorter thought it essential that designers and their salesmen be 'en rapport',[20] Clarice Cliff had some persuading to do. Oakes's misgivings were overruled and 'the largest car on the factory'[21] – driven by Shorter's chauffeur – was packed with samples of the bright new pottery. '[W]ithin two days they were back for more. So – "Bizarre" by Clarice Cliff was launched.'[22]

Oakes remembered soliciting orders in the autumn of 1928 for delivery the following spring. As 'Bizarre' was advertised to the trade for the first time in February 1928 and, according to a later advertisement, on sale from 1927 onwards,[23] Oakes must have misremembered the actual date. That he nevertheless recalled the correct season makes sense, given the dates of Clarice Cliff's London studies and the kind of tableware A.J. Wilkinson was producing shortly before 'Bizarre' was introduced.

The new patterns were promoted at the British Industries Fair in February 1928. A somewhat incongruous advertisement announced their presence, juxtaposing the word 'Bizarre' with a drawing of ornamental ware and a pair of kittens nestling in a floral tureen. The traditional and the modern had yet to work out their relationship within the factory. Within one month, all that had changed: '"Bizarre Ware" is made in every variety of Table and Fancy Goods,' retailers were instructed. 'Get Control for your Town.'[24] Initially, to promote the idea of exclusivity and encourage competition, 'Bizarre' was offered to only one retail outlet within each area, the first of many marketing ploys by Colley Shorter.

It must have taken a strong sense of bravado – and of fun – for Clarice Cliff to adopt the term 'Bizarre'. Patterns as demonstrative as these were as likely to attract criticism as praise, particularly within a conservative industrial environment. By claiming the definition for herself, Clarice Cliff pre-empted her detractors. 'They certainly were "bizarre",' she said of her new designs, 'hence the name of my pottery.'[25] In March 1928 an extensive appraisal appeared in the *Pottery Gazette*:

> There has recently been established at the Newport Pottery a special department which might almost be likened to a studio. It consists for the time being of a single room in which is to be found a group of young ladies working under the personal superintendence of a mistress instructor, who, whilst herself creating new freehand styles of decoration, and applying these direct to pieces of ornamental pottery, simultaneously holds a watching brief over what is being done by her apprentices. It is quite a delight to watch this coterie of handcraft decorators – for the most part, we believe, if not entirely, the product of the local art schools – giving free expression to their artistic inclinations direct upon pottery. They have no printer's guiding lines to hedge them round, no prescribed limitations; they simply brush away with colour upon pottery, producing designs which are never conventional, oft-times even whimsical, but full of life and, in the ultimate, attractive to a degree ... A new range of wares that has been produced under such conditions as we have endeavoured to depict has been styled 'Bizarre Ware', and if the name is intended to convey that the designs are singular and capricious, then it is, indeed, thoroughly apt ...
>
> Our advice to the buyer who sees this ware for the first time would be: Do not succumb to your first shock at what is undoubtedly a real blaze of colour, or the elementary simplicity of some of the designs; do not be too sure that the public taste is exactly what you believe it to be, but give the public taste a fair chance of expression ... After all, it is the feminine element which chiefly counts for innovations in our furnishing schemes, and no 'mere man' can be the arbiter of what is likely to please the gentler sex. One fact cannot be denied, and that is that the majority of women do like, and will have, colour, even though it may be simply riotous in its presentation.[26]

Looking at 'Bizarre' today, it is difficult to appreciate fully the impact Clarice Cliff's patterns made when they first appeared, but for

some years after 'Bizarre' was launched, the *Pottery Gazette* harked
back to the drama of that moment, and employed a succession of
superlatives with which to do so. Clarice Cliff's new tableware was
'extravagant and revolutionary' (1929); 'never before had such
powerful and intensive colouring been applied en masse in flat brushwork effects' (1930); here were 'colourings of undiluted forcefulness'
(1931), and so on. In 1932, four years after the initial launch, the
journal was still reeling at the memory: 'The colours, too; how daring
they were!'

It was not that bright colours had been absent from pottery decoration until now. A.J. Wilkinson itself had long been praised for its
innovative use of colour, which may have been one of the factors
that initially attracted Clarice Cliff to the firm.[27] The 'growing feeling
for colour in relation to domestic pottery' had been discussed within
the industry as early as 1920, but although the use of moderate
colouring was welcomed at that time, vivid colour had been characterised as 'a sort of jazz'[28] and greeted with much the same anxiety.
The critic and cartoonist Osbert Lancaster later defined 'jazz style'
as 'the fruit of a fearful union between the flashier side of Ballet
Russes and a hopelessly vulgarised version of Cubism'.[29] (Detractors
would say he characterised Clarice Cliff's early work to a T, although
in reviews of the period, 'Bizarre' did not acquire the epithet 'jazz',
but was generally described as 'modern', 'ultra-modern' or
'modernistic'; the latter would itself become a term of abuse in years
to come.)

Defined as 'a reaction from the sombreness of war',[30] 'violent
colouring' had been dismissed by the pottery industry as a passing
fancy. Now that was no longer possible. It was not necessarily depth
of colour that aroused such intense concern, as much as the manner
in which colour was applied. The decorations the majority of
manufacturers favoured tended towards diminutive, precise and
often repeating patterns which restrained even the most exhibitionist
of colours. Triangles had been seen on pottery before now – a
reflection of the growing influence of all things Egyptian – but their
treatment had been far more sober. A.J. Wilkinson's own 'Isis' shape,
a ewer introduced in 1920, had been decorated with a triangular
lotus-leaf motif which shows a family resemblance to 'Bizarre',

especially when seen in black and white reproduction. The ewer as actually produced, however, in traditional toilet ware, with white on a pink ground, or grey on black, for instance, was far from 'Bizarre' in impact and was not perceived as a significant departure for design.[31] Clarice Cliff's patterns were dynamic, their colouring dramatic, with background colour as intense as foreground. These decorations spoke not of the 'restfulness and repose'[32] for which the public had formerly been grateful, but of energy, freedom – and the future. Colour seemed to be breaking out of its former boundaries, just as women – with their shorter skirts, bobbed hair and growing clamour for the flapper vote – seemed to be breaking out of theirs.

'Bizarre' was launched into a changing world. 'The steady, and somewhat drab, existence that was sufficient for the majority before the war has disappeared,' the *Pottery Gazette* reported. 'Men who might, in the absence of the war, have been content to grow roses and don sombre attire on Sundays, now speed along the highways in a "sports" car, or array themselves in "plus fours" of diverse colours. Their wives, instead of knitting or sewing, may put on richly coloured coats and depart to the tennis courts. The upheaval in our habits seems to show itself in the effects with which we surround ourselves . . . the demand for colour is almost universal.'[33]

Clarice Cliff's designs 'certainly caught the public taste'.[34] Even she had not anticipated the strength of the response: 'To our surprise, the first pieces were an enormous success,' she told the *Daily Mirror*.[35] The *Pottery Gazette* described initial reactions among the trade: 'At first . . . the designs and colourings struck one as being so unlike anything previously attempted, and so revolutionary in character, as to be likely to prove short-lived . . . although many retailers who, when they saw the "Bizarre" ware for the first time, said that it was far too advanced for their particular market . . . were quick to change their minds when they saw how the bold colourings and whimsical decorations were finding a market in the shops of their more courageous competitors.'[36]

Faced with the unexpected enthusiasm of the female consumer, the *Pottery Gazette*'s reporter was reduced to describing himself as a 'mere man'. In this he was not alone. The 'mere man' had come into being after the First World War as a reaction against women's increasing emancipation. Whenever the status quo was threatened, and female behaviour proved startling or hard to fathom, the 'mere man' made his appearance. 'Courage' acquired new meaning too: it would figure repeatedly over the next few years, whenever the *Gazette*'s reporter was lost for words.

By the summer of 1928, Clarice Cliff's work was being marketed under her own name.[37] The use of a designer's name on tableware, though not without precedent, was infrequent and more likely to apply to studio pottery than commercial ware. 'The potter, not the designer, was the thing.'[38] Even on the occasions when a designer's signature was applied, the name itself was rarely promoted. One exception was William Moorcroft, whose signature gave his work its cachet, but then Moorcroft himself was a potter. It was not until the 1930s that arguments within the industry for designers' names to be more widely recognised took root. In one area, however, the promotion of names was already gaining ground. Tableware with nursery themes, made popular during the nineteenth century, was currently featuring designs by the children's illustrators Mabel Lucie Attwell, Hilda Cowham and Ernest H. Shepard, with their names publicised. Its increasing popularity was such that, over the next few years, several pottery manufacturers produced their own children's range, including A.J. Wilkinson, whose nursery ware was signed: 'Joan Shorter, Aged 8' – the name and age of Colley Shorter's youngest daughter.[39]

The use of Clarice Cliff's signature to promote 'Bizarre' brought naming up to the minute. Here was a woman designing pottery for the modern woman: consumers were buying not only her work, but all the connotations that went with it. Women were drawn to the possibilities suggested by the name Clarice Cliff – yearning, aspirational, seductive – the implied exoticism of those double, curling C's, particularly during an era that was beginning to succumb to film-star glamour. Here was a woman they had never met, but had nevertheless invited into their homes. They, too, were modern by association. The symmetry was perfect. In June 1928, women under thirty were finally awarded the vote. At last women and men were equally enfranchised. This seemed to mark the culmination of a decade of female achievements. According to the pages of the popular press, there was now little that women could not do. Clarice Cliff spoke to that moment. What better time to launch a woman designer? And what a name to launch; it would have been a dreadful shame to waste it.

In August 1928, Clarice Cliff and three of her young paintresses gathered in London to give the first of many demonstrations of 'Bizarre'. Though demonstrations had been a feature of pottery manufacture for some time, they were beginning to acquire a new momentum in pursuit of that new creature, modern woman. Manufacturers had long been aware of the need to appeal to women – Josiah Wedgwood himself deferred to 'the ladies of superior spirit who set the fashion'[40] – now they had to reach women in a rapidly changing world. Shorter knew very well that 'to sell goods nowadays . . . one must make them "the talk of the town".'[41] What better place to do so than Waring & Gillow which, inspired by the design studios of the leading Parisian stores, had just launched its own Modern Art Department to appeal to the design cognoscenti.[42]

One of the attractions of Clarice Cliff's decorated ware was the fact it was hand-painted: here was freedom of movement expressed through brushstrokes. Now members of the public could observe Clarice Cliff and her young team circle the rim of a vase with rings of tangerine, and trace green peaks before scaling them with loose brushstrokes of red. The Waring & Gillow foyer was transformed. The first trade buyer who saw 'Bizarre' was said to have been 'agog'.[43] The reactions of this audience were no doubt similiar. Unused to such a bold embrace of colour, some may have turned away; others, surely, were intrigued by this unexpected vision of modernity.

That autumn, Clarice Cliff's signature appeared in a trade advertisement for the first time.[44] The advertisement also introduced 'Miss Bizarre' or 'Bizooka', a curious creature which would feature as a ceramic model in future promotions.[45] A horse (or mule), whose limbs and bones and ligatures were composed entirely of pottery, 'Bizooka' was bizarre in every sense: its body a hectic blend of vases, dishes, plates; its ears protruding candlesticks; its tail a teapot spout. Its appearance was fantastic – exactly the effect Clarice Cliff intended. 'Bizooka', too, was credited to her name. What must she have thought, creating this strange creature and perfecting her own signature alongside? Seeing the letters circle, rise and fall, dot and curl, she must have felt her journey was as extraordinary as the creature curvetting beside them.

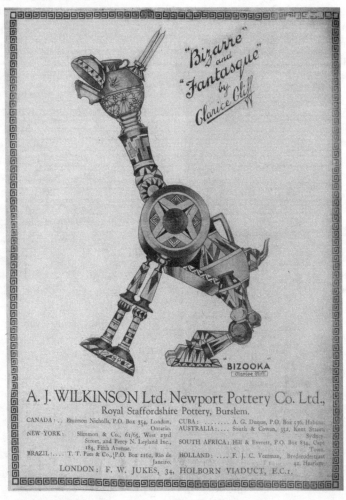

Advertisement showing 'Bizooka' and the 'Clarice Cliff' signature, *Pottery Gazette and Glass Trade Review*, October 1928

On the basis of her success, Clarice Cliff was taught to drive by Colley Shorter's chauffeur, Herbert Webb, and bought herself a car. There was no need to pass a driving test; she took to the road as soon as she felt confident to do so. A ruby-coloured Austin Seven, fondly christened 'Jinny', was her first car. Purchased from Holland & Hollinshead in Alsager, it was said to have cost £60, which suggests that the car was second-hand.[46] (In 1928, a brand-new Austin Seven cost £135 and upwards.) Even so, car ownership was the preserve of the upper and middle classes at this time. In 1922, 952,000 motor-vehicle licences were issued in Britain; by 1930, that figure had reached 2,218,000, representing approximately one vehicle to every five families. While the family car was becoming a possibility for many of the middle class, it remained 'a total improbability for almost all working-class families'[47]. What is more, within the Potteries working-class car ownership remained something of a rarity for years to come. 'The Potteries are just entering the motor age,' Mervyn Jones wrote in 1961, in his study of the area,[48] estimating that only one working-class family in ten owned a car. Though it is hardly surprising that Clarice Cliff hankered for the freedom driving would give her – not least the freedom to meet Colley Shorter some miles away from prying eyes – it is interesting that she so quickly asserted her new-found status. A car was her escape – out of Edwards Street and out of her class.

Cars spelled sophistication and self-assurance, as well as money. During the late 1920s, the *Lady* and *Homes and Gardens* ran articles for the well-heeled woman and her car. In 1928, the *Lady* published a weekly feature, alternating between the practical advice offered by 'The Lady and her Car: A Series of Articles on Choosing, Housing, Maintaining and Driving a Car' and the equally practical but rather more frothy instructions to 'The Woman in the Car – Her Part in Successful Motoring', which advised the female passenger against wearing long, fashionable scarves with fly-away ends – memories of Isadora Duncan's untimely death the year before were all too fresh – and against sporting the equally ubiquitous fur, 'waving paws and fluttering tails'[49] in the direction of the driver. Above all, the woman passenger was told that she must 'never, *never*, NEVER clutch the arm of the Man at the Wheel'.[50] Advertisements directed at the woman driver also veered between portraying her as capable or as inadequate. While some asserted a sense of adventure and derring-do – the Star Motor Company used Diana Strickland's '7,000-mile exploration through widest and wildest Africa'[51] to promote its cars – others played on the insecurities of 'the female driver'. 'Gear-changing, ladies? Why, nothing simpler!' an advertisement for the Vauxhall Cadet reassured them.[52]

'Ostentation is not in the pottery tradition',[53] but there was nothing more ostentatious than driving your own car. How the lace nets must have twitched when Clarice Cliff drove down Edwards Street the very first time – and countless times thereafter. There were unlikely to have been other privately owned cars in the vicinity. Women drivers were, anyway, something of a novelty: 'There's a woman driving that car!'[54] was the reaction of some in Stoke-on-Trent at the sight of Clarice Cliff behind the wheel. It took a while for her to get the hang of things, however. Taking a corner too fast in Burslem as a relatively new driver, she overturned the car and brought Colley rushing to her side. Fortunately, no damage was done, either to Clarice or the Austin Seven; from then on, she took corners more sedately.[55]

The 'New Austin Seven'. These proud owners sent this photograph as a
Christmas greeting, December 1928

Clarice Cliff's journey to Middleport was made easier with her own transport, but if eyebrows were raised in Edwards Street, they were surely raised still further at the factory. Years later, she remarked how thrilled she had been to save for and buy her own car,[56] but some may have interpreted things differently. Her situation was so unusual, few knew what to make of it – her growing prominence, her signature, and now a car. And all so quickly too.

If Clarice herself was taken aback by the speed of developments, her parents were surely uncomprehending. For Ann Cliff, it was not merely that someone in her family owned a car – and a daughter, at that – but the whole situation. Faced with the launch of 'Bizarre' and the 'Clarice Cliff' name, she was uncertain how to respond. Clarice's niece, Nancy, recalled that whenever her aunt tried to discuss her work, her mother refused to hear.[57] Perhaps she feared her daughter had 'ideas above her station'; 'getting above yourself' was not something to encourage and Clarice's achievements may have been brushed aside. Not knowing what to make of them, it was easier to make nothing at all.

Ann Cliff's feelings were possibly complicated by a sense of something 'not quite right' in her daughter's association with Colley Shorter. With so much shrouded in secrecy, and relationships outside marriage a source of scandal and shame, Clarice Cliff needed to deny the affair: anything the family overheard was simply gossip, she would tell them. It would hardly be the first time a family was presented with the version of events they found most palatable, the one guaranteed to cause least harm. If Clarice's mother preferred not to know, her sisters may have felt the same, or drawn their own conclusions, but said nothing. Habits learned in childhood – of not asking too many questions or speaking out of turn – extended into adult life as well. With so much left unsaid, awkward conversations could be side-stepped. Things were more difficult with Dorothy, however. She knew Clarice's daily life better than anyone. The change in her sister's status affected Dorothy as well. Her friends at the factory needed to be careful of their words within her hearing, and Dorothy had cause to be concerned for herself: if the rumours about her sister were correct, and the relationship with Shorter ended badly, she, too, would be looking for a new job.

Outside the home, there were the usual pleasantries to be answered and evaded – 'Not courting yet?' and so on – and Clarice's smart clothes, let alone her car, were likely to have been a source of speculation. It is easy to imagine the conversations in the corner shop, that bastion of community, where all was seen and heard and debated. The trappings of Clarice Cliff's success – the Liberty scarf, good leather shoes, good stockings – were enough to set her apart in themselves.

Clarice Cliff's paintresses described her very first patterns as 'V's and diamonds' or 'pyramids', a further affirmation of the popularity of the Egyptian.[58] Pattern books in the A.J. Wilkinson-Newport Archive feature a number of simple geometric designs which correspond with the early months of 'Bizarre' and show how effective a combination bold colour and pattern could be.[59] The simplicity of her early patterns enabled Clarice Cliff to train paintresses who had yet to become proficient in their craft; as her work evolved, so did their skills. Though within a short time her paintresses were dedicated to the creation of 'Bizarre', it was not their sole occupation in the beginning. A design dated 15 March 1928, 'Girl Calling Cows for Milking',[60] was painted by the 'Bizarre Girls' and may have been the first allusion to the name her paintresses acquired; the following month a description of a box decorated with bands of different colours was painted by the 'Freehand Girls'[62] – the label 'Bizarre Girls' had yet to stick.

Paintresses who worked on early 'Bizarre' patterns recall being instructed to keep their brushstrokes loose to emphasise the hand-painted effect. In later years, this requirement was dropped, although one paintress recalled being advised never to paint two pieces exactly alike in order to emphasise their individuality.[62] The phrase 'hand painted' was incorporated into Clarice Cliff's first backstamp (the potter's mark, usually on the underside of pottery), which read: 'Hand Painted Bizarre by Clarice Cliff, Newport Pottery, England'.[63] Although 'Clarice Cliff' patterns were painted in the Newport Pottery and her paintresses were Newport employees, the production and warehouse facilities were on the site of A.J. Wilkinson's Royal Staffordshire Pottery. Newport had its own office, however, and functioned as a separate unit for accounting as well as decorating purposes; the names of both or either of the potteries feature in contemporary press reviews.

The new visual language of the 1920s acquired vivid definition in the creation of 'Bizarre', but the impetus behind Clarice Cliff's new patterns was not purely aesthetic; commercial expedients also played their part. During the late 1920s, 'peasant pottery' from Eastern Europe was proving increasingly popular and British manufacturers needed to respond. The designer Susie Cooper ascribed the creation of her own colourful early work to an influx of cheap tableware from Czechoslovakia.[64] For the industrial designer, the market was always to the fore.

If 'Bizarre' was to be more than a momentary dazzle, Clarice Cliff needed to develop a range of tableware to satisfy a variety of tastes. By the autumn of 1928, she had designed a selection of Persian-type patterns, richly decorated in crimsons and purples, which were also promoted as 'Bizarre'. To capitalise on her initial success, Colley Shorter decided that the word should be adopted as a design label: future designs would bear their own names, but would also be labelled 'Bizarre'. That autumn also saw the launch of 'Crocus', a bright floral design for those who appreciated modern colouring but did not have the courage for geometrics. Adapted from a pattern created by John Butler some years earlier,[65] the impact of 'Crocus' lay in its simplicity: four upward strokes in tangerine created petals, four downward glancing strokes produced green leaves. Clarice Cliff completed the design with coloured bands: a band of brown beneath, to represent the earth, and a yellow band above – the sun. Later produced in blue and purple colourways, as well as the original orange, 'Crocus' became her most popular and enduring design, selling up to and beyond the Second World War. Ethel Cliff recalled seeing thirty girls painting the same springtime image. It was one of the 'Clarice Cliff' patterns that Queen Mary admired and purchased annually at the British Industries Fair, recalling the price she had paid the previous year.

Although the initial success of 'Bizarre' was seen in the UK, export markets were also a consideration. During the 1920s, A.J. Wilkinson had agents in Australia, Brazil, Canada, Cuba, Holland, New York and South Africa, as well as London. Belgium and Switzerland joined the list in 1931 and, although South Africa was later removed, Norway, the Argentine, Uruguay and New Zealand were added to it. New markets had to be sought and secured, existing markets nurtured. With overseas travel still a slow affair, and with Colley Shorter obeying his own creed of visiting key customers in person, he was away for long periods at a time. His absence lent a temporary security to his relationship with Clarice. No one could discover them, and any letters received at the factory could be easily explained. Clarice Cliff immersed herself in work, mixing shades of memory with splashes of anticipation.

NINE

Cup and Saucer Cubism

The order books swelled; the showroom swelled with them. An advertisement was placed in the *Evening Sentinel*, seeking new paintresses to decorate 'Bizarre', and an upstairs workshop in the Newport Pottery cleared to accommodate their growing numbers. Seeing the workshop taking shape, Clarice Cliff must have looked back to the moment when all she could be sure of was her private ambition; before she had a workshop crammed with paintresses, and buyers chasing orders, samples queuing to be photographed, new recruits to teach and new designs to contemplate – if only she could find the time. Within a year, her life had been transformed. A 'missus', Lily Slater, was appointed to oversee her paintresses and free Clarice Cliff to design.

'It would be difficult to advance a more striking illustration of how strong colouring can be applied to pottery, in styles which might almost be regarded as extravagant and revolutionary,' the *Pottery Gazette* reported in the spring of 1929.[1] The new thirst for pattern and colour emboldened Clarice Cliff to take her work still further, with designs that reach into the heart of Art Deco. The term 'Art Deco', which has come to identify much inter-war design, derives from the 1925 Exposition, but was not coined within the UK until the 1960s, with the revival of interest in the period. Art Deco drew on a number of diverse sources, reinterpreting them; Cubism, the Ballets Russes, the Bauhaus, folk art, classicism and the rectilinear aspects of Art Nouveau all formed part of this 'assertively modern' style.[2]

In the increasingly adventurous evolution of 'Bizarre' that year, Clarice Cliff's designs became all the more exuberant. Many were playful explorations of geometry, elaborations on the theme of line and colour, and increasingly more complex in their execution than the diagonals and stripes with which she initially made her name. Her method was not unlike that of the kaleidoscope she kept beside her in her office studio. In one design after another, patterns dissolve and then regroup; diagonals and blocks of colour overlap and intersect; bolts of lightning crackle on the glaze. Colours swirl like dizzy rainbows or speed towards the shoulder of a vase; castellated lines balance black and jade-green triangles. The descriptive pattern names they have acquired – 'Sliced Circle', 'Lightning', 'Diamonds', 'Blue W', etc. – demonstrate their vital configurations. 'Immobility is dead and this is the reign of movement,' Joseph Delteil declared in celebration of Sonia Delaunay;[3] the geometric patterns Clarice Cliff now produced radiate that energy.

Hers were eclectic, magpie tastes; nothing intimidated her. Over the next few years, she paid homage to the avant-garde, reinterpreting its message for the domestic. The pattern known as 'Cubist', with its slabs of diagonal colour, has been likened to Theo van Doesburg's *Counter Composition V*, and the one known as 'Mondrian' compared with Gerrit Rietveld's *Red/Blue Chair*.[4] The ease with which flat plains and surfaces could translate into ceramic patterns enabled Clarice Cliff to reproduce the language of abstraction. By now, the Cubist style – a generic term, taking in De Stijl, Fauvism, Futurism, Vorticism, et al. – was attracting the discerning; young people furnishing their homes in the modern manner were particularly keen on work by Clarice Cliff.[5] A dress design by Sonia Delaunay, whose 'simultaneous' fabrics had been acclaimed at the Paris Exposition and were favoured by such icons of the period as Gloria Swanson and Nancy Cunard, has been suggested as the inspiration for the pattern known as 'Circle Tree',[6] which makes use of paint and colour in ways unlike Clarice Cliff's other work. She may have been introduced to Sonia Delaunay's designs at Liberty, where her clothes were on sale in the years before the Depression. A later Clarice Cliff pattern, known as 'Tennis', also suggests an appreciation of Sonia Delaunay's work, resonating as it does with her *Designs for Fashion in an Interior*.[7]

The abstract patterns Clarice Cliff produced from 1929 were vibrant, supple, hot, and suggest an extraordinary confidence on her part. By now, she was not only certain of the direction she was taking, but was pushing herself forward all the time. This was not ornamental ware designed purely for display – although candlesticks and vases figured prominently – but earthenware designed for use. These patterns decorated cups and saucers, teapots, plates. Modernity was brought face to face with the kitchen sink.

Not all straight lines led to the avant-garde. Just as contemporary architecture, and much else besides, borrowed from classical influences, so too did Clarice Cliff with 'Archaic'. 'Realising how near to the original principles of art the designs of "Bizarre" ware really are,' a promotional brochure announced, 'we have dipped into archaeology to find that the Ancients had, in their day, almost identical styles. We have reproduced a number of ancient pillar heads, both in form and colour.'[8] Derived from *The Grammar of Ornament*, a nineteenth-century text by Owen Jones, taught in art schools of the period, 'Archaic' offered classicism a distinctly modern slant. The gaily coloured columns decorating numerous Alhambras and Astorias were similarly inspired by earlier motifs during a period in which the ancient could be transformed into the modern.[9] Despite its primary colouring, 'Archaic' was not widely popular, perhaps because its formal lines are more static than other Clarice Cliff patterns of the time.

Just as colourful abstracts conveyed the rhythm of modernity, so natural forms began to be portrayed in a new light. Clarice Cliff produced the first of many landscapes in 1929. An archive pattern book shows an early sketch for the pattern known as 'Trees and House',[10] whose final design was both more intricate and more fantastical than the pencilled concept. In the ceramic version, a row of whimsical trees is ranged across a hillside, their foliage the stuff of dreams, bubbling and frothing brightly, or else sloping towards the ground in a lazy triangle. A circle bush in bold, full bloom climbs the cottage walls, while enamel layers of stratus cloud promise eternally fine weather. The use of different colourways – trees blaze in red or tangerine or black – enabled the modern woman to colour her mood. 'Trees and House' among other patterns was sold under the design label 'Fantasque', not only a tempting name but a diversionary measure for tax purposes, which was introduced as early as the autumn of 1928 in response to the rapidly growing popularity of 'Bizarre'.[11]

Archive pattern book showing 'Trees and House'

Even the mundane acquired a fresh dimension. In 1929, an idea of umbrellas and rain was transformed into an image of spiky petalled flowers and outsize raindrops, and an early 1920s pattern, 'Broth', so-called because of the globules of fat which rise to the surface during cooking, revived with modern feeling. Quaint ceramic cats, originally conceived by Louis Wain years earlier, now acquired bright spots. There were further experiments with colour too: the pattern called 'Delecia' – pronounced Deleesha – took the concept of striated colour, first seen in A.J. Wilkinson's prize-winning 'Oriflamme', into a new register, its multi-coloured rivulets a vibrant declaration.[12] Every pattern and technique could be transformed, adapted or revitalised.

Bold, strong colours required new glazes to show them off to best effect. 'We were always experimenting with slips and glazes,'[13] Clarice Cliff explained, demonstrating the extent to which she immersed herself in technical as well as decorative aspects of the industry. That spring, 'a beautiful cream matt glaze',[14] 'Latona', was

introduced to give her colours depth and a new series of patterns
created especially for it, 'in the very best manner of . . . the modernist
vogue'.[15] Another new glaze came closer to art ware than anything
Clarice Cliff had yet produced. 'I call these vases . . . my
"Inspiration" pieces,' she told a reporter. 'A special firing process
makes the colours merge with dimming softness into one another.'[16]
'Inspiration' achieved its 'Ancient Egyptian . . . "Scarab" blue'[17]
colouring because of the chemical reactions of the metal oxides used
in its firing. The glaze was unstable and so difficult to produce and
therefore costly, but its effect was harmonious and comparatively
discreet and, as such, won Clarice Cliff new admirers.

In May 1929, the *Daily Mail* described some extraordinary scenes
at the general election: 'Women . . . led the way everywhere at the
polling stations . . . The crowds of women who voted on their way
to business were succeeded by servants who left their duties for a
few minutes and by housewives who polled before doing the
morning's shopping . . . In the Ripon Division of Yorkshire a young
men's flying squad of sixty motorcyclists conveyed women voters
by pillion from isolated spots on the moors. At Birmingham, family
party voting was a feature . . . women of all classes wore party
colours, some Socialist factory girls appearing in red dresses.'[18]
Women were marching into the future.

Clarice Cliff was doing the same, by designing dramatic shapes
to complement 'Bizarre'. Here was an opportunity to enhance and
amplify her thoughts, a chance to invent twice over – to create not
just the pattern, but the form it took as well. Her work 'cried aloud
for shapes other than the traditional',[19] as she herself explained. No
more hourglass waists and tight, ruched necks; she would replace
ceramic corsetry with freedom.

Though several years had passed since Clarice Cliff started
modelling, little had changed within the industry as a whole: on the
occasions women were allowed to design, they tended to be confined
to surface patterns. As the production of new shapes required a
considerable outlay on the manufacturer's part, any innovation was
generally greeted with caution. Not so for Clarice Cliff, who was given
a free rein to produce whatever she wished.

Some 'Bizarre' vases appeared in the autumn of 1928, but in 1929 Clarice Cliff's work acquired a new angularity. The intriguing bowls and vases which featured in the press that year offer a striking contrast to the shapes previously favoured for domestic tableware. Three suggest a close reading of *The Studio*: a conical bowl with squat triangular feet (shape 383) appears to have been based on a design in silver by the Budapest-born designer Ilonka Karasz,[20] and a small tiered vase comprising ever-widening circles (shape 366), on a design produced for the firm Zuid-Holland at Gouda.[21] An inverted square bowl (shape 367) may have been suggested by a Wiener Werkstätte shape conceived in brass, which featured in *The Studio Yearbook*.[22]

Clarice Cliff spoke of seeking 'inspiration and freshness of thought' from fellow designers;[23] Colley Shorter agreed on its importance. 'He could not see how any manufacturer could reasonably expect his designer to produce things which were going to sell, unless he permitted that designer . . . to get away from the factory and see what was being done in other industries . . . Pottery did not lead a fashion, it followed.'[24] It is interesting that Clarice Cliff was drawn to silverware, a medium so unlike her own, but one in which contemporary designers were achieving impressive results. She wanted to do the same, to produce something streamlined and immediate that would speak to modern women, as European designers spoke to her. It took confidence to believe that a novel shape conceived for a medium as malleable – and expensive – as silver could be adapted for one as inflexible and accessible as earthenware, with its very different stylistic connotations.

Some of Clarice Cliff's designs from 1929, and thereafter, drew on the work of French artists and designers who featured in the interiors magazine *Mobilier et Décoration, Revue Mensuelles Des Arts Décoratifs et de l'Architecture Moderne*, which she may have discovered in Paris.[25] 'I have only really visited one foreign country – France – and that for the briefest of holidays,' she told a reporter in 1931.[26] From that one sentence, much must be inferred. Clarice Cliff was speaking during the Depression, when 'continental influence' was not something to admit. Despite the evident impact of other cultures on her work, she claimed her designs were 'English right through'.[27] France need not mean Paris, but Paris was the place to be during the 1920s, for however short a time, and Clarice Cliff's designs from 1929, and her reading of *Mobilier et Décoration* during 1929 and 1930, allow for the possibility that she had visited the city by the beginning of that year.[28] The Modern Art Department at Waring & Gillow, where she had demonstrated 'Bizarre' the previous summer, had a sister branch in Paris, similarly inspired by the 1925 Exposition and the Parisian design studios.[29] This may have been the prompt for a short trip – if any prompt were needed. What could be more appropriate than a stolen weekend for two and a further chance to garner new ideas? The brevity of the visit can be accounted for by its clandestine nature: neither she nor Colley could stake lengthy alibis.

No definitive evidence points to 1929, however, and earlier dates should also be considered; 1925, the year of the Exposition and all its dazzle, has to be rejected because there is no record of A.J. Wilkinson's attendance and nothing in Clarice Cliff's work during that period to indicate her own presence at that event. A stronger contender is 1927, during the interval between her studies at the Royal College of Art and the emergence of 'Bizarre', although Clarice Cliff did not need to visit Paris to create 'Bizarre' when the visual language could be glimpsed in London.

Paris was a city of excitement, an impassioned mix of characters and cultures. What happened there and what Clarice Cliff saw can only be conjecture but, like London before it, Paris offered the chance to observe and absorb the new, and to visit possibilities of shape and form that were leaps ahead of anything she had seen. Here were galleries hung with rugs whose patterns, making abstract statements out of wool, insisted that rugs might also be paintings and paintings become rugs; smooth and softly angled chairs in different blends of wood invited the consideration that furniture might also become sculpture, while gleaming silverware whose decorations, in wood or stone or ebony or jade, appeared to evolve from the metal itself, suggested no distinction need be made between different materials. Even the most prosaic shops refused to disappoint: a string of galvanised watering cans strung together with chains was capable of forming a metallic picture in a doorway. 'Perhaps never before have I so definitely experienced the feeling of *entering a new world*,'

an observer wrote of the 1928 Paris Salons.[30] The city offered further
lessons in the willingness to dare; it also provided concrete ideas for
Clarice Cliff to develop and translate.

A cone-shaped silver goblet by the silversmith Desny, produced
as part of a cocktail set circa 1926–8,[31] is thought to have been the
starting point for 'Yo-Yo', a dramatic vase on sale by June 1929.[32]
In Desny's shape, a twisted cylinder forms two unequal cones,
supported by a silver blade; in Clarice Cliff's design, slip-sided cones
are held by angular fins, an elaboration on Desny's original theme.
A single cone-shaped vase was also produced that year, supported
by a single fin; another new shape, a globe, was arresting in its
simplicity and very much in vogue in 1929.[33] Geometry offered
boundless possibilities.[34]

Pleasing in their geometric solidity, Clarice Cliff's shapes were
practical as well as modern, enabling her to combine form and
colour in simple but effective ways. Hers were shapes without fuss
or frippery, squares and circles both. She drew them in tiers of
ascending or descending size and, recalling the work she had seen
as a young enameller, turned forms upside down to produce their
opposite image. Some shapes doubled in function: with the addition of a handle and an electro-plated silver lid, a stout vase could
become a biscuit barrel or, when accompanied by a shade, be transformed into a zany lamp. This was nimble thinking, extending a
design range with simple sleights of hand.

Clarice Cliff's most ambitious design to date was showcased at
two events in London that autumn. The British China, Earthenware
and Pottery Exhibition was held at the First Avenue Hotel, Holborn,
in September, and ran for several days. Here Clarice Cliff spoke to
the press for the first time and explained how crucial women were
to her success: 'Not until women buyers appeared was it realised
that women wanted bright and cheerful pottery and china in their
houses rather than the old-fashioned styles of circles or roses and
elaborate gold lines.'[35] Barely had the exhibition at the First Avenue
Hotel closed than she returned to London for a show of British
china and glass at Chesham House, Regent Street, in November.

Coming within a month of the Wall Street Crash, the mood of
the second event was less optimistic. Trade with America had

Town and Country Homes, September 1929, showing the new shapes, including 'Yo' and 'Yo Yo' vases, 'Conical' and 'Duo-conical' bowls and a 'Conical' tea set

ceased almost overnight; British manufacturing was seriously threatened. In response to this changing climate, the exhibition was intended to encourage the general public to buy British. Glass-cutting took place beside shelves of gleaming glassware; displays of pottery were complemented by those of plate-making, turning, throwing and casting; some of Clarice Cliff's paintresses demonstrated the intricacies of the hand-painted technique. The exhibition was an introduction to the potter's world (excepting silicosis and lead poisoning). In her opening address, Lady Cynthia Mosley, MP for Stoke-on-Trent, one of fourteen women MPs returned in that year's general election, spoke of the unemployment troubling the Potteries and went on to express the hope that 'firms would make use of the modern forms of expression in their decorations'. There was one caveat: 'By that, [she] did not mean "jazz".'[36]

The public knew exactly what was wanted: they demanded the 'gargantuan feast of colour'[37] that was 'Bizarre'. 'A girl artist Miss Clarice Cliff . . . is responsible for the most striking feature of the show,' the *Daily Mail* informed its readers.[38] Chief among the attractions was Clarice Cliff's latest design: a tea service that was 'all edges and angles',[39] and consisted of a teapot with a conical body, triangular spout and handles; a sugar bowl and milk jug with conical bodies and small triangular feet; and cups which took the shape to new limits by proposing solid triangles for handles. A novelty for Clarice Cliff's contemporaries and a source of amusement for design pundits thereafter, owing to her apparent disregard for the relationship between form and function, this development of her earlier conical theme took press and public by surprise. 'Cups with triangles for handles! Teapots with triangles for spouts! To many women these were the most interesting features of the British China and Glass Industries Exhibition,' the *Evening World* noted.[40] Not all reports were complimentary. 'Cup and saucer cubism is the latest cure for that early-morning drowsiness,' the *Daily Express* explained. 'This tea set . . . looks like a Russian ballet master's nightmare solidified . . . First-year geometry could be taught with a tea set instead of diagrams.'[41] Yet even so, the newspaper conceded that 'Bizarre' was 'proving unusually popular'.[42]

'Conical' was not without its problems. Its solid handles became 'hot and slippery'[43] and the design required modification. Impressed triangular handles were produced, before cut-out ones proved the most effective. With this problem solved, the shape went on to sell 'exceptionally well',[44] Clarice Cliff recalled with evident satisfaction. Within two years, the teapot shape was patented, presumably because A.J. Wilkinson feared imitators. The open triangular handle became a feature of 1930s tableware; it was adopted by Shelley for bone-china patterns such as 'Vogue', while a variation of the conical teapot was produced in 'Burleigh' ware.

Clarice Cliff's designs 'caught on at once' in the South of England.[45] 'The demand is so great that we can hardly keep up with it,' a Regent Street buyer told the *Express*.[46] 'Now they cannot design new shapes and patterns . . . quickly enough.'[47] The production of adventurous shapes as well as 'courageous' patterns confirmed that the creation of 'Bizarre' had been no happy accident. The boldness of Clarice Cliff's work and its impact on the public, supported by strong marketing, ensured that the designer herself began to be sought by the national press. 'I think a woman knows best the kinds of ornaments and articles for use in the modern home,' she told the *Evening News*. 'Women's homes are changing. The housewife nowadays demands more individuality about the articles she handles . . . yet each thing must be as useful as it is colourful.' She went on to describe the colours she particularly favoured: 'I advocate bright orange, clear cobalt and mauve blue, bright emerald and jade green and black.'[48] The reporter from the *Express* would have recoiled.

Individuality was now part of the vocabulary; uniformity was a thing of the past. Virginia Woolf spoke to the hopes of many women that year when she asserted: 'It is much more important to be oneself than anything else.'[49] One way in which Clarice Cliff responded to the assertion of individuality was by appealing to the growing passion for interior design. 'Why always buy your tea or dinner service with the pattern or design the maker has thought of? Why not have your own ideas worked on them?' one reviewer enquired.[50] Women could submit an illustration of their home, their favourite 'beauty spot', or their initials, and Clarice Cliff would produce a design or monogram to match. Each design was stamped – and thereby endorsed – with the 'Clarice Cliff' signature. Women were now their own interior designers. They could also embroider a tablecloth and napkins to match their best tea service: crocus petals picked out in tangerine-coloured silk, with tiny running stitches in leaf green.

*

Some forty reviews of Clarice Cliff's work appeared during 1929, almost half of which relate to the exhibition at Chesham House. This was an unprecedented response to a designer working in an industry which preferred anonymity. An earlier exception was Hannah Barlow, whose designs for Royal Doulton were reviewed in both the *Lady* and *Queen*. Interestingly, her profile was high during the 1880s, another period in which women were beginning to challenge expectations of their capabilities.

The Chesham House exhibition went some way towards educating the public about the changing role of women in the pottery industry. 'Pottery designing would seem to be pre-eminently a feminine talent,' the *Daily Sketch* reported. 'The most successful of the very modern designers is Miss Clarice Cliff, a pretty young woman whose wares have gone all over the world.'[51] 'Until recent years women have played a comparatively small part in the making of china,' the *Evening World* explained. 'Then came the war, and a shortage of boy-apprentices. Women made the most of the opportunity . . . Only in those factories making the highest grade of china is the designing solely confined to male craftsmen, and even here it is only a matter of time before the women come in,' its reporter concluded.[52] 'Girl artists are employed to give the pottery the finishing touch,' the *Birmingham Gazette* noted, illustrating the article with a photograph of one of Clarice Cliff's paintresses. 'In handwork of this kind, which requires a delicate touch and a true eye, they have few equals.'[53]

One of the earliest-known photographs of the 'Bizarre Girls' is thought to date from this period and shows a small group of paintresses posing in a corner of the workshop. Four of the Girls are seated; five make a row behind, as if posing for a school photograph. These paintresses are very much themselves – confident young women with bobbed hair and Marcel waves. The dresses glimpsed beneath their overalls – stripes and polka-dots among their fabrics – speak of an awareness of the latest styles, as far as they could be achieved on factory wages. In the middle of the back row stands Gladys Scarlett, a striking figure with peek-a-boo lips and buoyant hair. Her gaze issues a challenge to the photographer, who may have been Clarice Cliff. There was said to have been tension and some rivalry between them. Given her liking for pink dresses, Colley Shorter

'Bizarre Girls' c.1929: Back row: Florrie Eardley, Gertie Love?, Gladys Scarlett, Doris Bailey?, Sadie Maskrey? Front row: Hilda Peers?, Nancy Liversage, Annie Jackson, Ellen Browne

referred to Gladys as his 'little girl in pink',[54] and Scarlett said that Shorter would have also sent her to the Royal College of Art, had Clarice Cliff not objected.[55] The look the paintresses direct towards their photographer supports the view that they knew themselves to be 'special'.[56]

The paintresses who worked for Clarice Cliff were not known as 'Bizarre Girls' beyond the factory gates, but acquired the name within their workplace. 'The girls who worked in the warehouse at A.J. Wilkinson were rather jealous, like, "Oh, it's the 'Bizarre Girls,'" they said.'[57] With the revival of interest in Clarice Cliff's work, the phrase has reacquired its currency. 'Bizarre' – then pronounced 'Bizair' – 'Babes' was also an early epithet, as was the double entendre 'Bizookas'. The divide between the different areas of the factory becomes apparent.

Swifter than many of the paintresses who worked elsewhere in the factory, conscious that they were contributing to something entirely modern, they liked to consider themselves entirely modern too. They practised the latest dance steps and the words to popular tunes, which they sang at the top of their voices while they worked. Their workshop was a thing apart, in spirit as well as geographically. Already the 'Bizarre Girls' were becoming quite a clan.

Their days began at eight o'clock and ended at five-thirty, except on Saturdays when they finished work at lunchtime, with a week's wages in their pockets and an afternoon to spare, before church or chapel claimed them on Sunday mornings. Most came straight from school and, as the workshop grew, several Girls were joined by younger sisters; others had no immediate connection with potbanks, nor any prior thought of becoming paintresses. Some of Clarice Cliff's young apprentices, including three of four boys (who kept themselves 'a bit aloof'),[58] came from the Burslem School of Art, where they had completed the full-time pre-apprenticeship course in Design and Craftsmanship established by Gordon Forsyth in 1925. A letter offering students to A.J. Wilkinson – and other manufacturers – makes depressing reading: '20 girls and 20 boys – aged from 15 to 16 [will be] available for employment in various branches of the Pottery Industry,' Sidney Dodd, of the British Pottery Manufacturers Federation, informed the factory. 'The whole of the 20 girls wish to take up Pottery decoration; 8 of the boys wish to become Pottery Designers, 2 Throwers, 3 Modellers and Mould makers and 2 Engravers.'[59] So much for changing attitudes among young women.[60]

Like all paintresses before them, including Clarice Cliff herself as a young 'learner', the 'Bizarre Girls' were required to be proficient in a number of brushstrokes before they painted patterns for production. They learned to paint colour freehand and trained their brushes to stop sharp, clean, as if surprised by an edge the eye could not discern. Six months were spent acquiring the relevant skills and practising different brushstrokes, using Harrison's Red. 'Oh, I was sick of that red,' Doris Johnson complained. 'If only we could change to blue or another colour, but no . . . Red was the cheapest.'[61] Annie Beresford, one of the first paintresses to join Clarice Cliff, described her introduction to freehand work: 'I painted leaves, leaves and more leaves . . . I ran errands, mixed colours and did other odd jobs. Gradually, I started doing other things like tracing or outlining . . . I became a freehand paintress.'[62]

The Girls worked on top of paper which was spread across their benches to stop them being drenched with paint and, on summer days, fastened paper to the windows to minimise the glare. At twopence and even sixpence a time, their brushes were much cherished; they held on to their favourites for as long as possible. Clarice Cliff's paintresses were day-waged in the beginning and punched their hours into the clock. As elsewhere in the industry, anyone arriving more than ten minutes late was forced to wait until the clock struck nine and lost an hour's wages. Their weekly starting wage of five shillings and sixpence rose to seven and sixpence six months later, and ten shillings after a year. Older, more experienced Girls graduated to piecework and were paid by the dozen, though, like that of a baker, a pottery dozen is an invention of the industry. Some of the shapes Clarice Cliff went on to design were difficult to cost and so remained day-waged throughout.

The most dextrous of the 'Bizarre Girls' were assigned the task of outlining and worked to their own rhythm, defining each new pattern with steady lines of paint or Indian ink. Each outlined vase – or plate or cup – was passed to the other, waiting Girls, who filled in every pattern with vivid strokes of colour. Thick, thin, thick, thin, they brushed across the glaze, one Girl painting coral red, another cobalt blue, a third creating blades of green, and so on, down the rows, until each pattern was complete, and ready to be banded with the aid of a potter's wheel, the bander directing the wheel with one hand, while following its path with a paintbrush in the other.

The paintresses paused for a break mid-morning. Brushes lolled in turpentine, strips of banding grinned across unfinished plates. With turpentine-smeared fingers wiped on their pinafores, the Girls quickly ate a sandwich or a biscuit. Although they knew that the constant use of turpentine could lead to dermatitis, few seemed alert to the dangers of lead poisoning or other industrial hazards – one of the ways 'Bizarre' (and other designs of the period) achieved its vibrancy was the trace of uranium in yellow paint. A contraption 'akin to Stephenson's Rocket' provided water for their tea – which they drank from their own tea cups; no one was allowed to use 'Bizarre' – and occasionally, at lunchtime, kiln workers were persuaded to toast sandwiches or boil an egg in the mouth of one of the kilns. Threepence of brawn or pickled cabbage could be purchased from the shop on Prospect Street, which was owned by A.J. Wilkinson and decorated by Clarice Cliff herself with images of bottle ovens, paintresses and kilnmen, reminiscent of one of the early advertisements she created for 'Bizarre'.[63]

Conditions at the Newport Pottery were primitive – 'When I went there I thought, what have I come to?' said paintress Rene Dale[64] – though no worse than those at many other potbanks. Though calls for reductions in smoke were growing all the while, the kilns continued their disgorgings, and the 'Bizarre' shop was as dusty as any, if nowhere near as bad as the clay end. Dust was the paintresses' enemy, clinging ruinously to wet paint unless the workshop floors were regularly swept. The sink ran with rusty water; the lavatories did not flush, but discharged their waste into the Trent and Mersey Canal and were, anyway, a long walk from the 'Bizarre' shop. Some Girls sang and stamped their feet en route, a discerning few rattled biscuit-tin lids to scare the rats from the long grass at their approach. Rats notwithstanding, some of the younger paintresses found excuses to dawdle on their return.

Clarice Cliff's youngest sister, Ethel, was among those who joined her workshop in 1929: a freehand tulip pattern was credited to E. Cliff that spring.[65] It is interesting that Clarice Cliff ensured that her sister's contribution was noted in the pattern book, though whether the design was Ethel's, or merely its enamelling, is unclear. When Clarice Cliff introduced a new pattern to the workshop, she produced a watercolour sketch for her paintresses to copy or demonstrated the design herself. 'She'd have a plate in her hand and she'd come and use the pencils [brushes] and walk round with it,'[66] dressed in her white butcher's overall, buttons unfastened, pockets bulging, reaching across a bench to select a brush. Each pattern had to be adapted to fit a range of shapes and sizes – from the eighteen-inch charger, the largest piece of standard ware the factory produced, to the smallest, an ink well or decorative sabot. It was a question of proportion and of detail; each element needed to be as dramatic as the whole. Clarice Cliff demonstrated how to achieve the desired effect. '"Try it on this,"' she'd say, picking up a tea cup, and '"Try it on that [a plate] . . . No, bring the tree round this way"' – all little alterations, a paintress recalled, in order to achieve exactly what she wanted.[67]

After twelve hours in the enamel kiln*, the newly fired tableware was examined for imperfections before being transferred to the warehouse. This was a moment to be dreaded. 'We never knew what time Clarice Cliff was coming on to the kiln to sort the ware . . . She was there to pick a fault – especially if she'd been away for a few days. She'd perhaps bring four or five pieces into the shop. She more or less knew who'd done what . . . She knew her Girls.'[68] 'She used to pick up a plate or a vase and come in and say, "What happened to this?"'[69] if a line of paint bulged or a pattern tripped or ran. She was constantly watchful and 'very particular'.[70] If a pattern was unsatisfactory, she wanted it repainted – and painted yet again, if necessary – but did not raise her voice, preferring instead to exercise a quiet authority. Though evidently strict, she nevertheless conveyed a sense of achievement to her paintresses. 'She made us feel important,' Alice Andrews said.[71]

By now, Clarice Cliff's days were immensely crowded. She frequently worked late and asked Annie Beresford to sit with her, explaining how uncomfortable she felt in the empty factory after hours.[72] Which may have been the case – that warren of small rooms, one leading to another; those external, creaking stairs; and the inexplicable sighs an empty room can make. Plates towered ghostly white against the brickwork; pallets cast long surprising shadows across the floorboards. Annie Beresford lived close by and could ask her mother's permission during the lunch hour, or even dash home and back again at the end of the day. She mixed paints and generally busied herself while Clarice Cliff worked near by. But another of her paintresses suggested it was not the dark that Clarice was afraid of, but the gossips who would make much of her being there alone.[73] If that was her reasoning, she was wise. Any successful woman was prey to innuendo and there was already plenty for gossips to feast on. That there was a personal relationship between Clarice Cliff and

Colley Shorter only complicated matters further.

Inevitably, perhaps, Clarice Cliff's relationship with Jack Walker soured; likewise her relationship with Guy Shorter. How Colley responded to his family's disapproval is not known, although everything about him suggests he was a man who would always go his own way; few in the family would want to challenge him. For Clarice Cliff, however, the situation was different. She did not have his power, nor his standing, and, as the interloper and 'other woman', was likely to attract opprobrium. It must have been difficult for her to be set against those who had once supported her, especially Jack Walker, who had been so enthusiastic about her work. That was a snub she would have felt most keenly, unless she thought 'to hell with them'. That seems unlikely, though. In 1929, she did not know the end of her story.

TEN

A Woman Knows Best

In the spring of 1930, Clarice Cliff spoke to *Home Chat*. 'Housewives All Over the Country say "Thank you" for the new Pleasing Pottery,' the magazine announced, before going on to describe 'how a clever girl artist evolved a new type of pottery so that other women may have joyous chinaware'. The designer spoke of her impetus to create something 'quite modern as regards colour and form . . . which could be produced at a moderate cost to bring it within the reach of the great masses of the people . . . In addition to my first design – "Bizarre",' she told the magazine, 'I now have "Inspiration," "Fantasque" and the "Moderne" design in tableware.'

The 'Moderne' range, whose designs consisted of a small shoulder cartouche*, enabled Clarice Cliff to satisfy current tastes with the minimum of pattern. With individual pattern names such as 'Norge', 'Jewel', 'Paysanne' – French chic was everywhere apparent – 'Moderne' spoke of sophistication while delivering restraint. By contrast, 'Appliqué', a design range whose first patterns were issued later that year, was a further experiment in the possibilities of colour. Here pattern played across the whole ceramic surface: blue skies washed the lips of jugs, green hills ascended plates. Extraordinarily vibrant in their colouring, 'Appliqué' patterns – mostly landscapes, with names such as 'Avignon', 'Lucerne' and 'Lugano' – enticed the armchair traveller with picture-postcard scenes of castles, water-wheels and bridges, and were as notable for the simplicity of their folk-style images as their primary colours. The castle motif of

'Appliqué Lucerne' has been attributed to a pochoir print by Edouard Benedictus; copies of his *Variations* and *Nouvelle Variations* were among Clarice Cliff's studio possessions and are said to have provided motifs for other elements in her work. She may have become aware of the almost electric vitality of pochoir colouring at the V&A, when looking at Picasso's costume designs for Diaghilev three years earlier. Colourful landscapes and other pictorial images drawing on 'the peasant style' were fashionable. 'Quite the latest little *sac* from Paris,' the *Illustrated London News* advised, 'is made of flat wooden beads, forming gaily coloured landscapes with quaint little figures and houses, a different scene on each side.'[2]

'Colour seems to radiate happiness and the spirit of modern life and movement,' Clarice Cliff told the *Evening News*. 'I cannot put too much of it into my designs to please women.'[3] Now that the colour-loving woman could choose from a number of 'Clarice Cliff' styles, they ranged in price accordingly: a ten-inch vase in a 'Bizarre', 'Fantasque' or 'Crocus' pattern was priced seven shillings; the same vase decorated with 'Appliqué' cost nine shillings and sixpence, while 'Latona' glazed patterns retailed at ten shillings, and a vase bearing the sultry greens and blues of an 'Inspiration' glaze relieved the discerning buyer of fourteen shillings,[4] almost three times the weekly wage of one of Clarice Cliff's trainee paintresses or the price of a pair of glacé leather shoes with toe-cap stitching (fourteen shillings and ninepence).

The use of pattern names in preference to pattern numbers gave pottery design a new talking point.[5] Clarice Cliff and Colley Shorter chose the names between them. By now, Shorter took tea with Clarice in her studio every afternoon; what fun they must have had, selecting the latest name for her 'gay, many-coloured fantasies'.[6] 'Titania', 'Japonica', 'Poppyland' and 'Ravel' were among those introduced at the British Industries Fair that year. A shoulder motif*, reminiscent of the trailing ribbons of a kite, 'Ravel' satisfied the contemporary appetite for tangerine and jade, like 'Crocus' before it. Also like 'Crocus', the pattern proved extremely popular. 'Everything with a touch of orange in it . . . seemed to take people's fancy,' Clarice Cliff observed, 'while jade green was another winning colour.'[7] She might have been speaking literally: the famous Suzanne Lenglen played tennis wearing a bandeau of orange and jade.

Interviewers were keen to know how Clarice Cliff's patterns were conceived. 'I do not think of the designs at any time. They just "come" to me,' she told the *Evening News*,[8] casting aside hours of endeavour in favour of inspiration, before going on to explain, 'Birds, trees and flowers help and there is always something new to discover in the way of colour.' 'Ideas borrowed from meadow flowers, from gems, from bits of bright enamel such as were produced by old Italian craftsmen,'[9] were also cited. 'Each new design is modelled and painted by me before I pass it on to my staff to be copied,' Clarice Cliff told *Home Chat*.[10] 'I like to keep up with everything,' she informed the *Evening News*. 'It is so easy to lose touch and I have to take a practical part in the colour work.'[11] Keeping up with everything involved constantly looking out for new material. In addition to magazines such as *Mobilier et Décoration* and the *Studio*, Clarice Cliff collected botanical prints, perhaps emboldened by their precision to transform the natural into something stylised. With the pattern known as 'Picasso Flower', a simple bloom became monumental. Fruits were stylised too: when the patterns known as 'Melon', and 'Sliced Fruit' were applied to fruit bowls, the real and the abstract tempted one another.

Changes in fashion were closely observed: fashion's ability to translate the avant-garde into the accessible meant that dress design was always one step ahead. '[B]eing struck by a few coloured leaves or a rose'[12] also provided Clarice Cliff with new ideas. On one occasion, she adapted a floral pattern from a paintress's pinafore, and on another took the colour from a group of hydrangeas, probably to create the shade for a new glaze.[13] Other possibilities will have caught her eye – ideas for pattern, shape and colour – to be stored for future use: an empty cardboard box for soaps, perhaps, with a crazy pattern on its lid, or a scrap of textured linen. Private keepsakes may have joined her hoard, mementoes which held no special meaning for anyone other than herself, and so would not raise awkward questions if discovered: a twist of vermilion ribbon from the corner of a menu, a gardenia pressed between the pages of a novel.

By now, Clarice Cliff had an assistant, a young woman, Hilda Lovatt, who has been described as her 'right arm'. Lovatt's work 'took [her] to every department on the factory . . . There was always something different to do.'[14] As Clarice Cliff's reputation grew, Hilda Lovatt became responsible for an extensive press-cuttings file; a less onerous responsibility was that of dressing 'Phoebe', the nude some two and a half feet tall which Clarice had modelled at the Royal College of Art, and which now stood in a corner of her studio. 'We'd better make Phoebe respectable,' she would say, on the occasions provincial ladies paid a visit. And so the figure was tastefully swathed in tissue paper and tied with string, Grecian-style, to spare their blushes. There were always people calling: salesmen were a regular presence, examining new samples and reporting the reactions of buyers; students came to the factory; and, as Clarice Cliff's public profile grew, schoolchildren visited the workshop and painted their own plates; journalists also came by from time to time.

In May 1930, Wedgwood celebrated the bicentenary of its founder, Josiah Wedgwood, with a historical pageant recording the family's contribution to the industry and the history of the area so closely associated with its name. Schoolchildren as well as pottery workers took part in this celebration of industrial heritage; even Bernard Shaw returned to the district, despite his protestations years before. For one newspaper, the bicentenary provided a link between the traditional and the modern. 'Since this is "Wedgwood" week,' the *Evening News* remarked, 'it is particularly opportune to think of new pottery . . . Some of the most novel and attractive ideas in shape and colouring . . . have been created by a young girl, Miss Clarice Cliff.'[15] Clarice Cliff was singled out for attention again that month when her dinner ware, shown in Stoke-on-Trent as part of an exhibition of modern pottery linked to the bicentennial celebrations, was said by the *Pottery Gazette* to differ 'markedly from anything elsewhere shown in the pottery trade'.[16] Endorsements from both within and without the industry on such a historic occasion underlined Clarice Cliff's achievement. At the close of the exhibition, many of the exhibits transferred to Harrods and other major London department stores.

Clarice Cliff travelled to London herself the following month for the demonstration of hand-painting at Lawley's that was advertised in the *Daily Mail*.[17] Throughout the first week of June, the public watched her and four young paintresses bring tableware to life in a blaze of colour. Prior to the event, she wrote to the girls' mothers, asking if they could participate. Annie Beresford's mother was uncertain – she had heard rumours of the white slave trade. 'My mother gave me all sorts of lectures,'[18] Beresford recalled – but, with a promise that Clarice Cliff would look after her, she was allowed to attend and borrowed a yellow dress from Dorothy Cliff for the occasion. When they were not painting, Clarice showed the Girls the city and the sights she now knew well. Not so her paintresses. 'It was a new life altogether,' Annie Beresford said. 'You didn't travel in those days. London was like another country to me.'[19] The Girls stayed at a ladies' club in Russell Square whose doormat bore the warning: 'No men allowed past here.' A photograph shows them standing in the doorway. They smile, as if on holiday. It must have been a glorious adventure.

Lawley's 'new and handsomely appointed shop'[20] – the first china shop on Regent Street – had opened the previous year. Said to be the most ambitious of all the Lawley's stores – in 1930, 'Bizarre' was sold in twenty-two branches – the Regent Street store struck 'the latest note in modern shop fitting'.[21] How appropriate, then, that Clarice Cliff should demonstrate her latest patterns there in view of the national press. She spoke to the *Star*, whose reporter was beguiled by the 'large flowers, little weeping trees, fruits and geometrical designs'[22] on show and advised his readers to 'make a point' of seeing her work: it would change the minds of those who thought pottery 'unfinished' and 'inartistic'.[23] The *Daily Telegraph* was impressed by the proficiency of her paintresses and commented on the influence of Balkan and Russian 'peasant'[24] ware in her 'Fantasque' patterns. For the *Daily Mirror*, however, Clarice Cliff herself was the attraction: in less than three years she had become 'one of the romances of the pottery trade'.[25]

These were heady days for Clarice Cliff. However much faith she had in her own abilities, however determined she was to succeed,

she cannot have anticipated the level of achievement she would
attain, especially in such a short time. Not only within the industry
– her own design label, credited to her name – but within the wider
world. Whatever transformation Clarice Cliff envisaged for herself,
she cannot have foreseen that she would not only acquire a public
profile, but would quickly be characterised as 'the brilliant young
girl artist and sculptor'[26] whose presence at a London store was
something to be advertised in the national press. It was a good week
for women achievers: Amy Johnson, the first woman pilot to fly
alone to Australia, looked out from the front cover of the *Illustrated
London News* and national newspapers.

Clarice Cliff and Amy Johnson were among the exceptions of the
period. As far as most women were concerned, not all changes in
the changing world were for the better. Despite securing universal
female suffrage, few of the career gains women hoped for were
realised. The Sex Disqualification (Removal) Act, which had seemed
to promise so much in 1919, was never enforced, and the marriage
bars that operated within teaching, medicine and the civil service,
coupled with a diehard suspicion of the professional working
woman, restricted women's actual freedom. The pottery industry
was no more welcoming than others. In response to an article in
the *Manchester Guardian* describing women who were not only able
to 'completely furnish and equip a home' but could also 'mould
their own china', the *Pottery Gazette* responded: 'They had better
keep to their own work – moulding heirs.'[27] This from the journal
which, ten years earlier, had insisted that women had earned the
right to be considered in all future aspects of the pottery trade. The
position of the pottery designer continued to be a matter for debate
– 'No pottery of any importance should be without its trained
designer,'[28] the *Evening Sentinel* reminded manufacturers – and the
full-time course at the Burslem School of Art now offered workers
better training, but opportunities for either sex remained few. One
manufacturer observed that 'to "place" the young trained art
students in the industry as enamellers or paintresses should not be
difficult, but to find positions for them as highly paid designers is
quite another matter',[29] although the very fact that this comment
was made suggests a growing number of young women were now

at least considering the possibility.

While Clarice Cliff was making a career for herself – and being represented in aspirational terms by the press – the message the majority of women were receiving was the old one: a woman's place was in the home. For both working- and middle-class women, paid work was regarded as 'inferior to and preparatory to marriage',[30] and as far as middle-class women were concerned, the period between the wars saw their 'near-universal withdrawal . . . from the labour market – willingly or unwillingly – on marriage or at first pregnancy'.[31] Their best career was marriage and the home. 'The career of the homeworker is the finest in the world,' a popular magazine reassured them. 'If you can keep your husband's house efficiently, you can also keep his love.'[32]

Now that the role of home-maker was regarded as a career in itself, a new status was conferred upon it. 'It's not an easy business, running a house and servants; you've got to put brains into it, if it's to be done well,' a character in Rose Macaulay's novel *Crewe Train*, explained. '. . . The more intelligent a woman is, the more brains she ought to bring to bear on her home. The Cambridge and Oxford Colleges are excellent training schools for housewives.'[33] Although Rose Macaulay's comments were the stuff of satire, reality was in fact not far behind: at a service to bless the movement for higher education among women, the Bishop of London informed a group of Oxford students that they were 'all [*sic*] destined to become the wives of some good man'.[34]

Housecraft was now elevated into a science. For working-class girls, like Clarice Cliff before them, this meant special classes at school, where they learned to starch collars and make boot polish; for the middle classes, there was *Good Housekeeping*, with its white-coated advisers and (for those who could afford them) new labour-saving devices which reinforced the message of domestic economy and the importance of domestic work. The pressure on women to be good housewives – and nothing but – grew enormously between the wars. 'We Are Feminine Again,' *Home Chat* reported, with an almost audible sigh of relief.[35]

The middle-class woman who now found that her skills were best utilised at home faced a further problem: the decline in domestic servants prompted by the departure of working-class women for munitions factories during the First World War and their reluctance to return to ill-paid drudgery thereafter. Although significant numbers remained in service – domestic service continued to be the single most important semi-skilled work for women up to 1939 – jobs were becoming available in the new light industries and else-where. While most middle-class households retained some form of daily help, the live-in servant was becoming a thing of the past – hard to find and even harder to keep – and for those who were themselves in straitened circumstances as a consequence of the war, domestic help was now less affordable. The 'servant problem', and how to resolve it, filled numerous column inches in the press.

It also had a concomitant impact on designs for domestic table-ware. 'Owing to the modern servant problem, women are specially keen on china of good sensible shapes, easy to wash and hard to break,'[35] *Modern Home* noted, when reviewing the work of Clarice Cliff in 1930.[36] There was no longer the staff to wash a large dinner service, nor the cupboard space to store one. Although the inter-war years saw a considerable building programme,[37] the houses were smaller than those before the First World War. Changing habits also played their part. 'Modern conditions of life are all the time militating against our industry so far as the demand for [dinner] services is concerned,' a pottery manufacturer complained, '– smaller houses, the splitting up of country mansions, the craze for motoring, amusements, and so on.'[38]

Fewer servants, smaller houses, busier lives: all had to be acknowl-edged and accommodated by industrial designers. For Clarice Cliff, these changes provided opportunities to produce new shapes for tableware. In September 1930, her latest tea service was reviewed by the press. With its quadrant shape and flattened sides, 'Stamford' was tailored to the moment. 'It is to save space in the tiny modern flat or house,' Clarice Cliff informed the *Daily Mirror*.[39] 'It takes up far less room than a round or even a square set,' she explained, striking a blow against the 'Cube' teapot whose novel shape had been winning applause for some time.[40]

The shape known as 'Stamford' was originally created in silver by the French designers Tétard Frères, whose work was photographed in *Mobilier et Décoration*.[41] Their award-winning tea service was lean and compact, and could be tucked into a cupboard or slid on to a tea tray with ease. As with the designs Clarice Cliff had earlier adapted from Desny and Karasz – and, no doubt, buoyed up by their success – she was once again convinced that shapes conceived for silver could be achieved in earthenware, however novel their form. It was bold of her to respond to *Mobilier et Décoration* in the way she did. The magazine showcased some of the most stylish continental designers; the illustrations it carried of interiors alone – sleek, modern creations, fantasies in black and white – were enough to take away the breath. The sculptures, rugs and table lamps within its pages furnished the rooms of expensive apartments. These were nothing like a terraced house in Stoke-on-Trent, nor the middle-class homes in which 'Bizarre' found favour. Clarice Cliff made the leap required to translate the exclusive into the affordable and bring European influence to the high street.

As before, she looked to strong, original shapes for the experiment: curves and straight lines, a winning combination, and a recognition that the functional could also be adventurous. The *Pottery Gazette* reported Gordon Forsyth telling the North Staffordshire Art Society that year that 'Good ideas were even more important, to his mind, than technique. Self-expression was the thing which counted and it seemed to him as though the ablest of our men and women designers were seriously trying, through their work, to "say something".'[42] With her latest tea ware shape, Clarice Cliff spoke directly to the modern woman and indicated that flexibility was the way forward for domestic design. Another image drawn from *Mobilier et Décoration* in 1930 looks particularly effective when used to decorate 'Stamford', and may have been adapted with that in mind. The pattern known as 'Carpet', with its arcs of scarlet, grey and black, interspersed with scarlet dots, complements the teapot's unusual shape and was taken from a textile design by Éric Bagge, shown in black and white.[43] Much of the impact of 'Carpet' lay in the choice of colouring: had Clarice Cliff chosen differently, the effect would have been less chic.

A further teapot shape, 'Eton', joined Clarice Cliff's designs that year. With its cylindrical body and mortar-board lid, 'Eton' was

Silver tea set, Tétard Frères, the model for Clarice Cliff's 'Stamford' shape

more severe than either 'Conical' or 'Stamford' and offered a different take on geometry. These ultra-modern teapot shapes each acknowledged the thirst for tea which acquired a fashionable dimension during this decade. While early-morning sets proposed romance with tea for two, larger services satisfied the vogue for afternoon tea. Its popularity was such that Royal Doulton introduced an 'Afternoon Tea' figurine. The woman taking tea could now observe a china version of herself doing the same. And if she took her tea in a café, rather than at home, she could also purchase a model of an all-ladies orchestra, reminiscent of the ones performing in Kardoma cafés up and down the country at that time (and amusing Laura Jesson in *Brief Encounter*).

Part of the new ethos was to make the domestic desirable. How to dress the tea table became a matter for debate: 'You can go a long way to enchant your guests with your skill as a hostess,' *Ideal Home* informed its readers, 'if you know how to "stage" your meals with artistry.'[44] What's more, 'Anyone who allows their breakfast or lunch or dinner-table to be charged with unattractive crockery must be extraordinarily negligent or extraordinarily insensitive to beauty,' according to the *Morning Post*.[45] For the middle-class

'Fantasque Trees and House' on a 'Stamford' tea set

woman, the domestic was itself fashionable. 'The china that is making the tea tray in a smart house as much a matter of fashion as the hostess gown can be seen in . . . shapes of utter modernity,' *Woman and Beauty* announced.[46] The emphasis on tableware as fashion gave *Punch* the opportunity to mock: 'What kind of joint do you think would go best with a blue-and-gold dinner service?' a young housewife enquires of her butcher.[47]

The battle was now on to 'lure the Modern Eve'.[48] No self-respecting pottery manufacturer could ignore the growing demands of the female consumer. Over the next few years, bids to tempt her ranged from the saccharine appeal of an advertisement featuring 'The Marriage of Royal Doulton Ware to Miss Dainty Tablecloth',[49] to a national newspaper campaign conducted by Shelley. Clarice Cliff had a significant advantage. While the directors of Wedgwood consulted their wives and sisters for 'the feminine point of view',[50] she had first-hand knowledge – 'A woman knows best.'[51]

Now that the modern woman was judged by her domestic arrangements, the shift from live-in servants to daily help was presented as a form of liberation. 'The mistress of daily servants will find first and foremost that the morning and evening journey infuse a new tone and vigour into the daily round,' *Good Housekeeping* advised. 'Best of all ... as the door closes finally *the chancellor of the domestic exchequer* may sigh with contentment for she knows that below stairs everything invites inspection.' [my italics][52] This spirit of cheerful management extended to the middle-class woman who lacked domestic help altogether, if she was fortunate enough to purchase tableware designed by Clarice Cliff. 'If it is possible to imagine that the task of washing up can have anything *likeable* about it, I could bring myself to think that any woman could positively *enjoy* even washing up such colourful plates and dishes as I saw today,' the editress of the Home Page told readers of the *Evening News*.[53] As Clarice Cliff's career blossomed, other women were encouraged to put their hands into the soap suds.

The *Evening News* was commenting on a display of 'Bizarre' ware staged in London at the First Avenue Hotel, Holborn, in September 1930. It now became the habit of the three factories beneath the Shorters' umbrella – the Royal Staffordshire Pottery, the Newport Pottery and Shorter & Son – to show their latest productions in the capital each autumn, assisted by their London agent W.H. Jukes. 'Miss Cliff was never stuck for ideas when the September show ... was drawing near,' said Hilda Lovatt, recalling some of Clarice Cliff's preparations: 'We created table mats with crêpe paper ... to match the bands of the ware ... she had dock leaves painted in colours to match one pattern and ... sprayed with clear varnish. [On] plywood table tops we used fabric dyes ... so we could get the same colour as the bands on the plates. Anything to make something different.'[54] At one London display, the walls were decorated in turquoise and gold, while an iridescent palm tree with a miniature stalk of bananas took the place of table-centre flowers at another.

Clarice Cliff applied the same spirit of novelty to the decorative pieces she produced in 1930. Pleasure was not restricted to the tea table, but now extended to the cocktail hour. That autumn, 'Subway Sadie', a 'jaunty top-hatted maid in orange, honey-colour and mauve',[55] made her appearance in the national press. 'The chief feature' of an equally colourful dish designed to hold 'cocktail sandwiches or cheese straws', she took her name from a popular film and was greeted as 'an amusing possession for any hostess to own!'[56] The changing habits and increased informality of the period meant that while formal dinner parties were on the wane – 'Nobody has "grand food" anymore,' *Vogue* insisted[57] – cocktail food was becoming more substantial.

The cocktail hour was taken up by Clarice Cliff in other ways that year. A set of figures modelled in clay were also designed to appeal to the cocktail set, or to the suburban couple with social aspirations. These ceramic figures, the 'Age of Jazz', comprise pairs of musicians – a drummer and saxophonist, pianist and banjo player – and dancing couples. 'Listening to the jazz dance music on the wireless after dinner inspired Clarice Cliff's new dancing figures,' the *Daily Sketch* reported.[58] The impetus behind her Jazz Age models has been ascribed to an evening at the Café de Paris, where she and Colley Shorter were 'discovered', dining à deux, by a Potteries businessman and his wife, who were themselves spending an evening in London. Although the occasion doubtless caused embarrassment all round, the ensuing conversation between Clarice Cliff and the businessman, a wireless manufacturer, led to the suggestion that she 'design a centrepiece' to capture the spirit of the age.[59] For the past few years, the BBC Dance Orchestra, with Jack Payne at the helm, had been lending a new dignity to the jazz-band craze and bringing ballroom dancing into the home. Thanks to the increasing afford-ability of the wireless, a growing middle-class audience was being instructed to 'roll back the carpet and take a few steps'.[60]

The flat-sided figures of Clarice Cliff's 'Age of Jazz' are similar in concept to 'Les Arbres', the ceramic trees modelled by Robert Lallement which had appeared in *Mobilier et Décoration* the year before.[61] 'Les Arbres' were likely to have been the source for the ceramic flowers giving 'all-year colour' that Clarice Cliff produced in 1930, and probably provided the form for her group of figures. Clarice Cliff's were not the first musicians to be modelled in clay. The Parisian retailer Robj produced a set of 'Jazz Musicians' circa 1925,[62] although Clarice Cliff need not have been aware of Robj's work when her own figures were conceived: by now, the craze for dancing was such that images of dancers and musicians – saxophonists in particular – were ubiquitous, appearing everywhere from *Punch* cartoons to backcloths. Dancers swirled on dress fabrics and on posters for the London Underground; instructions for the latest dance steps appeared in women's magazines. Although the tunes of the day were slower than those of the previous decade, and the steps less frenetic, dancing remained very much the rage. Even Stoke-on-Trent acquired a new, large dance hall during the 1930s.

Whatever the impetus behind Clarice Cliff's Jazz Age decorations, she made the theme her own. With backless evening gowns sweeping an imaginary dance floor, and long bodices accentuating their slender figures, her ceramic women subscribe to the latest fashions as they surrender to the drum and saxophone. Intended for a 'dance supper',[63] placed, perhaps, between the galantine of chicken and the plates of petits fours, the figures struck the latest note in cocktail sophistication. The concept was, perhaps, too bold – 'The cocktail habit was confined to a very tiny sector of society'[64] – which may have been why they were not recalled as being strong sellers.

An 'original notion'[65] that autumn was the use of a different design for each plate within a dinner service. Picture a dining-table set for six in the traditional manner. Thereafter, tradition departs and bravado takes its place. Sunspots and bolts of lightning challenge one another; vibrant abstracts face them, as if a Picasso were placed beside a Mondrian, with a Theo van Doesburg to the left. Imagine matching candlesticks, their candles blazing orange, blue and yellow, alternating with tureens, each describing their own pattern in the centre of the table. Embroidered napkins mirror each design, while the honey-coloured tablecloth imitates the underlying glaze. Function and flamboyance – a conversation piece. The artistic and the domestic, side by side.

With displays and exhibitions requiring Clarice Cliff to travel to London three or four times a year, a pattern was beginning to emerge. London offered the best chance for Clarice and Colley to be alone together, even if their time was largely occupied by professional commitments. The capital, at least, allowed the two of them to stay together, even if propriety required them to book separate hotel rooms, or register under a false name; employees who travelled with them stayed in a different hotel. Clarice Cliff surely felt audacious, standing next to Mr Shorter, sales director, throughout the long and public days, behaving with polite formality, feeling far from polite, conscious of the secret they shared. This was where they belonged, their world and no one else's: showing off 'Bizarre' to their agents and to buyers, judging their reactions to the latest styles, exhilarated by the looks on people's faces. Handshakes, nods and smiles all round, assessing other factories all the while. They, too, were on show. Not just the latest 'Clarice Cliff', but Clarice Cliff herself and Colley Shorter, in full view of the hall and of those who could so easily carry tales back to the Potteries. Did they dance together at the Benevolent Institution's dinner, a regular fixture at the opening of the British Industries Fair? Most likely they sat out the foxtrots and the tangos, conscious that their easy movements would be all too compromising.

Trade fairs required months of organisation, the elaborate preparations for the exhibition stand itself, let alone each season's new designs – twenty-four in sixteen hours on one occasion, if Shorter's hyperbolic assessment can be trusted.[66] (Clarice Cliff herself spoke of creating twelve new designs in one particular week.) Then the actual exhibition, the reporters and photographers. And afterwards the journey home, and separation – Colley to 'Chetwynd' and his wife and family; Clarice to Edwards Street and a life hedged in with caution and pretence. There would be months to wait before they could as easily spend time together again, each trip a pungent blend of exhilaration, achievement and loss.

In October 1930, the *Pottery Gazette* listed 'Clarice Cliff' among the names recently registered as trademarks. Trade press advertisements the following spring advised buyers to 'look for the original signature',[67] a combination of events which suggests that Clarice Cliff's work was being copied and that A.J. Wilkinson was taking steps to prevent this. A number of 'Clarice Cliff' designs were patented during this period, including a display case for 'Bizarre'.[68] 'We were copied by so many that we had eventually to patent many shapes,' Clarice Cliff later remarked. 'Even the Japanese copied some.'[69]

Copying had long been part of the pottery tradition, hence the testing of innovative designs behind locked doors. 'We have been infringing one another's moral copyright ever since potteries of any importance existed,' the *Pottery Gazette* reported. 'It has become a second nature with us . . . in Meteyard's *Life of Wedgwood*, there are accounts of that eminent potter ransacking Europe for examples of inspiration, only to find that the results of these efforts were promptly annexed by inferior competitors.'[70] Imitation was, of course, the highest compliment which could be paid to Clarice Cliff; she herself borrowed from other designers, although mostly from other mediums, and in doing so gave new meaning to their work.

Clarice Cliff was not the only pottery designer with access to the motifs of modernity and, over the next few years, pendulous trees, zany patterns and so on grew in number. Nevertheless, the trade press highlighted her influence. 'A.J. Wilkinson's of recent years have . . . almost established new fashions in pottery,' the *Pottery Gazette* observed in 1932. 'It is common knowledge today that the new line caught the public eye . . . so much so, that other manufacturers, not blind to what was going on, decided to institute something similiar.'[71] *Woman's Life* agreed: 'As with all pioneers, where she led, others have followed.'[72] One example may have been Barker Brothers, who 'threw themselves into the new movement with zest',[73] but whose first 'ultra-modern' patterns followed the launch of 'Bizarre'.[74]

Clarice Cliff's own keynote at this time was abundance – an abundance of pattern, shape and colour. And, by applying traditional patterns to modern shapes, and vice versa, she was continually able to extend her design range. Not only did this flexibility ensure a healthy turnover – slow-selling, old-fashioned shapes could be enlivened, modern ones toned down – it allowed her to appeal to as many different temperaments as possible. Even the most tentative of modern women could cope with a 'Conical' teapot if it bloomed with crocuses, or risk a clash of colourful abstracts if they circled the traditional 'Globe'. A contemporary review of Clarice Cliff's work from *Modern Home* offers a glimpse of that abundance and of the variety of designs with which she greeted the new decade:

'Happy china' is how one might describe the fascinating modern ware called 'Bizarre' . . . To begin the day with a smile, [Clarice Cliff] has designed amusing early morning tea sets, painted to suggest cottages and country landscapes . . . Zinnias & marigolds blaze on the honey-coloured ground of the 'Gayday' service, and one uncommonly lovely dinner set has a drooping spray of Solomon's seal, suggested in orange and jade . . . The china itself is honey-coloured with a painted border of narrow jade, fuschia and cobalt-blue bands . . . A natural linen cloth, with a design of one of the plates, embroidered in colours in the centre accompanies the set.

The cloth-to-match idea is only one of Miss Cliff's typically modern and practical touches. All her dinner services have combined ashtrays and cigarette stands in matching china; wee saucers for individual butter pats; toast racks (with breakfast sets) and grapefruit holders which stand firm on squared bases, and can also be used for cereals.

Designs with more than one use are a speciality; for instance, delightful covered dishes which will serve equally well for porridge, hot tea-cakes, or vegetables, and large shallow chargers for fruit, bread, cakes or floating flowers according to the mood and needs of the moment!

The decorative pieces – such as flower-vases, book ends, lamps, candlesticks and table ornaments – provide perfect finishing touches for modern rooms. A beautiful bowl of 'Dreamland' china, suggested to the artist by fish rising, will pick up all the colours in cretonne curtains without introducing any actual pattern. Shallow flower bowls, in 'trough' or other unusual shapes, have pierced flower holders, of matching china, exactly fitting them. Long-handled china baskets . . . are another charming idea.

When fresh flowers are scarce, or you want 'something different', you can decorate your table with a china 'cut out' of tulips or other conventionalised blossoms, standing in a squared pot that matches your dinner service.

For a dance supper, there are table groups of modern musicians and dancers, looking very much alive in their smart black and scarlet costumes, made to match a dessert service which is complete down to the low candlesticks, designed to catch any drips from your scarlet candles in their black bowls.

From this you may turn to admire a bowl in which the swirling rings of colour suggest water ripples; little honey pots with an inquisitive bee making the compact handle for the lid; a cruet set like an upturned mushroom – with the salt, pepper and mustard pots grouped on a pinkish ground round the fat white stalk which serves for [the] handle!

Everything Miss Cliff sees, or (as she says) 'thinks of as she goes along', suggests a new design to this poet in pottery.[75]

ELEVEN

The Art Director of a Famous Firm

'What usually happens to the woman who becomes absorbed in a career is that when her appetite for work is satisfied, her sex instinct is roused by a man who has contracted obligations much earlier. That he may be through with these emotionally only adds to the complications,' wrote the MP Ellen Wilkinson, who knew what she was talking about.[1] By the beginning of the 1930s, Clarice Cliff's personal and professional lives were inextricably entwined. Although her relationship with Colley Shorter offered all the professional support she could wish for and a design freedom few enjoyed, it was accompanied by a life of secrecy and evasion. If London offered anonymity, Stoke-on-Trent did not. When asked to consider 'Modern Freedom', E.M. Delafield could only reflect that 'it doesn't exist in the Provinces'.[2]

In a community in which Church and Chapel held sway, and the only thing a woman had was her reputation, Clarice Cliff did her best to protect herself. 'It was Jekyll and Hyde,' employee Eric Grindley recalled. 'She treated you as an equal on your own. But when you went into the studio and Shorter was there she was quite aloof. They gave the impression that it was purely a business asso-ciation. I think she did care what people thought.'[3] The 'Bizarre Girls' were protective of their employer. 'We knew Clarice Cliff was talked about,' said Annie Beresford, 'but none of us saw anything and I don't think we would have said if we did.'[4] And, at fourteen, fifteen, sixteen, the majority were anyway 'more interested in our

own lads'[5] than in noting the relationship between the factory's
designer – who was now in her mid-thirties and so considered old
by them – and its owner who, at nearly fifty, was even older. 'There
was probably more gossip on the other side of the factory,' Alice
Andrews said.[6]

'We heard the Shorters didn't get on very well,' kiln man Jim Hall
recalled. 'Colley was a member of the Conservative Club. He'd go
there for a drink on Saturday lunchtime and didn't seem to go home
much.'[7] Whatever the truth behind the factory gossip, unintentional
gestures and moments of exaggerated caution inevitably drew attention to otherwise innocuous events, such as Colley speaking to
Clarice, and moving away too quickly at someone's approach. The
need to be on guard, and to avoid careless remarks or over-
familiarity whenever in the presence of her lover, was a constant
strain for Clarice. She learned to conceal her emotions. 'She was
always reticent,' an employee who knew her later has said, 'always
shying away from showing her true self.'[8]

By the 1930s, Colley and Annie Shorter were fastened in a
marriage neither could easily leave. Colley was raised a Methodist
and, whatever his feelings for Clarice, accepted his responsibilities
to his family. Within the small, tight-knit community of the Potteries,
he was a respected figure, a successful manufacturer and fox-hunting
Freemason, best friends with the bank manager and others, great
and good. 'Everybody knew Colley Shorter.'[9] Within that closed
world – his world – blind eyes were turned as long as his relationship with Clarice did not cause social embarrassment. Life was less
straightforward for Colley's wife. Though technically able to divorce
her husband – the Matrimonial Causes Act of 1923 equalised
grounds for divorce on the basis of adultery; prior to that date,
women needed to prove desertion or cruelty in addition – the stigma
was such that Annie Shorter was unlikely to have entertained the
possibility. As the journalist Mary Stott explained, 'In my young
days divorce was an unthinkable disgrace for a woman, however
virtuous, and however guilty her husband.'[10] Although the changes
in the law saw a rise in the numbers of those petitioning, the overall
figure remained low, with fewer than 4,000 decree absolutes granted
each year.[11] Legal proceedings were both complex and costly. In

practice, divorce was the preserve of the wealthy and the brave – proceedings made front-page news in the *Evening Sentinel* – and was rarely considered by a middle-class woman with two children. Wives were expected to adopt the view expressed in Somerset Maugham's play *The Constant Wife* and 'remember that they have their homes and their name and position and their family, and they should learn to close their eyes when it's possible they may see something they are not meant to'.[12] That Annie Shorter probably had to deal with other people's knowledge of the relationship, as well as her own, can only have made her predicament more painful. Over the years, the view that she was ill acquired a certain currency, albeit a debased one; she was not an invalid.[13] Yet it is not difficult to see how that notion might develop into a convenience for the lovers themselves.

The situation in which Clarice Cliff and Colley Shorter found themselves was far from unique, although, with adultery attracting loud condemnation, actual figures are impossible to calculate. In professions such as banking and insurance, any hint of 'sexual impropriety' brought all prospects of promotion to a halt, while, at the BBC, Lord Reith refused to allow divorcees across the threshold. Newspapers, meanwhile, thrilled to ever more lurid tales of adulterous affairs gone wrong. Suicide pacts and lovers shot by jealous husbands provided material for the prurient to debate the behaviour of immoral women, brazen hussies, and others who were no better than they should be. Even the 'Court' columns of *The Times* exposed the smallest details of private lives. During the Cunningham–Reid divorce case towards the end of the 1930s, the minutiae of Society life – gambling at Le Touquet, jewellery valued at over £30,000, and other financial details – tantalised the broadsheet public for four consecutive days.[14] Women's magazines made their own contribution: 'My dear,' 'Mrs Jim' counselled 'distressed Isobel', 'it would be a dastardly thing to break up his home.'[15] Had Clarice Cliff looked beyond the pages of *Home Chat* in which she was interviewed, she would have seen herself advised against her 'foolish action' and warned that she could not 'build happiness on another woman's tragedy'.[16] Everyone had an opinion, even if it was rarely expressed within her hearing.

*

At the beginning of 1931, the *Pottery Gazette* toured the Royal Staffordshire and Newport Potteries once again and was surprised to note that 'the output of the new lines is altogether overpowering that of the more conservative productions . . . Shapes that are startling in their originality, and colourings that are daring, are doing more to keep the workers busily employed than all the rest.'[17] Clarice Cliff's work was leading the factory.

Advertisement, *Pottery Gazette and Glass Trade Review*, November 1930–March 1931, including Clarice Cliff's ceramic flowers designed to bring 'all-year colour' to the home

Her success was at odds with the prevailing climate. As the Newport Pottery reported vigorous sales, with its southern representative's figures showing a 50 per cent increase on the first week of January the previous year,[18] the *Pottery Gazette* was describing 'the Army of the Unemployed' in the region.[19] Already, unemployment levels in the Potteries were approximately double those of 1930. By June, 20,126 pottery workers were registered at employment exchanges. The fall-off in American trade was a particular cause for concern – one large firm which regularly received American buyers reported 'not a single call' that season – with the state of the London market running 'a good second in disappointments' for many.[20] There were wage cuts throughout the district, with a general reduction of 10 per cent across the industry. This was 'a year of crisis'[21] all round: in 1931, armed forces and public sector salaries were also cut and unemployment benefit reduced by two shillings in the pound.

And yet. 'Despite the trade depression the demand continues,' Clarice Cliff told the *Daily Sketch* during a brief visit to London that summer.[22] Not all areas were equally affected by the Depression. Though regions of 'old' industry – coal mining, heavy engineering, textiles, ship-building and pottery – suffered high levels of unemployment, in areas of 'new' industry, such as electrical goods and car manufacture, unemployment was comparatively low. Indeed, the newer industries fared 'rather better'[23] during the 1930s than in the previous decade, and the construction industry positively boomed. With 'new' and 'old' industries situated in different parts of the country, unemployment showed a strong regional bias. While the hardship experienced by the unemployed was severe, for many standards of living were rising.

Speaking to the press in June, Colley Shorter spoke of pottery 'reflecting the phase of curves and curls in the feminine fashions of dress and house decoration. There is,' he said, 'a definite breaking away from the hard, severe lines, which have been the vogue in pottery as well as in everything else, and the autumn designs are all on soft and beautiful lines.'[24] He may have been thinking of the new pink glaze, 'Damask Rose', when applied to the 'Daffodil' tea set, whose curves owed a debt to Art Nouveau, but whose execution was nevertheless contemporary, or the narrow, tube-shaped vase, supported by soft and sweeping ceramic curves, which Clarice Cliff introduced that year 'to show single blooms to advantage'.[25] Other women designers were also producing work that reflected a new sensuality: Betty Joel's furniture echoed 'the Feminine form'.[26] Gone were the 'slate-pencil silhouette, the cloche hat, the cropped hair . . . Breasts, hips and bottoms made a sudden and welcome comeback,'[27] while in hairdressing salons far and wide, women requested the curls of the permanent wave. Gradually, tastes were changing, moving away from the energetic and confrontational. While Clarice Cliff continued to appeal to the liking for the futurist with abstract patterns, softer images were also being introduced. Although the ballooning trees of 'Autumn' (attributed to 1930) are extravagant in concept, their luscious foliage marks a departure from the assertively geometrical: Clarice Cliff's 'Autumn' trees are softly rounded. Landscape patterns issued from now on were mostly quieter in tone and full of yearning, as the winding path and red-roofed cottage at the heart of 'House and Bridge' suggests. These are images of reassurance, not adventure.

In the midst of the Depression, Clarice Cliff produced what was perhaps her most sentimental image, 'Appliqué Idyll'.[28] A 'crinoline lady', the embroidered subject of antimacassars, tea cosies and tray cloths throughout the land, provides the focus of this romantic pattern. With flowers decorating her hat and a posy held between gloved hands, she is shaded by a tree in a picture-book garden. In some versions, she reaches up to pluck the blossom from its branches, and in others stands erect, as if waiting for an unseen suitor. To ensure the pattern's swift decoration, the crinoline lady has no face – it is concealed beneath her hat, hinting at a delicate femininity. Bands of colour frame and complete the image and, in some colourings, suggest a rainbow. What could be more reassuring?

By the late summer of 1931, nearly 24,000 pottery workers were unemployed, with more than 40,000 out of work within the region as a whole. Withdrawal from the Gold Standard that September and the consequent run on the pound fuelled concern. While A.J. Wilkinson continued to proclaim Clarice Cliff's success, it did so that autumn with an old-fashioned appeal: 'Bizarre holds Miladyes [*sic*] Favours Against All Comers'²⁹ the advertisement announced, illustrating the statement with a drawing of a knight on horseback (Clarice Cliff's 'Knight Errant')³⁰, with the word 'Bizarre' unfurling on his standard. In the face of economic threat, traditional values were being reasserted.

Though Clarice Cliff was introducing 'soft lines and curves' to her tableware, the novelty lines she created that year were 'fearlessly handled as regards shape and colouring'.³¹ As the economic climate worsened, those who could afford distraction welcomed its ever more extravagant features. 'It is significant that the old English fondness for disguising everything as something else now attained the dimensions of a serious pathological affliction,' Osbert Lancaster observed. 'Gramophones masquerade as cocktail cabinets; cocktail cabinets as book-cases; radios lurk in tea-caddies and bronze nudes burst asunder at the waist-line to reveal cigarette lighters; and nothing is what it seems.'³² Although Clarice Cliff was not responsible for the offences described above, she nevertheless responded to the frivolity the public mood demanded.

One of the freedoms the inter-war years offered women was the freedom to smoke in public. They took this up with such alacrity that characters in a *Punch* cartoon were able to joke: '"There's a woman over there not smoking."' "My dear, there are some people who'll do anything to be conspicuous."'³³ Like others of the period, cigarette manufacturers courted the female consumer. Abdullah cigarettes, in particular, ran a witty series of cartoon and verse advertisements directed at the discerning female smoker, featuring such compelling contemporary issues as the woman's right to vote and the Bolshevik threat, as well as the growing passion for interior decoration. Clarice Cliff made her own appeal to the design-conscious smoker with a range of cigarette- and match-holders and ashtrays to complement her dinner services. No service was complete without its smoking apparatus; the matches themselves, their sulphurous tips mirroring the colours of her dinner ware, added a new dimension to the word 'striking'. Of all her smokers' designs, Clarice Cliff's 'Lido Lady' or 'Bathing Belle'³⁴ ashtray was her most jaunty. With her baggy, loose-fitting trousers, the figure captured 'the pyjama vogue' which had originated at the Lido and on the Côte d'Azur, and, according to 'Mr

Gossip' of the *Daily Sketch*, was now spreading 'all over the
Continent'.[35] The pyjama vogue had done much to alter travelling
fashions. 'Pyjamas have definitely supplanted evening dresses on the
Riviera,' Mr Gossip told his readers, 'and more than two-thirds of
the women at the various dinners dansants and galas wear them in
pastel colours.'[36] Clarice Cliff's ceramic models were equally fashion-
conscious. Their pyjamas came in the latest shades. One stylish 'Belle'
wore spots, while a more audacious figure coupled spots with the
floral pattern 'Chintz'. If Clarice Cliff's smoking paraphernalia
followed the latest word in fashion, the contemporary fantasy of
luxury and escapism was satisfied by her 'Ocean Liner' vase. This
transatlantic liner, its prow the sharpest of straight lines, offered innu-
merable voyages to those who journeyed only in their imagination.

In defiance of the increasingly austere demands made by
Modernists of the period, the buying public seemed to be engaged
in a quest to maintain the 'colour, fizz and bubble'[37] of the previous
decade for as long as possible. During the early 1930s, quirky figures
reappeared, reminiscent of those produced by Clarice Cliff some
years earlier, while supper plates for bridge parties proclaimed that
poverty was 'the banana skin on the doorstep of romance'[38] and
similar dinky aphorisms suited to the mood of the day. Clarice Cliff
was enjoying herself immensely. Critics of what she called 'innocent
tomfoolery' – and they termed 'low comedy' – were seen off with
the reminder that her business had increased steadily over recent
years. 'Having a little fun at my work doesn't make me less of an
artist,' she said.[39] Among her novelties were a series of wall masks
– women's faces, whose fixed enamel smiles and brilliant lips puck-
ered into perfect cupid's bows: the perfectly made-up face, glimpsed
on cinema screens in every town. Though her ceramic portraiture
could not come close to that of the Wiener Werkstätte, it nevertheless added a note of sophistication to the suburban sitting-room.
Not all masks spoke of Hollywood, although all had a contemporary appeal. 'It's all a question of masks, really; brittle, painted
masks,' Noël Coward informed his audience in *Design for Living*.
'We all wear them as a form of protection; modern life forces us
to.'[40] Clarice Cliff knew that better than most.

*

The 'Lido Lady' or 'Bathing Belle' ashtray

The 1920s and '30s raised unsettling possibilities for social class. With the aristocracy and the traditional middle class weakened by the First World War, manufacturers and industrialists benefiting from it, and a new lower-middle class of white-collar workers emerging, the period was one of social flux. Newspapers and magazines were quick to highlight social advancement. Social mobility was at its most appealing when it concerned the working-class young woman.

'Until a few months ago,' the *Sunday Chronicle* explained, 'Miss Barbara Wells, the mezzo-soprano, who was heard broadcasting in *One Crowded Hour* [on the BBC] last evening, was a factory worker at Woolwich. She helped in the manufacture of tennis rackets.'[41] Advertisements likewise pandered to the notion of girl-next-door makes good, albeit in a more traditional manner: 'How I married a millionaire – though I was poor,' an advertisement for Creme Tokalon Skinfood informed future hopefuls, with the additional encouragement that '(On account of the high international social prominence of the woman referred to above she does not want her name printed).'[42] Domestic tableware had its part to play. 'Best' tea and dinner services were themselves aspirational, promising entertainment and leisure, and perhaps furthering social ambition along the way. One writer linked domestic skills with social standing: 'There are many ambitious young hostesses today, in flats, in small houses, in suburban villas, who want to know more about Good Food, for their own and their friends' pleasure, and possibly – who will blame them? – with an eye to social advancement.'[43] Yet the parenthetic question says it all. There were plenty who were willing to lay blame.

In 1931, Clarice Cliff was appointed art director.[44] 'She is now the art director of a famous firm,' the *Yorkshire Evening News* reported that September, 'her name is known all over the world.'[45] By December, the *Daily Sketch* was describing Clarice Cliff as 'the only woman art director in the Potteries'.[46] From gilder to art director was newsworthy indeed. To be the only woman art director of a large commercial concern was an even greater achievement. Clarice Cliff had apparently attained the unattainable. Pottery companies were generally family-owned and family-run, and nearly always by the men of the family. Although Colley Shorter's mother attended board meetings occasionally, the decisions made within them were not hers. Even Susie Cooper who, in another highly unusual and significant achievement of that decade, had recently established and supervised a business of her own, did so with family backing and support, from within a business background and a different social class.[47]

Clarice Cliff's name was not listed on the company letterhead during this period, which suggests hers was a courtesy title rather than an office with financial liabilities. John Butler had been art director before her, in the same way. Butler left A.J. Wilkinson during this period; Clarice Cliff's growing prominence within the factory may have had a bearing on his decision. Her directorship was likely to have created further problems among the Shorters. It is difficult to imagine Guy being comfortable with the new arrangement; the wives and sisters of the family would also have had a view, particularly Annie Shorter, Colley's wife. Although Clarice Cliff's appointment formalised design freedoms and responsibilities she already enjoyed, it considerably extended her credibility. Perhaps, by default, it also appeared to confer respectability upon her relationship with Colley, which can only have affronted the family.

Clarice Cliff's professional advancement confirmed she was moving out of her social class. The Shorters probably considered her an upstart, as well as an outsider. If so, their response was symptomatic of broader class anxieties of the time. Their steady world was shaken – Clarice Cliff was not only disturbing a marriage, but unsettling alliances within the family firm. Though her relationship with Colley could be more or less ignored – like anything else that offended social mores – her status as director was a different matter. Her new role threatened the family firm in a way Butler's could never do: while his appointment sustained the status quo, hers showed how precarious that was. The family group that had looked so solid in the photograph circa 1926 was no longer so secure.

From her indenture as a modeller, through her studies at the Royal College of Art and appointment as director, each step took Clarice Cliff further from her roots. Social advancement was rarely as smooth as newspaper accounts liked to suggest. Despite the apparent mobility of the period, class remained an indelible marker; snobbery was rife (and continues to inform responses to Clarice Cliff's work today, for those who regard bold colouring as nothing short of vulgar). It was not simply a matter of professional achievement; there was the correct vocabulary to acquire, the right table manners and intonation, and all the other nuances that determine acceptability and are monitored by those reluctant to admit outsiders to their ranks. The transition required a continuing transformation and the confidence to carry a new role. René Cutforth described the

'Miss Clarice Cliff, the remarkable young artist who creates "Bizarre Ware" for a famous Burslem pottery firm', *Modern Home*, November 1930

strain that decade imposed: 'There was a Thirties face, a Thirties expression . . . and it went with an assessing, a sitting-in-judgment eye . . . you were on stage the whole time and tense with the effort of playing the part of a thoroughly relaxed and secure individual. The universal game was class assessment and judgment.'[48] With each advance in her professional status, Clarice Cliff's social position became both more certain and more unsteady.

In the early days of 'Bizarre', Clarice Cliff was known to her young charges by her first name. As the number of Girls in the workshop grew – girls of fourteen and fifteen joining paintresses two or three years older than themselves – and Clarice Cliff gained in stature, she asked to be known as 'Miss Cliff'. Paintresses who had always called her 'Clarice' were now required to adopt her formal title. One day she entered the warehouse, where women inspecting dinner ware were calling out to one another across the room. Some of them she had known for years – as some, perhaps, were only too pleased to remind her. 'What should I do with this, Clarice?' Someone jogged her elbow, waved a damaged plate. Her remonstrance was immediate: 'Don't you think it's time you started to call me Miss Cliff?'[49]

The woman in authority was still a rarity. 'The woman boss is a matter for comic pictures and music-hall jokes and sly banter,[50] the writer Winifred Holtby complained; and when women MPs sat for their first all-night parliamentary session, the *Daily Mail* was more concerned to describe their clothing than their words.[51] For Clarice Cliff's 'Bizarre Girls' – and paintresses throughout the industry – there was nothing unusual in having a woman boss: the 'missus' had long ruled the workshop. Though they were unused to women designers, they recognised female authority. More difficult was Clarice Cliff's relationship with the rest of the factory.

Success and changing status do not necessarily bring popularity, particularly if envy sometimes plays a part, and Clarice Cliff's situation was further complicated by the disapproval of some of those with knowledge of her relationship with Colley Shorter. She was said to be unpopular with his secretary, that guardian of Colley's days, and with Harry Steele, the general manager of Shorter & Son, while more than one employee recalled Guy Shorter speaking to her only when necessary. Surrounded by suspicion and distrust, she probably defended herself to such a degree that many of her exchanges were combative. On top of which, she was a designer who sometimes faced resistance to her ideas. There were myriad ways in which designers could be undermined; some subtle, others less so: experimental glazes thrown away 'by accident' because the general manager did not like the look of them; or the kiln set early on a day the designer was known to be rushing to fire new sample pieces – sleights of hand that could make life difficult. Designing in the face of opposition could require an equal cussedness on the designer's part.

Recollections of Clarice Cliff suggest she did not try hard to win allies beyond the decorating shop. She already had the best ally, after all, and was not seeking friendship, but respect. That did not always make her easy to work with. An employee who was overheard criticising her designs was told her opinion did not matter because they sold.[52] In pushing the boundaries of design, Clarice Cliff pushed the factory too, particularly the men who assisted in the creation of her more complex shapes, the head modeller, Joe Woolliscroft, and the clay manager, Bill Lunt, whose relationship with 'that bloody woman'[53] could be stormy. Lunt's was not a lone voice. Most likely there were occasions when, walking through a workshop or crossing the factory yard, Clarice heard a whisper fade at her approach or caught the edge of an oath. Even those who were unaware of any thread of gossip connecting her with Colley knew she was Shorter's designer, protected by his smile, an occurrence sufficiently rare they would not wish to jeopardise it, nor indeed themselves, by speaking out of turn within her hearing. Did she read the suspicion on their faces, see the way they did not like to catch her eye or say more than they felt was necessary? The older men, in particular, must have found it hard, taking orders from a woman, especially one whom they had known as some young slip of a lass. At times, hers was a steely progress through the factory.

In the autumn of 1931, Clarice Cliff spoke to the *Bristol Times*. 'I love mixing bold tints – rich oranges, reds, greens, blues and mauves,' she told Millicent Hardiman. 'These make a glorious riot of colour on large articles of pottery. On breakfast, dinner and tea sets, though, too much design is not effective, but harmony of colours is most important.'[54] She also appealed directly to the ways in which women's lives were changing: 'In these times of money scarcity, articles that have a useful as well as a decorative purpose have a more general appeal. Labour-saving is another important factor . . . my table china is designed on lines that simplify its cleaning.'[55] Women were responding to these changes throughout the world of design: they were to the fore in adapting their work to meet the new domestic climate.[56]

The *Bristol Times* interview took place during an exhibition for which A.J. Wilkinson joined forces with Paragon China, with which the firm shared a London agent, to display a series of table settings arranged by 'well-known editresses of national women's magazines'.[57] The exhibition, which ran for a fortnight, took place in Fleet Street, thus guaranteeing strong interest from the press. The link between pottery manufacturers and 'several accepted leaders of feminine thought'[58] was timely. The period between the wars saw a significant rise in the number of women's magazines. Between 1922 and 1939, more than eleven new monthly periodicals emerged, the majority of which were directed at middle- and lower-middle-class women.[59] A.J. Wilkinson further strengthened the relationship by offering *Woman's Journal*, one of the more upmarket of the new magazines, a tea set with an exclusive 'Clarice Cliff' pattern: 'Conical' tea cups decorated with brightly coloured flowers provided the latest word in afternoon tea. As Clarice Cliff's popularity grew, women were invited to write to the Newport Pottery for information and a young woman was employed to respond to their enquiries.

The magazine which featured Clarice Cliff's work most frequently during this period was *Modern Home*. Launched in October 1928, priced sixpence, this was one of the new titles directed at the middle-class woman. This 'Magazine of New Ideas' provided 'technical pages to assist with 'every aspect of home planning and equipment', 'entertainment features' and a 'craft section', together with 'more intimate articles [to] discuss the subtle side of "home-making" upon which the charm of the house depends'.[60] Practical advice for the modern hostess sat side by side with fiction. *Modern Home*'s first issue introduced the reader to a serial by the popular romantic novelist Ruby M. Ayres (who led her fictional heroines to the bedroom door, but no further) and three short stories, among them 'Glamour' by Storm Jameson: 'Each month a leading authoress . . . will contribute what she considers to be her most "true-to-life" romance',[61] the editor advised her readers. Their escapism was to be tempered by reality.

Modern Home was directed at the woman with little or no domestic help. 'Take Care of your Floors' and 'How to Use Paint' were among the articles in its first issue.[62] (Magazines and advertisements of the inter-war years assumed decorating was solely a woman's responsibility.) A photogravure supplement – a regular feature of the magazine and the era – offered readers the inspiration of 'Other People's Homes'. Like other magazines of the time, *Modern Home* proffered mixed messages. 'The girl who is out at business all day', and lucky enough to enjoy the benefits of 'An Up-to-the-Minute Town Flat', with its 'central heating, constant hot water, gas, electric light and power and a restaurant', was unlikely to spend her evenings making appliqué dinner mats or 'New Cushions for Old', though readers who struggled to afford the labour-saving devices advertised within the magazine's pages must have often wished themselves transported to a similar mansion flat. Help was close at hand, however. 'Buying "On the Nod"' advised readers about hire purchase, which was fast transforming consumer spending at this time. The woman who read *Modern Home* was a home-*maker*, concerned with every aspect of domestic life. And when her floors were clean and her walls freshly painted, a piece of the latest 'Clarice Cliff' added the finishing touch to her interior scheme.

In 1931, the *Daily Mail* reported that Clarice Cliff was designing for three factories.[63] In addition to her work for the Newport Pottery, she was also producing designs for A.J. Wilkinson and Shorter & Son. Although her Newport patterns – 'Bizarre', 'Fantasque', etc. – bore the 'Clarice Cliff' signature, her designs for the other companies did not (though those originally marketed as A.J. Wilkinson occasionally transferred to Newport if it was felt a particular design would benefit from her trademark). A.J. Wilkinson continued to produce an extensive range of lithograph and print-and-enamel patterns, as well as fancies; Shorter & Son, originally noted for its production of majolica*, was now developing a range of matt-glaze earthenware, much of which was also ornamental.[64] For a designer who was as playful as she was inventive, there was plenty of scope to explore new possibilities.

Designing for three factories gave Clarice Cliff considerable flexibility and even greater power but, inevitably, made further demands upon her time. 'It would be of course impossible for me to do it all now,' she told the *Bristol Times*, 'so I teach boys and girls who show aptitude for design my own methods.'[65] How many employee designs reached production and were sold as 'Clarice Cliff' is impossible to know; some have been identified, however. A 'Grotesque' face mask created in 1929 was credited to Ron Birks, who received a royalty for his work,[66] and an apprentice, Fred Salmon, was allowed to sign a small number of patterns he created, although their tone was more traditional than that normally produced by the 'Bizarre' shop;[67] a pattern book includes 'Hand Painted Scenes' by Harold Walker, another workshop boy.[68] While a small number of 'Bizarre Girls' also recall creating designs which were issued under Clarice Cliff's name – Margery Higginson produced a floral pattern made by finger painting, for example – others counter that there was no opportunity for employees to produce their own work.[69] Some 270-plus patterns were marketed as 'Bizarre' during the late 1920s and 1930s and it has not yet been established that any well-known pattern was conceived by an employee, which suggests that such designs were either few or not manufactured in great quantity. One thing is certain: however many employees created their own designs, decisions about their production were Clarice Cliff's.

A press report at the end of 1931 showed how far she had come. On 4 December, the back page of the northern edition of the *Daily Sketch* was dedicated to 'Bizarre'. (The frequency of *Daily Sketch* reports and its ability to pick up the latest developments suggests a particularly enthusiastic correspondent on the paper.) Beneath the banner headline, 'How Famous Bizarre Ware is Made at Stoke', a special feature page illustrated the workings of the Newport and Royal Staffordshire Potteries with eight grainy photographs and captions. The most appealing of these shows the 'Bizarre' shop itself: row after row of paintresses, heads bent low over cotton pinafores.

Back-cover feature, *Daily Sketch*, 4 December 1931

With brushes poised above their work, they present a picture of
absolute concentration. Clarice Cliff's popular status was thus
confirmed – as was Shorter's salesmanship: 1,000 copies of the *Sketch*
were delivered to key customers.[70]

The feature offered Clarice Cliff the perfect photo opportunity,
one she evidently declined. Despite the focus of the piece, there is no
accompanying photograph of Clarice Cliff herself, which must have
disappointed the newspaper. Faced with the colourful exclamations
of 'Clarice Cliff', designs, interviewers anticipated the same of their
creator and were surprised to discover that she was not as bold or
outrageous as her work. Although she spoke to the press on numerous
occasions, she did not court publicity for herself. One reviewer was
'astonished to find a shy girl';[71] she was also said to be 'quiet,
restrained and earnest, with a feminine charm' that another thought
'sweetly "old-fashioned" despite the extreme modernism of her decorative ideas'.[72] What is more, she was 'singularly modest'.[73] Clarice
Cliff claimed 'no special personal merit for the happy revolution she
has brought about';[74] there was 'no hint of pride in her tone',[75] which
was not what reviewers expected. Repeatedly, the designer was
confused with her designs.

From the earliest appearances of 'Bizarre', Clarice Cliff was a
subject of press interest; particularly fascinating – along with the

exuberance of her work – was the capacity for romance within her story, as the *Daily Mirror* noted: 'One of the romances of the pottery trade has been that of Miss Clarice Cliff, who a short time back was a modeller for a pottery firm.'[76] For the *Daily Telegraph*, her achievements were simply 'phenomenal'.[77] That Clarice Cliff's success continued to be something of a novelty was underlined when a photograph illustrating her work was captioned: 'A modern pottery tea set designed by a woman'.[78]

'Until I saw her picture,' one interviewer remarked, 'I imagined her as being tall, fragile, having an aesthetic faraway kind of look in her eyes, but . . . she is short, plump, and oh, so merry looking.'[79] Judged by her appearance, Clarice Cliff was an unlikely symbol for the times. Not for her the sleek athleticism of the women who stride across period bronzes with their borzoi hounds, nor the slim figure seen to best effect in the short, cylindrical frocks of the 1920s and the satin evening gowns of the following decade. This period saw the first pangs of weight consciousness. 'And do you drink at meals?' a doctor asks his patient, in a contemporary cartoon. 'Don't be silly, Doctor. Why, I don't even *eat* at meals,' is her reply.[80] Though curves were making a comeback, fashion still dictated to the slimmer figure and, from the end of the 1920s, skirts lengthened, much to the consternation of those with no desire to return to the imprisonment of longer clothes. In an extended correspondence on the *Guardian* Women's Page, the writer Naomi Mitchison and others of like mind argued for the shorter hemline and the freedoms that went with it.[81] E.M. Delafield's Provincial Lady typified the confusion of the times. 'Women will never again submit to long skirts in the day-time,'[82] she confidently asserted; only to 'Perceive that Everybody in the World except myself is wearing long skirts, a tiny hat on extreme back of head, and vermilion lipstick'[83] two years later.

The longer skirt and tiny hat suited Clarice Cliff. Hers was the figure of the matron, not the vamp, although the addition of a cigarette and holder in years to come doubtless added a vampish quality to her image. Interviews were sometimes accompanied by her photograph: the factory took its own pictures too. Increasingly, she appeared looking smart and in later photographs, was mostly seen without an overall. One picture shows her in a dark dress with leg-of-mutton sleeves and a lengthy string of pearls, possibly a gift from Colley Shorter. A black skull cap sits snugly on her head. Elsewhere, she is wearing one of the Liberty scarves she favoured. (In a Liberty advertising brochure, a modern young woman meets HIM at a country-house weekend, with her Liberty scarf draped across her shoulders.)[84] Newspaper photographs of Clarice Cliff were taken at exhibitions, mostly, and so gave the lie to the soot and dust of factory life. The idea of female pottery designers being 'fragile . . . aesthetic' creatures may have suited the mythology of the time, but could not have been further from the truth. Potting was hard and heavy work which required strong hands.

Clarice Cliff's employees say no photograph did her justice. She had 'a most charming smile',[85] 'very blue eyes and long dark lashes'.[86] Interviewers agreed that she was pretty. She was variously said to have 'merry eyes that seem to dance',[87] and to be 'happy as a lark',[88] which suggests she was frequently amused by proceedings. If, in manner and appearance, Clarice Cliff surprised her interviewers, the comment that she had 'a delightfully calm expression, which hints at a tremendous reserve of strength of purpose'[89] was one of their more perceptive remarks. She was described as a 'vivacious, very alive-looking girl'.[90] Again and again, one senses her vitality.

Like many who find popular success, reports of Clarice Cliff's swift ascent disguised years of dedication. Yet the story of her hard work was also part of her appeal. As with many romances, the truth was sometimes blurred. One press report offered this version of her 'discovery': 'The manager . . . decided that here was a girl worth watching, and, one day, he took her away from the kilns and set her to work in the midst of the clay. She had never had a lesson in modelling but he gave orders that she was to be left entirely to her own devices for a month. At the end of that time, she brought him some original designs that surprised even the man who had such faith in her, and from that day her future was assured.'[91] The notion of Clarice Cliff being left to her own devices for a month as a young factory worker seems improbable, to say the least. It is notable that this formed part of an overseas promotion.

Although Clarice Cliff and Colley Shorter were adept at securing attention for 'Bizarre', they were sometimes inconsistent in their conversations with the press. The number said to work with her varied from one press report to another and was, at times, said to be as high as 200. This figure may have included those engaged in the production of 'Bizarre' who were not actually paintresses, or may have been an instance of Clarice Cliff bolstering the size of her workforce. 'Bizarre Girls' themselves recall their number to have been in the region of sixty much of the time (and employment dates suggest the total reached the seventies).[92]

In a bid to underline Clarice Cliff's modernity, the idea of her youth was promoted. In one review, 'a representative' of A.J. Wilkinson – Colley Shorter, most likely – described her as being 'scarcely out of her teens'[93] when she was already in her thirties; she was frequently presented as being younger than her years. In the argot of the times, Clarice Cliff was, anyway, generally represented as a 'girl', a description which makes her achievements sound all the more remarkable and up to the minute. Her story had all the ingredients to tempt the national press, suggesting that ordinary women could succeed against the odds, could rise in a profession if they dedicated themselves, even, perhaps, find fame, as she had done. But behind the newspaper reports lay some of the contradictions of the period, and of Clarice Cliff's own life, not least the fact that her work sustained the domestic ideology she herself resisted.

The designs themselves unsettled notions of female behaviour, speaking as they did to a modernity that was far from decorous. Clarice Cliff's work did not sit quietly on a table in the corner of a room, but called out 'look at me', at a time when, despite press reports to the contrary and women's aspirations, women were expected to sit quietly at home. At home with their husband and family. Not stay late in a factory creating patterns some thought brash, nor give rise to speculation about the nature of their relationship with their employer. Though Clarice Cliff designed tableware to complement a home, the Mrs Grundys of the period would have thought her a home-wrecker, had they known the details of her private life. On this matter, Clarice Cliff was silent. 'She simply refused to talk about herself,' *Woman's Life* reported, before concluding that she was 'wedded to her art'.[94] As was, indeed, the case. But Clarice Cliff had another reason for remaining silent: modernity had its limits, especially where women were concerned.

TWELVE

A Furore of Colouring

By 1932, the issue of women designers in the pottery industry was becoming a matter of debate. In the spring of that year, Gordon Forsyth addressed the Design and Industries Association on the subject: 'It [is] a singular thing that there [are] so few women designers in the pottery trade,' he told them. 'There [is] room for more. It would be thought that an educated woman of first-class intelligence would be the one to cater for her own sex, that she would understand the feminine mind and their desire for fresh ideas.'[1] Forsyth went on to praise the work of Susie Cooper, before continuing that the only other two women he could think of as having served a long and arduous apprenticeship to the pottery trade, and who were now actually producing good work, were 'Miss Rogers of Clifton Junction and Miss Clarice Cliffe [*sic*] of Wilkinson . . . There [is] also Mrs Carter.'[2]

Forsyth might also have mentioned Charlotte Rhead at the Gordon Pottery and Millicent Taplin who, as foremistress of the decorating department at Wedgwood, was producing her own patterns. Nevertheless, the naming of a mere handful of women from within an industrial district of some 300 potteries indicates how few there were at the time. (Their numbers were, at least, an improvement on the past, when even fewer women could have been named.)[3] Not that the industry was inundated with male designers either: 90 per cent of pottery firms had no designated designer in their employ. Under Forsyth's direction, a younger generation of women designers was emerging from the Burslem School of Art, among them Mabel Leigh, who would soon join Shorter & Son, but their names were not yet known – nor would they ever attain as high a public profile as Clarice Cliff. Yet Forsyth had a word of caution for aspirant designers. 'Because . . . there was room for more ladies in the pottery trade, they must not rush into it and think they were going at once to be pottery designers. They would have to serve many years of very earnest work first.'[4]

Earnest work was continuing for Clarice Cliff. Colley Shorter gave some indication of the extent of her responsibilities when he addressed a meeting of the Society of Industrial Artists.[5] In semi-humorous vein, he listed some of the skills 'the average pottery manufacturer expects from his designer'. His demands were extensive and would have taxed the most efficient of designers, hence his tone. They included settling prices for printing, enamelling and gilding, writing up description books, estimating the costs of decoration, designing shapes – and preferably modelling them personally – spending time with salesmen each week and seeing the commercial principal of the firm daily, as well as keeping an eye on the work of competitors and beating their prices. Was Shorter not asking 'a little too much', a member of his audience enquired. The *Pottery Gazette* reported:

> [He replied that] they might well think it was impossible for anyone to do what he had suggested, but he would like to say that he knew of one of the most successful designers in the Potteries, whose work during the last five years had sold as well as, and probably better than, most, who was determined, when starting in the decorating department of a pottery many years ago, to master every branch of pottery decoration. After starting at gilding at one shilling a week, that designer stayed at that job until able to earn full wages at gilding. This was followed by another place at which enamelling was tackled. This, again, was followed by a period of hand-painting, lithographing, printing, and even throwing. The result was that, today, that person, in the event of there being any query as to how much should be paid for a particular job, and the possibility of earning wages at it, would sit down, take a dozen plates, and enamel, paint, gild or trace-and-line them, in order to test the position. And the firm

employing that designer was then perfectly happy to settle the price for the respective jobs judged by those results. It seemed a big thing to contemplate, but it was not impossible, and it was even desirable. He was almost omitting to say that the same designer had studied at the Royal College of Art in South Kensington, and could model in addition to wielding the brush.[6]

Though Shorter did not name the designer he praised so highly, her identity is as clear as his admiration for her.

Retail order books from 1932 give some insight into the extensive range and scope of Clarice Cliff's work during this period. Together, they cover orders placed between early March and the end of October; one, in particular, which runs from June, shows how colourful that summer was for Clarice Cliff.[7] Here are page after page of hand-written orders, their lists scrubbed through with pale blue pencil, once dispatched. Their pattern names convey a feast of colour and display – 'Blue Palermo', 'Fantasque Summerhouse', 'Sungay', 'Inspiration', 'Blue Chintz', 'Citrus', 'Red Fuschia', 'Pastelle Fruit', to name but some of them. 'What was at first a very small department has grown into a very big one,' the *Pottery Gazette* observed that year. 'New shapes, new patterns, new flashes of colour, are constantly being introduced.'[8]

Although the London branches of department stores feature prominently – Maple & Co., Lawley's, Bon Marché, John Lewis, Peter Robinson, Selfridges, John Barker & Co., Waring & Gillow, Gorringe Ltd, Harrods, etc; one extensive Harrods' order covers three dates in September, suggesting that stock levels were constantly replenished – provincial department stores, such as Griffin & Spalding in Nottingham and Harrogate's Marshall & Snelgrove, also figure. Contrary to a popular misconception, Woolworth's does not: Clarice Cliff's work was not on sale there.[9]

Orders placed during this period were mostly for small quantities – typically, ones, or twos and threes – in an extensive range of shapes and patterns, indicating that part of Clarice Cliff's success lay in the variety she offered, a variety at one with the growing tendency for a wider choice of small 'editions' that emerged within that decade. Showcards and 'Bizarre' banners also make appearances – the summer of 1932 may have seen a particular marketing push or, just as likely, demonstrate the vehemence with which 'Bizarre' was regularly marketed. There are extensive orders from individual shops as well as department stores: Miss Mussell of Kay's Pantry, Petts Wood, near Orpington in Kent, was obviously making something of a splash with Clarice Cliff that June – her order included two showcards, together with an extensive list of tableware whose very names beguile: 'Crocus' teapots in assorted shapes – 'Conical', 'Stamford' and 'Globe' – honeys in 'Café au lait Green' and 'Nuage Orange'; bowls in 'Red Trees and House', 'Fantasque Orange Mosaic' and 'Pastel Autumn', together with numerous fancies, three 'Bathing Belle' ashtrays among them.

Stockists were countrywide – from Glasgow to Exmouth, from Merthyr Tydfil to Norwich – in large and small towns, as well as cities, confirming that those in full employment still had money to spend. Shops in the north of England and in Scotland ordered a range of patterns, indicating that the original division between Clarice Cliff's appeal in the north and south had long since healed. Seaside resorts figure prominently. The summer of 1932 was particularly hot. Southern England and London experienced 'a heat wave of unusual intensity' that year, with London, especially, enjoying 'a succession of almost tropical nights'.[10] '[I]t blazes; swoons; the heat,' Virginia Woolf wrote in her diary.[11] The temperature was such that the usual codes of dress were 'considerably modified': even the appearance of beach trousers on Oxford Street and 'bright yellow pyjamas' on Tottenham Court Road did not cause a 'riot [nor] even a shower of protesting letters to the newspapers'.[12] No wonder the 'Bathing Belle' was in demand. So, too, was 'Gibraltar', a pattern whose sailing boats and shimmering seas offered an escape from the city.

Items ordered by Aspinall & Son, in Barmouth, in July included sugar sifters, cruet sets and honey pots – ideal gifts or treats, small enough to be tucked into a suitcase and carried home as mementoes of the perfect summer holiday. 'For Presents Give "Bizarre",' A.J. Wilkinson advised.[13] Evidently, its words were being heeded. Other seaside shops also tended towards small items, sometimes in large quantity – Messrs D.C. Shimmin, from Douglas, on the Isle of Man, for instance, ordered thirty-six ashtrays and honies, and forty-eight muffineers, all decorated in 'Crocus'. Individuals placed small orders – Miss N. Young of Ashley Road, Hale, Cheshire required four plates in 'Damask Rose' – as did small shops, including one in London's Palmers Green. Perhaps the poet Stevie Smith paused before its window, startled by the latest 'Clarice Cliff'. Domestic middle-class life during the 1930s is writ large between these pages: here are tea sets sold in Forest Gate, ink wells and toast racks on sale in Ambleside, and mustard pots in Bromley, together with 26-piece dinner services and coffee cans displayed in Oxford Street. There are also repeat orders from a branch of Lawley's in Stoke-on-Trent, despite the belief of Clarice Cliff's paintresses that her designs were not available locally.

The 1932 order books point up some of the contrasts of the Depression years, the discrepancy between the haves and the have-nots, of whom there were so many during that period. Between 1932 and 1933, 23 per cent of the labour force was unemployed, and September 1932 – the month in which the *Pottery Gazette* commended Clarice Cliff's constantly expanding lines of tableware – saw unemployment peak at 3.75 million. In contrast to colourful days at A.J. Wilkinson, the early 1930s saw Wedgwood on the verge of bankruptcy. With a considerable proportion of its turnover dependent on American trade, the firm was one of the first and hardest hit by the Wall Street Crash; its European sales also suffered. In 1931, Wedgwood's total sales fell by 40 per cent; during the first half of 1932, sales of china dropped by a further 50 per cent.[14] 'Times were bad when I started at the Etruria Works in 1932,' a Wedgwood cup-handler recalled. 'Potbanks were closing down because of the recession . . . we had a boy . . . who couldn't afford a good pair of shoes. Mrs Cecil Wedgwood . . . straightaway bought him a new pair of clogs.'[15] 'It wasn't easy to find work in the 1930s,' a lithographer agreed, 'so I counted myself lucky to get a job doing three days a week at Minton's when I left school.'[16] Seniority was not exempt from hardship: the wages of senior staff were cut at Wedgwood. Groups of unemployed men stood hunched and brooding on street corners, children begged for bread (and hoped for cake), as they had when Clarice Cliff was a young factory worker, and, just beyond the reach of A.J. Wilkinson, the Trent and Mersey Canal was said to provide a final, filthy resting place for those who found the Slump too hard to bear.

'We were never on the dole,' one 'Bizarre Girl' said, with evident relief.[17] She recalled occasions when Clarice Cliff 'had the girls painting anything', however old-fashioned – pitchers, ewers, etc. – to ensure their constant occupation, and to make use of everything to hand. Having witnessed the hardship of unemployment as a young gilder, Clarice Cliff was no doubt all the more determined to protect her own workforce. She succeeded: 75 per cent of 'Bizarre' was sold in the home market during this period. A.J. Wilkinson was not the only pottery manufacturer to buck the Depression. Shelley managed to do so, while the downturn in trade actually helped Susie Cooper establish her own company – 'If things were buoyant no factory would have given me premises,' she said – even if business got off to a chequered start because of it.[18] Manufacturers who appealed to modern tastes and trends rode the difficult climate; Wedgwood was saved from bankruptcy by 'unexpected but crucial business from Cadbury's'.[19] The company noted for its delicate Jasper ware received an order for earthenware beakers and saucers which could be exchanged for labels from Bournvita drinking chocolate. 'New' England came to the rescue of the 'old' industrial one, and saved 200 jobs.

The Depression still prompted narratives of escapism and cheer, and the reassuring security of 'Home Sweet Home'. Further 'Clarice Cliff' patterns featured quaint cottages as motifs; flowers were abidingly popular. The evolution of floral patterns during the 1930s was such that, within a relatively short time, modern tableware became a horticulturalist's delight, as manufacturers vied with one another to produce yet more colourful foliage. (Though there was surely a note of desperation behind one manufacturer's decision to decorate his ware with 'an interesting rendering of a spray of deadly nightshade'.)[20]

There was nothing naturalistic about the flowers that bloomed on Clarice Cliff's tableware. For the most part, these were large and stylised, with extravagant petals roaming the surface of a tea cup or jug. Unlike the delicate rosebuds and forget-me-nots of old, these flowers had presence and, above all, colour. 'As regards the intensity of colouring,' the *Pottery Gazette* remarked that year of Clarice Cliff's 'Nasturtium', 'it might be difficult, if one searched the trade throughout, to find its equal.'[21] Painted cheer was everywhere, and could be purchased in the very latest styles.

As the contrasts of the decade become more pronounced, so did the gap between image and reality, particularly in relation to women's lives. Not least of the contradictions was the way in which women's professional horizons were shrinking at a time when, socially and culturally, their world was otherwise expanding.[22] The increasing popularity of sport and other leisure activities – the rise in the readership of novels and the number of women writers, for example – all served to broaden women's lives. The cinema introduced a new democracy – 'factory workers, shop girls and debs went to the same films'.[23] On screen, the same dreams were available to all.

Reality was slow to catch up with fantasy, as commentators of the period were aware. 'Except for the comparatively fortunate owners of modern tenement flats,' Vera Brittain observed in 1932, 'the wage-earning classes of this country still live in badly planned, inconvenient little houses which harbour dirt, involve incessant labour, and are totally unequipped with the most elementary devices for saving time and toil.'[24] Rose Macaulay described the multiple and frequently conflicting messages directed at women at this time: 'How to dress the kiddies, keep the home nice, make your husband comfortable, succeed in business or at the Bar, use your vote, choose a car . . . What a life is this into which we have been flung!'[25] No wonder the writer Mary Borden referred to the 'chaos of illogical notions, contradictory longings and confused images'[26] with which women were constantly bombarded.

If the majority of women discovered that reality did not match the visions promoted by the popular press and cinema screen, their lives were nevertheless more colourful in a variety of ways. Cheaper, brighter clothing and the vogue for painted furnishings and colourful tableware were radical departures from the past and Clarice Cliff was at the forefront of this change. 'Miss Cliff has probably done more to bring colour into the homes of the middle classes than anyone else,' the *Daily Sketch* concluded.[27] The alacrity with which women responded to her work underlined the extent to which they had previously felt 'starved of colour'.[28] The release from drab into colour, and the new possibilities afforded by wider choice, gave greater numbers of women a sense of flexibility and freedom, even if that freedom was largely circumscribed. In an era that perpetuated a domestic ideology, the ways of alleviating and personalising its codes became all the more important.

No contrasts of the decade were more pronounced than those within Clarice Cliff's own life: the independent professional woman and company director who shared a terraced house with her parents; the newsworthy designer whose story was widely told, but not wholly revealed. As the 1930s progressed, the differences between Clarice's life and that of her sisters became increasingly apparent – though less so with Dorothy, perhaps, who, like Clarice, was independent, albeit on a different scale. Hannah and Ethel now had children of their own, while, for Sarah, the contrast was particularly striking. With their parents now in their sixties, exhausted by long years of work, the responsibilities of the household increasingly fell to her. She probably lost count of the occasions when she had just finished the dishes and put Nancy to bed as Clarice arrived home from some professional event, wearing a diamond eternity ring and a dress from a London store.

Contrasts cut both ways, of course. For Clarice Cliff, weekdays of professional satisfaction and excitement were followed by weekends and holidays which accentuated the gap between her public and private life. Long and varied hours offered few chances to socialise[29] and friendships within the Potteries were, anyway, made difficult for Clarice because of her relationship with Colley. One of her few friends, Gertie Langford, was a buyer at Griffin & Spalding, whom she drove to Nottingham to see. Wakes Week, the annual August celebration when pottery workers holidayed and the accumulated filth of an industrial year disappeared beneath a coat of whitewash, was likely to have been especially difficult, and the experience heightened by the fact that the towns themselves acquired a look of abandonment when the kilns stopped firing.[30]

Equally pronounced was the difference between Clarice Cliff's home life and Colley Shorter's, not just his wife and daughters, but the trappings of a manufacturer's household – the governess, the horses, the games of tennis played on his own court – plus 'Chetwynd' itself which, in July 1932, was the subject of a feature in *Town and Country Homes*, as if to underline their different circumstances.[31] Like the majority of manufacturers, Colley lived in one of the outlying Staffordshire villages 'from which the Potteries are only seen as a distant haze'.[32] 'Chetwynd' itself, which occupies land originally owned by the Duke of Sutherland, is a classic of the Arts and Crafts style, and was built by Barry Parker and Raymond Unwin, who set out their principles in *The Art of Building a Home: A Collection of Lectures and Illustrations* (1901), written while the house was under construction; the book features a detailed account of the property and its floor plan.

However strong the temptation, Clarice needed to resist the desire to turn her car in this direction and take her thoughts through the front door and into Colley's home, or pause outside the stable yard and peer inside the gates. On one occasion, she delivered something there, taking Nancy with her as companion and safety net.[33] It cannot have been an easy experience. If Clarice did not see how Colley lived, it was easier to maintain no other life existed that was as real as the one they shared. She must have longed for their next trip to London.

In the late summer of 1932, A.J. Wilkinson 'went "all out"' with a 'memorable exhibition'[34] at the Throne Room of the Holborn Restaurant, where Clarice Cliff and Colley Shorter were joined by several 'personalities' of the moment – the stage actresses Adrienne Allen, Marion Lorne and Marie Tempest, the BBC presenter Christopher Stone, theatrical producer Leslie Henson, and musical comedy star, Bobby Howes. As a marketing ploy, this was exceedingly inventive. 'Three of the most popular actresses in London chose new pottery ware for their own homes this week,' the *Daily Mirror* reported,[35] while the *Daily Sketch* informed its readers that 'Bobby Howes ordered dinner ware as well as a nursery service for his children.'[36] Marion Lorne's presence at the autumn display ensured that the 'ideal tea and breakfast set for her topmost flat in Piccadilly'[37] attracted the attention of not only the national press,

Marion Lorne

LAYS HER TABLE *Like This!*

Photo by Paul Tanqueray

THIS set of six plates and a fruit bowl designed for Miss Lorne, by Clarice Cliff, can be bought for 21s.

ISN'T this table gay and inviting? It was specially arranged by Miss Marion Lorne.

MISS MARION LORNE, who in her own inimitable way, has delighted thousands of playgoers by her acting in *Road House*, at the Whitehall Theatre, takes a great interest in her home, and loves to go out in search of pretty accessories to add to the charm of her rooms.

She chose this lovely fruit set, she says, "because it was so gay—not strikingly modern, but just beautifully colourful." The set consists of six plates and a fruit bowl, designed specially for Miss Lorne, by Clarice Cliff. The background is cream with a design of orange and yellow citron fruits, and leaves of smoky blue and light and dark green outlined in a soft shade of brown.

Although she is a real home-lover, Marion Lorne is a thoroughly out-of-door person, and every Saturday she and her playwright husband, Walter Hackett, motor down to their bungalow in Sussex.

Even when she is in London, Marion Lorne never misses her daily walk. Wet or fine, she and Ambrose, her dog, set out solemnly to do their regulation mile and a half. But don't expect to meet them in the streets or the park—you must look upwards if you want to see them. For their route is always the same—up and down the balcony of the flat overlooking Piccadilly.

Ambrose is a devoted companion, and goes everywhere with his mistress. He even accompanies her to the theatre—in fact, it is sometimes said that Ambrose simply runs the theatre!

Modern China

Modern Home, January 1933

Colley Shorter with Sir Malcolm Campbell at the First Avenue Hotel, London

but of *Woman's Life* and *Modern Home*, thus extending the promotion into the following year. 'I think this dessert set is the loveliest I have seen and it is most awfully sweet of Miss Clarice Cliff to design it specially for me,' she wrote to A.J. Wilkinson,[38] referring to a pattern which combined citrus fruits with 'Delecia'-style streams. 'The colouring is wonderful. Very many thanks, Marion Lorne.' It was probably only a matter of hours before Shorter dispatched copies of her note to significant retailers. Future invitations were extended to Gertrude Lawrence and members of the Crazy Gang, as well as to Sir Malcolm Campbell, whose ability to break his own land speed record, year on year, made him a national hero, and ensured that 'Bizarre' continued to be associated with the absolutely up to the minute.

These initiatives have the ring of Colley Shorter, although, by now, Clarice Cliff must have been equally well informed. Whenever time permitted, she had London to explore: like Waring & Gillow, Peter Jones had its own modern furnishing department, and Liberty and Selfridges continued to be a draw, particularly after the latter's refurbishment. For anyone interested in the latest styles, Marion Dorn Ltd was situated off Bond Street, while Dunbar Hay yielded fabrics designed by Vanessa Bell and Duncan Grant, and Gordon Russell's furniture shop on Wigmore Street, together with Heal's, offered much to examine, and Knightsbridge housed Betty Joel's showroom. If Clarice Cliff found herself alone, however, or in the company of another woman late one evening – if she and Hilda Lovatt wanted to find a restaurant after preparing for the Throne Room display – her enjoyment of the city may have been curtailed. In 1930, Winifred Holtby denounced the number of restaurants and cafés which, after certain hours, refused to admit women unaccompanied by men.[39] Though the professional woman was no longer such a rarity, thoughts of the oldest profession still held sway.

Trips to London provided opportunities to see the latest plays – perhaps Clarice and Colley were fortunate enough to see Gertrude Lawrence star in *Private Lives* – while all wireless listeners knew of Christopher Stone, whose name, for many at this time, was practically synonymous with the BBC. An archive photograph shows Adrienne Allen draped in a fox-fur stole, and Marie Tempest in a pert hat and gloves, her clutch bag resting beside her on the table; in another picture of the same period Clarice Cliff wears a coat with a fur collar. For those with money, and the time to spend it, 1930s London was a city of excitement, even during the Depression. The West End 'seemed, and was . . . fabulously wealthy'.[40] Fashionable restaurants were frequently redecorated to keep up with the latest styles and there were night clubs, cocktail bars and cabarets for entertainment. After its own refurbishment in 1929–30, the interior of Claridge's became a hymn to Art Deco, while the entrance to the Savoy Hotel was a seductive mix of chrome, soft light and glass. Just to glimpse this world was to taste glamour. Nothing could be further from the Potteries.

Back in Stoke-on-Trent, the fashions of the day were continuing to cause alarm, albeit expressed in tones of some amusement. In a debate on 'Modern Art and Pottery Manufacture' that year, Major Wade, from the company of that name, informed his audience: 'Modernistic art [is] a disease . . . specially noticeable in a particular class of young ladies; one [can] always tell when they [have] it by the shortness of their hair, the length of their cigarette-holders, and the fact that they invariably [sit] in rooms with black walls, purple ceilings, and orange-coloured chrysanthemums in the background.' He went on to remonstrate that, in the name of 'Modern Art', manufacturers felt obliged to decorate their ware with 'cubes or triangles, or question marks, or influenza germs, or a thousand and one other things', before warning them of 'the deadly peril which lurk[s] . . . in the guise of the Eton-cropped flapper. To those who [are] unsophisticated she might be very appealing, but,' he advised, 'she [is] a deadly and paralysing influence, and they [have] got to steer clear of her.'[41] Such was the siren call of the modern woman.

THIRTEEN

Thoroughly Individualistic

Purple ceilings and orange-coloured chrysanthemums notwith-standing, a quieter style was emerging as a counterpoint to the exuberances of colour. 'The "jazz" period may be said to be over,' *The Studio Yearbook* announced in 1932. 'Art and fashion alike have begun to retrench ... Just as music is beginning to be more tuneful, as women are beginning to be more feminine ... so in decorative art we may expect, and already begin to find, a more decorous and refined style than has for some time past been prevalent.'[1] The *Morning Post* concurred, when reviewing some of Clarice Cliff's 'frankly modern' designs that autumn. 'This year the colours are chosen to harmonise and tone.'[2] Harmony increasingly became a watchword.

'Since the last [British Industries] Fair interesting developments have taken place in the well-known Bizarre ware,' the *Pottery and Glass Record* reported in the spring of 1933, 'the decorations being to a large extent in soft pastel shades. This was so with the novel and pleasing Holly Rose decoration, as well as the landscape and cottage pattern called Secrets. A tree design called Solitude was shown on graceful vases ... and a tree study in orange and black was called Wyndbells, while Oasis was in soft blues, pinks and greens.'[3] Texture began to figure as much as pattern; one reviewer commented on 'a texture effect ... something similar to that which one encounters in connection with linens, or carpets, or even an artist's canvas ... something *really* new it would appear to be'.[4] Slubbed linen and bouclé wool, crêpe de chine and astrakhan testified to texture's hold on fashion; knitting patterns favoured textured effects.

The extravagances of 'Le Bon Dieu' also reflected this new feeling. 'I conceived the idea . . . by chancing to find a tree bole of curious formation, which I thought might serve as a mould,' Clarice Cliff informed the *Star*.[5] 'In the reproduction process, quaint animal shapes, and even gnomes and pixies are revealed.'[6] The new design, which was indeed the exact shape of a tree bole, complete with nodules and indentations, was described as 'remarkable'[7] by the trade press, although this was definitely one occasion when the word 'courageous' would have been apt. To borrow another word from the period, 'Le Bon Dieu' was venturesome, to say the least. Nothing could better indicate that Clarice Cliff had absolute design freedom. Though some of her customers shared her courage – requests for 'Le Bon Dieu' feature in the order books for 1932 – any pleasure they derived was surely fleeting. By contrast, a winning new design was 'Biarritz', a dinner-ware shape whose square plates – 'for square meals' – according to one wag – with impressed circular centres proved extremely popular.[8] Sales of 'Biarritz' were put through A.J.

'Le Bon Dieu'

Wilkinson because the 'Newport Pottery Company were making too
much profit'⁹ – not a bad position for a manufacturer to be in
towards the end of the Depression.

A further new shape, 'Bon Jour', also made an appearance around
this time.¹⁰ Its teapot, a complete, flat-sided circle, balanced on cylindrical feet; its flat-sided, circular vase – available as a single, double
or even triple circle – was 'specially designed to stand on the narrow
modern mantelpieces in new labour-saving houses and flats'.¹¹ Like
the 'Stamford' shape before it, the 'Bon Jour' teapot owed a debt
to the silversmiths Tétard Frères; Colley Shorter is said to have
negotiated a copyright fee for its translation into earthenware. The
creation of 'Bon Jour' was a further exercise in persistence. Although
the circular shape appealed to the latest trends, its flat sides tended
to collapse during firing and the men responsible for its production
'played merry hell'.¹² The public, who knew nothing of such
struggles, was much taken with the new design: when decorated
with the hands and numerals of a clock, 'Bon Jour' made the perfect
early-morning tea set.

Not all pottery manufacturers were keeping pace with changing
fashions, as J.B. Priestley observed when he visited the Potteries as
part of his *English Journey*:

> I went through one long clayey slippery room after another, and saw
> ladies and gentlemen . . . painting gilt lines or green leaves or pink
> roses on the superior ware, most of which, I think, would be still
> more superior if it did not reflect the taste of the Fifties and the Great
> Exhibition. Some of these better firms are now beginning to make
> use of the services of real artists, but they have still a good deal to
> learn about the aesthetic demands of this present decade . . . these
> firms are at their worst when they are told to spare no expense, for
> then they fairly riot in artiness, in dreadful elaborations of cupids
> and roses. The craftsmanship behind these pieces of super-ware is
> astonishing, but, unfortunately, so are the pieces themselves.¹³

Priestley did not restrict his criticisms to manufacture, but confessed
himself to be both 'fascinated and repelled' by the appearance of the
pottery towns themselves, which resembled no other industrial area he

knew. 'For a man of the Potteries, it must be either work or misery,' he noted. '[A]s a district to do anything but work in, it has nothing to recommend it . . . the general impression is of an exceptionally mean, dingy provinciality, of Victorian industrialism in its dirtiest and most cynical aspects . . . the Potteries are not worthy of the potter.'[14] Outsiders' views are rarely welcome and the inhabitants of the Potteries had long defended 'Smoke-on-Stench' from brickbats, but it was not only Priestley who objected to the appearance of the six towns. 'Will the various factories comprising the Potteries always be huddled together, cribbed, combined and confined between rows of smoke-grimed cottages in an atmosphere which is diametrically opposed to an elaborate scheme of city beautification?' the *Pottery Gazette* complained in a contemporary editorial.[15]

Small wonder, then, that Clarice Cliff sought the diversion of the countryside – 'The moorlands around Leek – Axe Edge and Gunn and Morridge, or . . . the Churnet Valley beyond Cheadle with the wild woods of the bird sanctuary and the long drive to Alton Towers',[16] plus the Dove and Manifold Valleys and the solemn beauty of the Dark Peak. Years after leaving the area, Vera Brittain held fond memories of 'the beauty of the wild countryside between Staffordshire and Derbyshire'.[17] Despite industrialisation, and unlike many industrial towns, the Potteries had countryside within easy reach. Some of the 'Bizarre Girls' hiked at weekends, spurred on by the urge towards health and fitness that was a feature of the decade, and which Clarice Cliff reflected in pattern names such as 'Sunspot' and 'Sunrise' which suggested the health-giving properties of the sun.[18] For Clarice Cliff herself, the countryside was a short drive away, and an essential means of occupying weekends.

'If that car was on the road, I was in it,' Nancy Craddock said.[19] A regular companion on her aunt's country drives, she numbered Alton Towers, Moreton Old Hall and Trentham Gardens among their journeyings: 'Anywhere within a thirty-mile radius.'[20] There was also the hillside folly and site of Primitive Methodism, Mow Cop, the 'steep wooded banks' and picnic areas of Rudyard Lake, the bluebell woods at Moddershall, and Biddulph Grange, that testament to High Victoriana, with its Chinese pagoda, Egyptian Court and willow-pattern bridge. All were accessible; some gave both names and images to designs by Clarice Cliff. The landscapes 'Mow Cop' and 'Alton' were among the 'Bizarre' patterns shown at the 1933 September display.

Also seen that year was 'May Avenue', one of Clarice Cliff's most notable landscape patterns, a stippled image which, with its arcade of trees tapering along an avenue of red-roofed houses, reinterprets Modigliani's *Landscape at Cagnes*. It is strange that this dreamy landscape acquired a Potteries street-name. There were two May Avenues in the area: one in nearby Newcastle-under-Lyme, the other in Clarice Cliff's home town of Tunstall. Newcastle's May Avenue, with its row of 1930s mock-Tudor housing, seems the more likely candidate of the two, although the association of Modigliani with either is incongruous. 'May Avenue' has become one of Clarice Cliff's most coveted patterns: in 2003, an eighteen-inch charger, priced in the region of twenty-five shillings when new, sold at auction for nearly £40,000, four times its sales estimate and a world record among the already steep and rising prices for her work.

One of the archive pattern books demonstrates the progress of Clarice Cliff's designs through the 'Bizarre' years.[21] Here are bursts of water-colour, surely as bright now as when they were first painted tangerine, Sèvres green, or the intense heat of Persian reds and purples. Geometric abstract patterns give way to flowers – lupins, with blobs of colour rising from bright stems; nearby, the crimson arcs of parrot tulips. Images fixed for ever on biscuit-coloured paper offer water-colour promises whose names – 'Latona', 'Lily', 'Broth', painted on dark afternoons in Stoke-on-Trent and examined on dark afternoons years later – show how quickly Clarice Cliff progressed from stripes and jagged lines to more demanding abstracts – swirls that are almost psychedelic in intensity – and from the graphic simplicity of a pattern such as 'Lupin', to more detailed florals, like the radiant bursts of orange that form 'Erin'. Not all Clarice Cliff patterns are colourfully described: faint lines outline pendulous blooms fading on pencil trees, labelled 'Solitude' or 'Wyndbells', while the beautiful arc of a 'Stamford' teapot, compass-drawn, suggests early possibilities of line and form. Here, too, are sketches marked 'For Lawley's only': signif-icant retailers, Harrods among them, were provided with exclusive

'Clarice Cliff' designs. As a record of 'Bizarre', the book is incomplete. Inevitably, it offers a mere sample. Nevertheless, its contents give some indication of the journey Clarice Cliff took from simple colour to complexity, and from the abstract to the narrative, and beyond. Elsewhere in the archive are more formal pattern books, in which pages of copperplate, written by several hands, offer explicit instructions to her paintresses, such as: 'Roof of cottage and chimney pencilled in tangerine.'[22]

Increasingly, Clarice Cliff was able to develop patterns that catered for a range of decorating skills as well as appealing to a variety of tastes. 'More and more work is being found both for beginners and more experienced workers,'[23] she told a magazine, conscious always of the need to occupy her workforce. Complex landscape patterns called for painterly control and a sense of perspective. Trees and houses taper and expand within the cones of conical bowls; geometrical vases require curving foliage to negotiate different plains and surfaces without any pause or tremor in their brushstrokes. The square-sided plates of 'Biarritz' dinner ware offered opportunities to place and frame an image – the pattern known as 'Blue Firs', for example, striking a cool, elegant note to one side. These designs are compositions, requiring decisions to be made about the amount and weight of colour, as well as pattern, and how best to apply it – garlands drape the top half of a pot destined for preserves while, in another version of the same shape, luscious gardenias play across the whole. This was modern art for the tea table, statements of sophistication for the corner of a room, whose achievement required technical ability and discernment. 'Undoubtedly this lady has a versatility that is quite exceptional,' the *Pottery Gazette* reported.[24] Whatever the decoration – be it pastel-coloured or bold – by 1933, Clarice Cliff's 'Bizarre' ware was said to be 'more popular than ever'.[25] The whole factory revolved around her work.

With a workshop of young paintresses, Clarice Cliff's was an ever-vigilant eye. Rene Dale recalled herself as a young learner, turning in her seat to watch the 'Bizarre Girl' behind her work, and hearing her name called out. 'I was only doing what she had done,' Rene defended herself, remembering how Clarice Cliff had learned by watching those around her. 'It was the work I was interested in, not the girl.'[26] On another occasion, the paintress Nora Dabbs was caught flickering a piece of tin to catch the light and dazzle those near by, and was foolhardy enough to try the trick a second time as soon as her employer left the room. However, Clarice Cliff had

'Bizarre Girls' posing in artists' smocks in front of the Newport Pottery float at a charity event

Stoke-on-Trent City Archives

Clarice Cliff decorating a charger, early 1930s

Charlotte Shorter and Ann and Martin Harris

The Shorter family, 'Chetwynd', c. 1926

Standing, back row: Austin Walker[?], Nora Crawford (née Shorter), S.A. Lett, Arthur Shorter, Jack Walker, L.A. Lett

Seated, middle row, from left to right: Elsie Shorter, John Brereton Shorter, Mabel Walker (née Shorter), Joan Shorter; Noreen Crawford, Henrietta Shorter, Colley Shorter, unidentified woman, Annie Shorter

Seated, front steps: Guy Shorter; Margaret Shorter

Christie's Images

The 'Tibetan' ginger jar gilded by Clarice
Cliff; her signature is on the base in gold

Maureen and Harold Woodworth

'Girl Figure Early Victorian' modelled by
Clarice Cliff, dated 1925 on the base

V&A Picture Library

The spirit of the age: Vladimir Polunin's theatre design for a drop scene representing George and the Dragon, created for the Diaghilev Ballet Season at the London Coliseum, 1925, and seen by Clarice Cliff at the exhibition of Modern French and Russian Designs for Costume and Scenery, V&A, 1927

Christie's Images

Selection of original 'Bizarre' vases

Stoke-on-Trent City Archives

Archive pattern book showing watercolours of Fantasque designs, late 1928–29
Clockwise from top left: 'Lily', 'Fruit', 'Lily', 'Pebbles', 'Umbrellas and Rain', 'Broth'

Stoke-on-Trent City Archives

Archive pattern book: 'Kew'

Stoke-on-Trent City Archive

Archive pattern book: 'Erin'

Stoke-on-Trent City Archives

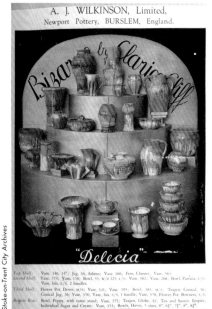

A. J. WILKINSON, Limited,
Newport Pottery, BURSLEM, England.

"Delecia"

Top Shelf: Vase, 14th, 14"; Jug, 36; Athens; Vase, 586; Fern, Chester; Vase, 563.
Second Shelf: Vase, 574; Vase, 158; Bowl, 55, w/r 225, i/s; Vase, 562; Vase, 268; Bowl, Patricia, i/s; Vase, Isis, ii/s, 2 handles.
Third Shelf: Flower Pot, Dover, M/S; Vase, 341; Vase, 195; Bowl, 583, M/S; Teapot, Conical, 50; Conical Jug, 56; Vase, 356; Vase, Isis, s/s, 1 handle; Vase, 370, Flower Pot, Bowness, s/s.
Bottom Row: Bowl, Poppy, with rustic stand; Vase, 575; Teapot, Globe, 42; Tea and Saucer, Empire, Individual Sugar and Cream; Vase, 555; Bowls, Havre, 5 sizes, 6", 64", 7½", 8", 8½".

Archive promotional
photograph showing
'Delecia' on a display stand
designed by Clarice Cliff

Stoke-on-Trent City Archives

Archive promotional photograph, showing patterns on sale in the early 1930s
Back row, left to right: Charger in 'Oranges and Lemons'; double inkwell in 'Farmhouse';
vase in 'Café au lait' landscape pattern; double-handled 'Lotus' jug in 'Limberlost';
banded tube-shaped vase; 'Stamford' tureen in 'Orange Chintz'; banded graduated bowl
Front row, left to right: pastel-coloured honey pot; vase in 'Blue Chintz'; sugar sifter
in 'Oranges and Lemons'; 'Mango' vase; 'Stamford' teapot, milk jug and sugar bowl,
and 'Conical' tea cup in 'House and Bridge'; vase in 'Café'; butter dish in 'Blue Chintz';
cruet set; banded preserve pot

Christie's Images

Selection of abstract patterns, introduced 1929 and 1930
Clockwise from top left: octagonal candlesticks in 'Football'; 'Meiping'
vase in 'Sunray'; 'Conical' cup and saucer in 'Diamonds'; trumpet vase
in 'Sunburst'; plate in 'Diamonds'; globe vase in abstract foliate design;
trumpet vase in 'Sunburst'; 'Conical' tea set in 'Diamonds'

Christie's Images

Selection of patterns introduced between 1929 and 1933
Clockwise from top left: 'Biarritz' plate in 'May Avenue'; 'Isis' vase in 'Tennis'; plate in 'Pastel Mountain'; pair of vases in 'Blue Firs'; vase in 'Sunray'; 'Conical' jug in 'Appliqué Lucerne'; sugar sifter in 'House and Bridge'; vase in 'Sunray'; single-handled 'Lotus' vase in 'Autumn'; 'Dover' jardinière in 'Gibraltar'

Christie's Images

'Age of Jazz' dancers

'Conical' tea set in 'Orange
Picasso Flower'

'Stamford' teapots, and other 'Bizarre'
ware in 'Crocus'

'Daffodil' tea set in 'Orange Hydrangea'

'Bon Jour' tea set in 'Yellow Cowslip'

Christie's Images

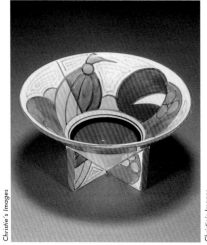

Christie's Images

'Conical' bowl in 'Melon'

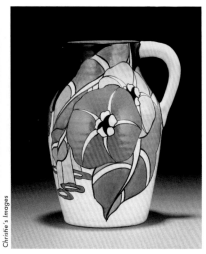

Christie's Images

Single-handled 'Lotus' vase in 'Latona Bouquet'

Christie's Images

A 1928 vase in 'Solitude'

Christie's Images

'Conical' biscuit barrel in 'Oranges'

Christie's Images

Single 'Bon Jour' candlestick in 'Honolulu'

Christie's Images

'Stamford' tea set in 'Solomon's Seal'

Christie's Images

'Marilyn' face mask

Christie's Images

Double-handled 'Lotus' vase
in 'Appliqué Idyll'

Stoke-on-Trent City Archive

Leaflet advertising 'Modern Art for the Table', Harrods, 1934

Stoke-on-Trent City Archive

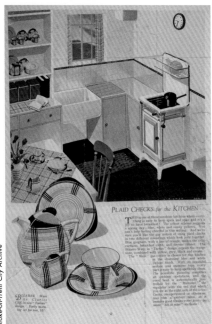

Photogravure feature, Modern Home, March 1936, showing a 'Trieste' tea set in 'Tartan'

Clarice Cliff on the terrace at the Hotel Miramar,
Napoli, 1953

Clarice Cliff, stylish and light-hearted at the Surf Club,
Bermuda, 1953 (the legs are Colley's)

Leonard Griffin. www.clarice.cliff.com

Clarice Cliff with a kitten at 'Chetwynd', 1951.
The original slide, in Colley Shorter's handwriting, was captioned:
'Two reasons for going back to England'

a knack of appearing when least expected – perhaps borne out of her own experiences of the factory floor – and sent the girl home for misbehaviour. The loss of an afternoon's wages during the Depression years was not insignificant: Nora had to pretend there was no work in order to avoid a beating from her mother.[27]

More than one 'Bizarre Girl' noted that, like Colley Shorter, Clarice Cliff was 'cute' about time and money. She came into their workshop at the end of the lunchbreak to ensure her paintresses were settling back to work and sometimes watched their arrival, one day standing in wait for those who had slipped into the habit of clocking-on in outdoor clothes before changing into their overall, and thereby gaining some minutes of factory time. She waited out of sight and then confronted them: 'Coats off in your time, not in mine.'[28] The installation of a wireless was reported in the press. 'Working to music has increased output by 25 per cent at least,' Guy Shorter told the *Daily Sketch*. 'Somehow, the music blends with the artistry of the work. Brighter working hours have created brighter minds and increased efficiency.'[29] Singing paintresses could not chat or distract one another.

That Clarice Cliff was strict is not surprising – the 'Bizarre Girls' were all in their teens – but although she demanded concentration, she was nevertheless considerate if her Girls were ill, sending cards and enquiring after them; she even paid for a holiday for a paintress who was sick. She attended the parties held in the workshop on their birthdays, after hours, and, with Colley Shorter, took her paintresses on a day trip to Llangollen: a thank you for their hard work, or a holiday in lieu of overtime payment, depending on who is speaking. Either way, the outing showed consideration.

Memories of the 'Bizarre' shop were happy, for the most part. 'We had such fun,' said Mollie Browne. 'I always said we ought to have paid them to go there.'[30] 'I'd go back now, if I could,' said Doris Johnson.[31] The Ovalteenies tune acquired new lyrics and became their workshop song – 'We are the gay Bizookas, happy girls are we . . .' Their singing served as an early-warning system as well as keeping them amused, their L-shaped workshop allowing the paintress at the topmost corner to alert the others as soon as Clarice Cliff appeared. If 'The Wedding of the Painted Doll' changed to 'Bread of Heaven', with barely pause for breath, her paintresses were immediately forewarned.

The 'Bizarre Girls' tell a familiar tale of young women of the time. Edna Cheetham, who had enjoyed evening classes in French and English Appreciation prior to joining the 'Bizarre' shop, later asked her parents why they had not considered entering her for a scholarship at school. 'They just looked blank at me. It wasn't the sort of thing people did.'[32] Some of the Girls initially had jobs in shops; a couple started out in tailoring. 'Nobody wanted to go on potbanks,' one of them recalled. 'They wanted something different – making tea in offices, or shops.'[33] They had hopes of joining the expanding modern economy, of becoming part of the new England J.B. Priestley defined, not the old industrial one they had inherited. But potbanks continued to be the largest employer of young women in North Staffordshire and the job of paintress retained its cachet, just as the clay end continued to be out of the question. And working for Clarice Cliff had its privileges – 'even if we didn't know what they were'.[34] Despite her success, paintresses did not see that Clarice Cliff could be a role model. 'We girls realised how clever she was,' said Annie Beresford. 'We couldn't have done what she did.'[35] Mollie Browne agreed: 'She was a bit different.'

One of the ways the 'Bizarre Girls' extended their horizons was by taking part in the pottery demonstrations that were now 'a great draw to many ladies'.[36] A particular effort was made in the autumn of 1932, when Clarice Cliff and her paintresses spent a week in South Kensington, as part of an extensive promotion at Barker's department store that was much appreciated by the press. 'To see this modern display . . . is to take a mental leap into the future,' the *Evening Standard* noted.[37]

Large London demonstrations were supervised by Clarice Cliff, with Colley Shorter making a brief appearance, but for other, smaller events, in London and elsewhere, the 'Bizarre Girls' were taken under the wing of individual store managers. Clarice Cliff nevertheless remained responsible for their welfare and continued to ask permission of their mothers. When Rene Dale was required to stay by herself in Liverpool because her companion was called to a demonstration in Scotland, she received a note from Clarice, thanking her for staying on alone, and suggesting she take one or two of the shop girls to the cinema at the factory's expense;[38] Clarice also advised two paintresses travelling by train to Dundee not to take their tea in the dining car, but to ask the attendant to bring refreshments to their carriage.[39] Of course, they ignored her. Demonstrations were adventures and they wanted to make the most of them. Their pleasures were innocent ones, nonetheless, and the Girls were always met at railway stations and chaperoned.

'Bizarre Girls' Lily Barrow and Nancy Dale at a demonstration, Bath, 1936

Though London offered the greatest contrast to the Potteries, all demonstrations allowed them to visit towns and cities they would not otherwise have seen. Hastings, Great Yarmouth, Manchester, Welwyn Garden City and Plymouth were among the other places also holding in-store demonstrations. Some of the 'Bizarre Girls' grew homesick and returned to the Potteries, others were sent on trips time and time again, but not all Girls were lucky. Ethel Barrow, the paintress initially responsible for decorating 'Crocus', longed to go on a demonstration but was never asked: 'Clarice Cliff had her favourites and I wasn't one.'[40]

As the 'Bizarre Girls' grew older, some married. The first to do so was Annie Beresford; Clarice Cliff told the workshop that Annie must be known by her married name from then on, until Annie herself insisted she was perfectly happy being 'Annie'.[41] For a woman who consistently resisted boundaries, Clarice Cliff was remarkably traditional in some ways, perhaps because aspects of her own life would otherwise have been open to scrutiny. On her marriage, Annie Beresford's attendance at 'Bizarre' demonstrations came to a halt. 'Clarice Cliff wouldn't let married women go,' Rene Dale explained. 'I was enjoying myself too much . . . I was thirty-two when I married. That was old in those days . . . Normally I wouldn't have gone to those places. It would have been hard to give that up and think: Now I'm going to be a wife . . . It was an opportunity to see these places and meet people as well . . . We saw more of life than we would have done in our small village.'[42]

Seeing more of life included lessons in sophistication, observing women dressed in the 'latest modes' wafting Ashes of Roses through Selfridges and Peter Robinson. Demonstrations were not simply lessons in the unattainable, however; they also supplied ideas to imitate. In London, at least, make-up had acquired respectability – in 1931, 1,500 lipsticks were sold for every one purchased a decade earlier – and if the confections sold by Yardley and Revlon were beyond the purse of a 'Bizarre Girl', a splash of Woolworth's scent and a dab of powder were affordable, if not encouraged by Clarice Cliff: 'That will rot your eyelashes, you know,' she told one of her paintresses at the end of a workshop day, having observed her 'secretly' applying mascara some time earlier.[43]

The high street was now a place of heightened consumerism; Marks & Spencer doubled its shops during the 1930s, the decade which saw the rise of the mass market. With the aid of high-street retailers, improved paper patterns and efficient sewing machines, young women were able to copy the latest styles. Some commentators were remarking on the difficulty of distinguishing 'a factory girl from the unoccupied daughter of an urban landowner'.[44] Increasingly, they took their lead from Hollywood. 'Mimetic images of Harlow, Garbo and Crawford paraded in the high street, as they glowed across the cinema screen.'[45]

In her analysis of the period, Diana Gittins asserts that, by now, the married woman was, in many ways, more useful to the economy as an unemployed consumer than as a producer.[46] She could spend

'Miss Clarice Cliff ... makes an appeal to women who like individuality in their home,' *Modern Home*, October 1933

her morning browsing the shops, before treating herself to one of
the new designs by Clarice Cliff, as demonstrated to her that very
day and, after a café lunch, could sink into a seat in the one-and-
nines, with a box of peppermint creams and an afternoon of cinema
ahead of her. Though unable to compete with the heroine's celluloid
glamour, she could nevertheless transport herself to another world
and later, at home that evening, continue to dream, with the aid of
the 'Fantasque' tea set for which she had paid fourteen shillings and
sixpence that morning.[47]

FOURTEEN

Art *Out* of Industry

By the early 1930s, 'in small ways and in great . . . art and industry were approaching one another: if not with arms outstretched, at least with some politeness'. Cadbury's commissioned designs for chocolate boxes from nine well-known painters, including Dame Laura Knight; Shell-Mex Ltd commissioned a series of paintings which could be reproduced on its lorries to advertise the English countryside and Shell petroleum: Vanessa Bell and Duncan Grant were two of the first artists approached. Later that decade, Yardley invited Reco Capey to design packaging for its toiletries, perfumes and cosmetics. The mood was contagious. In 1933, the BBC devoted a series of programmes to educating the British public on *Design in Modern Life*: Gordon Russell spoke on 'The Living-Room and Furniture', Frank Pick discussed 'The Street', Elizabeth M. Denby 'The Kitchen', and so on. New habits required new rules: with the old formalities disappearing, the public was thought to require instruction. This was the essence of the Gorrell Report, a Board of Trade investigation into art and education, published the previous year, which recommended that 'the citizen must be made design-conscious'.[2] Exhibitions were particularly favoured: 'EXHIBITIONS mania', John Betjeman dubbed the report.[3]

Clarice Cliff and Colley Shorter needed no instruction. They were already involved in their own experiment with art and industry. In 1932, Colley Shorter joined with Thomas Acland Fennemore, an 'energetic and progressive'[4] director of E. Brain & Co. Ltd, the manufacturer of Foley China, to commission a number of British artists to produce designs for tableware. A.J. Wilkinson was to make breakfast, dinner and dessert services in earthenware, with E. Brain & Co. making breakfast, tea and coffee sets in china. The manufacturer Stuart & Sons also participated by commissioning designs for glass.

An initial list of twelve artists, selected by Fennemore, together with the designer Milner Gray and the painter Graham Sutherland, focused on the avant-garde and included Barbara Hepworth and Ben Nicholson, who were currently showing their work as part of Unit One, a group of English artists who were said 'to stand for the expression of . . . that which is recognised as peculiarly *of today* in painting, sculpture and architecture'.[5] The intention was to take 'the first big step forward in the intelligent use of British artists in designing for industrial production'.[6] This was advanced thinking on the part of two pottery manufacturers who had long been aware of the importance of making modern design accessible and who needed no encouragement from officialdom. Although the project was conceived in advance of the government-sponsored collaborations between art and industry that took place over the next three years, as with many experiments its execution proved more complicated than its inception. It was 1934 before the results of the collaboration were exhibited at Harrods in an exhibition of china, pottery and glass called 'Modern Art for the Table'.

Before the project was complete, A.J. Wilkinson participated in the government-sponsored exhibition that was the natural consequence of the Gorrell Report. In June 1933, the exhibition, 'British Industrial Art in Relation to the Home' took place at Dorland Hall, Regent Street. Visitors were greeted in the vestibule by the sculpted figures of *Man* and *Woman* by Eric Gill and Charles Wheeler which, when seen in juxtaposition with examples of industrial design, introduced them to 'the genesis of art and industry'.[7] A series of rooms, each by a different designer – a dining-room by Sir Ambrose Heal, a 'minimum flat' by Wells Coates, and a weekend house with garden and terrace by Serge Chermayeff, for instance – led off from the main hall. 'The surprises will be in the sections of silver, pottery and glass in the front gallery on the first floor,' *The Times* informed its readers. 'The sections named are a revelation.'[8] Chief among them was surely Oliver Hill's all-glass room, featuring a glass bed and glass table on a glass floor. This was industrial design for the future.

Among the 'striking new designs of daring impulse'[9] exhibited by A.J. Wilkinson were those of Clarice Cliff and Milner Gray; these would feature again the following year as part of 'Modern Art for the Table'. Gray's design, 'Whoopee', an early-morning tea set consisting of 'a light-hearted set of designs featuring various means of locomotion – balloons, bicycles, boats, horses, etc.'[10] somewhat overwhelmed the *Pottery Gazette*: 'To describe this pattern as fantastic,' it complained, 'would be to exercise a full measure of restraint.' 'Much more acceptable' was Clarice Cliff's 'Hello', a banded pattern consisting of black circles relieved by green or coral spots, which the *Gazette* considered 'modern without being so trying to our patience'.[11] Modernity was the key to 'this remarkable exhibition' which, *The Times* acknowledged, was likely to 'frighten some and excite others'.[12]

Art and industry was now the theme on every designer's lips. For Clarice Cliff, this union involved a further project in 1933, when a series of replica plaques of the 'Brangwyn Panels' were created under her direction. The evolution of the original panels dated back to 1925 and Frank Brangwyn's commission to produce a set of murals for the Royal Gallery in the House of Lords to commemorate the peers who lost their lives in the First World War. The resulting panels were rejected and ultimately housed by the Guildhall, Swansea, South Wales. Clarice Cliff's replica plaques, reproducing their lush colouring, were prepared with Brangwyn's approval and produced in limited numbers, priced ten guineas.

By now, the mood of design in general was said to be one of quietude. As if to echo this assertion, Clarice Cliff took part in an exhibition at Waring & Gillow in the spring of 1934, 'The New Idea in Tableware'. Together with Susie Cooper, Crown-Ducal, Doulton, A.E. Gray, Poole, Spode-Copeland and Wedgwood, she showed a 'feast of designs, which represented the feeling of today'. All were described as 'simple and sensible'.[13] 'Now we have come into our own,' the *Pottery Gazette* declared, casting aside 'feverish . . . Continental fashions' in favour of ideas that 'express the British spirit, charming in colour and restful in design'.[14] Even tableware was becoming nationalistic.

By contrast, that spring Clarice Cliff also introduced 'My Garden'. With embossed flowers clustering at their base and handles, and colourful streams trickling down the glaze, this series of highly decorative jugs and vases launched a combination of pattern and form that would prove extremely popular for years to come. New floral decorations, 'Rhodanthe', 'Daphne' and 'Christine' also emerged that year, as did 'As You Like It', a series of ceramic flower troughs which could be arranged to form various table-centre shapes, and was generally considered 'ingenious'.[15] Regardless of the increasing emphasis on simplicity, flowers retained their appeal, albeit with less bravado than formerly.

The pressures on Clarice Cliff were now considerable. In 1934, the *Pottery Gazette* observed that few manufacturers produced 'such an astounding variety of pieces',[16] but to do so required constant innovation, conscious always of the timetable imposed by trade fairs and annual displays, let alone other major exhibitions. Clarice Cliff was not able to devote herself to her own work during this period, however. The Foley China/A.J. Wilkinson project was nearing completion and responsibility for A.J. Wilkinson's contribution fell to her.

By now, the list of artists had grown to twenty-seven – more than double the original number – with the intention of embracing 'all sections of contemporary design'[17] and ensuring the experiment's wide appeal. The aim was to be 'as catholic as possible'.[18] The final selection included John Armstrong, Freda Beardmore (a young designer employed by Foley China, who oversaw their part in the venture), Vanessa Bell, Frank Brangwyn, Clarice Cliff, Gordon Forsyth, Duncan Grant, Milner Gray, Barbara Hepworth, Laura Knight, Paul Nash, Ben Nicholson, Dod and Ernest Proctor and Graham Sutherland.[19] The youngest contributor was Angelica Bell, aged fourteen when commissioned, who made her début with 'a gay assurance'.[20] Forsyth was extremely optimistic: 'My dear Taf,' he wrote to Fennemore, 'I bet you all I possess that it will be a great

Dame Laura Knight visiting A.J. Wilkinson during preparations for 'Modern Art for the Table'

success in every way . . . It has been a great adventure and one that will rebound to the credit of Staffordshire potters.'[21]

Clarice Cliff was less enthusiastic. 'I remember what headaches we had over the reproduction,' she said, looking back on the experiment years later.[22] One of the 'Bizarre Girls' described the project as 'a nuisance. It . . . took a lot of doing and had to be fired separately and in between [other] orders.'[23] Each artist had 'absolute freedom'[24] in creating his or her designs, but the application of a variety of patterns to pre-existing shapes was not straightforward (and the cost of producing dedicated shapes would have been prohibitive). The patterns submitted were not always suited to the pieces they were required to decorate and, in some instances, needed considerable adjustment.[25] There were 'endless conferences' about technical details over the two years in which 'Modern Art for the Table' came to fruition.[26]

Clarice Cliff and Colley Shorter were said to have disagreed over the project – the idea to extend the list of contributors was his.[27] It was more likely to appeal to Shorter: he was more interested in public debate and more concerned with acceptance by the design fraternity.[28] For Clarice Cliff, the experiment occupied time she would otherwise have devoted to her own designs. Like all pioneers, she was single-minded, with little desire to be a conduit for other people's work. To liaise with and keep abreast of twenty-seven designers, many of whom lacked direct experience of the pottery industry, entailed immense effort and probably considerable frustration.

Although few took up the offer, all the artists/designers were invited to Stoke-on-Trent. Milner Gray, Graham Sutherland and Laura Knight were among those who met and worked with Clarice Cliff. A chance meeting on a train is said to have been responsible for Laura Knight's involvement, when she responded enthusiastically to Colley Shorter's suggestion that she 'try her hand at pottery design'.[29] Her 'Circus' tableware, which drew on her observation of Carmo's Circus, also seen in her paintings of the period, is perhaps the best known of the work exhibited. Her tumbling clowns, horses, acrobats and ballerinas are confident studies in colour and invention. Whereas other artists produced only patterns, Laura Knight also conceived shapes.[30] In one example, a clown kneels at the base of a lamp stand, while a second balances on top of him, supporting a third, who grasps the knees of a group of trapeze artists stretching their arms towards the filament. Laura Knight initially modelled the lamp in plasticine, from which a mould was made;[31] Clarice Cliff and her modeller Joe Woolliscroft were responsible for its translation into earthenware thereafter, and were said to have worked for months to achieve the desired effect.[32]

Laura Knight's designs exhibit humour as well as grace: elsewhere, a smiling clown performing the splits provides the handle for a tureen lid. By contrast, Ben Nicholson's and Barbara Hepworth's patterns were austere, each making use of a grey background. For her part, Clarice Cliff exhibited the designs already seen at Dorland Hall, together with samples of her 'Biarritz' tableware, 'creamy-coloured square plates, edged with gold and treated with small, neat black spots scattered around the border'.[33]

'Modern Art for the Table' was opened at Harrods on 22 October by Sir William Rothenstein, principal of the Royal College of Art, and ran until 10 November. Most designs were exhibited alongside their original drawings, with twelve sets of each design offered as limited editions; Virginia Woolf and the actor Charles Laughton were among those who reserved them. For *The Times*, the number of artists represented was 'the outstanding feature of the display'.

Leaflet advertising Harrods' exhibition of china, pottery and glass,
'Modern Art for the Table'

Although manufacturers had commissioned work by individual artists in the past, 'now there is a battalion, and the result is amazing in its vividness and beauty'.[34] 'No one should miss the show at Harrods,' the *Observer* insisted, 'it represents a marriage of ideas,'[35] while the *Evening Standard* reassured its readers: 'There is no need to be frightened by the word "modern".'[36]

The aim was to sell work by distinguished artists 'at very reasonable sums',[37] to show the public that 'art' need not mean exclusivity. In price, the services ranged from two pounds, seven shillings and sixpence for a tea set to thirty-five pounds for a 52-piece dinner service. Raymond Mortimer thought the prices reasonable, but noted, 'There is still a long way to go before pottery of this sort can be marketed at prices possible to the great mass of the public. But how can it ever reach them,' he concluded, 'unless the intelligentsia have the intelligence to give a lead?'[38] Writing in the *Spectator*, Anthony Blunt thought that the right kind of compromise had been reached between art and industry. Commercially, he thought, the project unlikely to fail.[39]

The most popular design was John Armstrong's 'Chaldean' or 'Chevaux', a primitive cave-like drawing which caused considerable amusement when shown to a group of pottery manufacturers in Stoke-on-Trent, but sold more than twenty services during the exhibition. His was also one of the least expensive, retailing at three pounds and five shillings for twenty-six pieces. Gracie Fields, currently the nation's darling, at the height of her success with the film *Sing as We Go*, whose theme tune became a factory workers' song, bought a 52-piece dinner service in Laura Knight's 'Circus' ware, a purchase which united one of the best-known women painters of the period with the most popular British film star, and the best-known ceramic designer. Gracie Fields's motto, 'Hard work and plenty of it',[40] seems suitable for all three.

Despite the favourable review coverage, and fervent hopes for future experiments, 'Modern Art for the Table' was not the commercial success envisaged. Although Harrods was delighted, retailers thereafter were less enthusiastic. Milner Gray told the familiar tale of buyers who were reluctant to take a risk with something new. The project had been conceived as a commercial venture, after all, with

Harrods as its showcase, not its *raison d'être*. Forsyth remained optimistic. Acknowledging his own 'modest' involvement, he 'ventured to think that the exhibition, regarded broadly, was one of the most exciting things which the pottery industry had witnessed of recent times . . . it had suggested to his mind at least half a dozen means of decorating pottery which had not yet been fully explored'.[41]

Reflecting on the experiment nearly twenty years later, the potter Reginald Haggar concluded that 'the shock of many of the exhibits . . . had a salutary effect upon ceramic design'.[42] Looking back herself, Clarice Cliff's own assessment was mixed. Although she described 'Modern Art for the Table' as 'a show which, I believe, probably created more interest than any before or since . . . [and] undoubtedly changed the trend of thought in design throughout the pottery district', she added that, 'sad to relate, from a commercial point of view, i.e. sales to the public, it was so disappointing that it was the closest thing to a flop that, I am glad to say, I have ever been associated with'.[43]

The project was further complicated by the use of Clarice Cliff's signature. All the artists retained their own copyright and received a small fee and royalties for their work but, in addition to the artist's own name, each piece of tableware A.J. Wilkinson produced for the experiment bore the trademark 'Clarice Cliff'. Perhaps Clarice Cliff insisted her time should be repaid in this way. Just as likely, the idea was Colley Shorter's. This was a decision in which his salesmanship was wholly to the fore. Clarice Cliff's name was an obvious spur to the buying public, but in a climate in which the use of artists' signatures was becoming increasingly pressing, it was not the wisest decision, and was one to which Gordon Forsyth objected. 'I do hope Colley will not use such a distinguished bunch of artists to advertise Clarice Cliff,' he told Fennemore. 'No one could object to Newport Pottery by Frank Brangwyn RA, but he should not use Clarice Cliff's name except for pottery designed by her.'[44]

Some months later, Forsyth was involved with the recently established Council for Art and Industry in setting up a committee to look into the work of pottery designers. He proposed Susie Cooper and Shelley's designer, Eric Slater, but, when asked about Clarice Cliff, is reported to have said 'that he doubted very much whether

Miss Clarice Cliff would be of the slightest use for our purpose'.[45]
A surprising response, given her profile and her unusual progress
through the industry, and particularly surprising when Forsyth had
publicly commended her work two years earlier. *Modern Art for
the Table* had evidently soured his view. While Forsyth was
promoting the need for individual artists and designers to be credited for their work – an argument that, in 1934, still had some
ground to gain – Colley Shorter had moved beyond that point to
conclude that a designer whose name was already established could
also be effective as a brandname. This was a reflection of the
commercial success Clarice Cliff now enjoyed, but a decision that
generated bad feeling. The conflict between art and industry was
articulated in the very experiment designed to unite them.

The 1930s were years in which design theories clashed and coexisted.
While some embraced the style now called Art Deco, others, since
defined as Modernists, took their lead from the Bauhaus, 'the alternative modernism'[46] of the period, and argued for the elimination
of ornament. Although Clarice Cliff responded to the increasing
desire for quietude from the mid-1930s on, 50 per cent of her work
remained colourful[47] and humour was close to hand. Variety and
an ability to seize and interpret different trends had always been
her keynote. As ever, she resisted pigeon-holing. Clarice Cliff was
not alone in evading definition. 'Style and the so-called "modern
movement" in design don't really matter in a woman's home,' the
furniture designer Betty Joel insisted, arguing that women should
construct a composite style that satisfied their personal taste, rather
than respond to design diktats. 'This age moves with such rapidity
that styles are merely fashions which change faster than our tastes
can possibly follow.'[48]

That the decade was awash with factionalism was exemplified by
the exasperation expressed by the *Pottery Gazette* in the run-up to
the exhibition of industrial art which took place at the beginning
of 1935: 'We shall have the advocates of "simplicity in outline"; the
advocates of "fitness for purpose"; the advocates of "best-sellers";
and many others in groups not easily defined,' it complained,[49] for
once expressing an understandable frustration. Created under the

auspices of the Royal Society of Arts and the Royal Academy, 'British Art in Industry' took place at Burlington House and was opened by the Prince of Wales. Since its announcement two years earlier, its principles had been repeatedly rehearsed. The intention was to establish links between designers and manufacturers, and to impress upon the public the importance of good design. The help of 'women experts' was enlisted 'on the domestic side of the exhibition' and a series of window displays created as an enticement – 'what could more delight the heart of Woman?' *The Studio* enquired.[50]

As with Dorland Hall, *The Times* considered the ceramics to be among the 'most encouraging' of the exhibits.[51] The assistant keeper of ceramics at the V&A was particularly impressed by some of the banding: 'It was this that really excited me . . . some six or eight examples are the best I have seen. Susie Cooper is admirable with her frugal "chalky" line set off with green and with brown . . . Clarice Cliff has a lovely spiral movement which uses body and glaze tones with great skill; a service of hers at Harrods combined this effect with rim banding in colours, and ought to have been here too . . . This is what is wanted, art *out* of industry.'[52]

On the first day the exhibition opened to the public, 3,000 visitors passed through its doors, but, whatever their response, most arbiters of design were not impressed. Writing in the *New Statesman and Nation*, Raymond Mortimer named A.J. Wilkinson as one of the few manufacturers worthy of 'special praise', but complained that the exhibition as a whole revealed 'the extreme poverty of the designs which British workmen have to execute'.[53] Like other commentators, he saw it as a lost opportunity. 'Good industrial art is being produced in England,' Clive Bell observed, 'but you will see little of it in the Royal Academy Exhibition.'[54] The *Pottery Gazette* voiced a shared concern: 'The industry caters for the multitude and the multitude does not go to Burlington House.'[55]

That Clarice Cliff was impatient of some of the debates taking place was evidenced by her words when she was asked about 'good' and 'bad' design some twenty years later. 'I have always had a considerable amount of satisfaction in looking back,' she replied, referring to the Harrods experiment, 'Modern Art for the Table'. 'It proved that what is aesthetically known as good design has not arrived at the position where a manufacturer distributing bulk goods could really use that type of design to keep his workpeople busy or, in fact, to continue producing for very long.'[56] Having come to ceramics without an ideology or theoretical view, Clarice Cliff disliked design hierarchies. She had spent her life resisting definition and, as someone who aimed to satisfy women's individuality, did not welcome constraint. Her responses to design were born of the marketplace and, importantly, the factory floor, and, like those of other women designers of the period, included a knowledge and understanding of the domestic that male ideologues could never share.

FIFTEEN

Women Who Make Money

Beyond the walls of the Royal Academy, the public was looking to be soothed. *The Studio Yearbook* expressed a general hope: 'The *crise*, the present discontents, bewilderments and privations demand some kind of counterpoise. The home, at least, should provide comfort, some anodyne for the cares of the day.'[1] Home was unlikely to provide much comfort for Clarice Cliff in 1935. Towards the end of January, Colley Shorter sailed for Australia, the start of an overseas trip which occupied much of the year. The reasons for his departure were not commercial, as the *Pottery Gazette* explained: 'Mr Shorter has not been enjoying the best of health for some time past, and a change and rest have been medically prescribed for him. Being of a particularly active temperament, however, Mr Shorter does not relish the idea of rest, pure and unalloyed. He is expecting, therefore . . . to undertake a complete tour of the Dominion before returning to England in the autumn.'[2] According to a further press report, the trip took Shorter around the world.[3] He was recovering from an operation for cancer, hence his extensive convalescence.[4]

Illness did not put Colley Shorter off his stride. He made his travels work for him. The tableware shown at Harrods the previous year was high on his agenda, with samples of each design taken to 'the best china store . . . in every city he stayed in'.[5] He also took the chance to speak of Clarice Cliff to overseas reporters who were as captivated by her rise to prominence as British journalists before them. 'No great movie star can tell a more romantic story of "How I Was Discovered",' the *Australian Woman's Weekly* felt certain.[6] Clarice Cliff's work was already known in Australia, but the personal note added a new dimension. Once again, a reporter remarked that Clarice Cliff was 'oh, so merry looking',[7] either Colley was carrying her photograph, or a copy of a British press report.

With Shorter out of the country, the regular commitments of factory life demanded more of Clarice Cliff's time during a period of increasing distraction. Not only was there Colley's health and prolonged absence to consider but, in April 1935, her father died. The cause of death was myocarditis (inflammation of the heart muscle), probably exacerbated by the asthma from which he had suffered for some years, a legacy of his work at the foundry. Harry Cliff was sixty-five: statistically a good age in Stoke-on-Trent during the 1930s.

For the first time since the beginning of that decade, August 1935 saw unemployment fall below 2 million. That economic confidence was returning to the middle classes in full employment was evidenced by the increasing number of tableware designs reintroducing gold and other metals during this period. A review of Clarice Cliff's work that year showed a new treatment of her 'Autumn' pattern, which now appeared as an outline, 'in jade green with platinum decoration',[8] a quite different presentation of a once-colourful design. With contemporary fashion emphasising the female silhouette, it was not surprising that ceramics followed suit. Simplicity and sophistication were now very much the thing, as was a new formality, underlined by the growing demand for dinner services in bone china and the increasing popularity of monograms.

'The craze for monograms has spread to china,' the *Manchester Evening News* reported,[9] demonstrating how advanced Clarice Cliff had been when she introduced personalised dinner ware in 1929. What could be more desirable for the modern interior than 'a platinum

'Even the early-morning tea-set flaunts its owner's initials nowadays.' Cream 'Lynton' tea set decorated with gold bands and black lettering, priced 14/-, *Woman and Home*, April 1935

dinner service initialled in black'?[10] The liking for two-colour designs, often featuring black, corresponded with the era's continuing fascination with monochrome glamour; throughout the 1930s, weekly cinema admissions were between 18 and 19 million.[11] Owners of the new personalised dinner ware paid higher prices for the privilege:

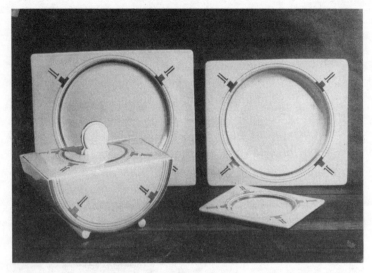

'Biarritz' tableware: 'severe lines to suit a modern scheme'

while a 32-piece 'Biarritz' dinner service decorated in soft browns and greens cost two pounds, nine shillings and sixpence, a 24-piece service, banded in gold and featuring the owner's initials, retailed at four pounds.

Design broke out in spots during the mid-1930s – lemonade sets with green spots and dinner services in a 'pin spot' design, like those exhibited at Harrods, in a choice of black or gold, were among the patterns produced by Clarice Cliff in 1935, while the fashion house Jaeger, which opened its Regent Street store that year, was also advertising 'Spots for the London Season'.[12] The liking for texture continued with the introduction of 'designs imitating raffia'[13] and a range of tableware, 'Lynton', 'with a ribbed surface suggestive of unturned, hand-thrown pottery',[14] whose teapot shape, a softened cone, demonstrated how the sharp lines of geometry could be tamed. By the end of the year, tartans were 'very much in vogue'.[15] Monograms, spots, tartans and textured dinner ware – plus banded ware in every shade and combination – here was modernity with the minimum of pattern. With 'much less flamboyance'[16] favoured for interior colours, too, Clarice Cliff's mushroom tones and pale pink grounds were popular. Yet, despite the increasing sobriety of her dinner ware, colour remained essential to Clarice Cliff's palette. Jade green continued to find favour, flowers still bloomed effusively, while patterns as bright as 'Sungold' and 'Killarney' – designs of interlocking triangles – were among those reviewed that year.

A.J. Wilkinson was congratulated for its 'real breadth of vision' during 1935,[17] but, with a reduced demand for colour, the Newport Pottery was less busy. New trends in tableware design called for new directions: Clarice Cliff's geometric shapes began to be phased out; the soft curves of 'Bon Jour' and 'Biarritz' dinner ware, and the newly introduced 'Lynton', were better suited to the present mood than the more demanding 'Conical' and 'Stamford'. Even so, 'Bizarre' continued to beguile. 'The decorating rooms fascinate you most,' the journalist Dorothy Critchlow observed, on visiting the workshop in May.

> You open the door and find that somehow the sunshine has pierced the haze and is streaming through the windows on to the endless benches and the girls' bent, glossy heads. The room is filled with singing, which does not stop . . . By one bench where the wheels turn quickly a girl holds a brush in her thin fingers. With quick, light touches she dips it in the colour on the tile beside her, lays the tip of the brush against the whirling saucer. Sure, even, and steady the band appears. On another bench a girl is sketching a flower pattern on to vases with Indian ink, working with a speed which would surprise some lightning artists. The next girl, just as quickly, is filling in her sketches with broad strokes of a colour-filled brush. No wonder they all look so happy.[18]

Little had changed since Arnold Bennett penned his own description. Were it not for the introduction of a wireless, it might have been the 1890s.

Such publicity affected the 'Bizarre Girls' themselves. Others in the Potteries were aware that Clarice Cliff's paintresses featured in the press from time to time, and there was evidently an element of rivalry between them. 'We felt that we were an élite, certainly on a par with Clarice Cliff's "Bizarre Girls", who got more publicity than us,' a figure-paintress from Royal Doulton said,[19] while a 'Bizarre Girl' countered, 'Doulton's always thought they were the best.'[20] The painting of figures was intricate and painstaking. 'You wouldn't find many figure-painters singing in the workshop or listening to the radio,' a Doulton paintress remarked,[21] alluding to the publicised wireless in the 'Bizarre' shop. Not surprisingly, given the competitive interest that exists between collectors of Clarice Cliff's and Susie Cooper's work today, a similar rivalry existed between their employees. Most 'Bizarre Girls' knew of Susie Cooper – 'We were very partisan,' said one.[22] 'The Girls would say, "She's copying off Clarice,"' said another.[23] No doubt Susie Cooper's paintresses were equally disparaging. At least one of the 'Bizarre Girls' later worked for Susie Cooper; another enquired about work, but was sent back to the Newport Pottery when Clarice Cliff intervened, which suggests neither designer wanted to step on the other's toes. Although conscious of their status, the 'Bizarre Girls' did not feel a particular affinity with Clarice Cliff's designs: 'It was just a job.'[24] On her marriage, one paintress asked her sister (also a 'Bizarre Girl') for 'a plain white china tea set, with a gold line'.[25]

'The designer's recent trip in seach of new ideas on the Continent is reflected in her new designs,' a journalist observed in the autumn of 1935, which suggests Clarice Cliff had joined Colley for part of the European leg of his travels. 'She has abandoned to some extent the conventional modern forms with which we became familiar in her earlier designs, and natural flowers and leaf patterns are largely used in her new ware, though still used with the simplicity that is essential to the modern mood.'[26] 'She travels frequently to Europe,' another reporter noted, 'visiting the art centres of Prague, Paris, Vienna, Brussels and Berlin and has even been so far afield as America.'[27] Now that Colley's children were older – his youngest daughter was now fifteen; his oldest married (against her father's wishes) in 1935 – he and Clarice may anyway, have, started travelling much more frequently. Trips abroad reduced the need for discretion as well as providing Clarice with new ideas. A further press report that year referred to her 'long working holidays',[28] and paintress Rene Dale recalled her being away for weeks at a time.

'Italy's art is reflected in pieces featuring a beautiful opaque glaze, pale lemon in colour,' one newspaper explained.[29] Foreign travel provided design names too: the names for the teapot shape 'Trieste', and the pattern 'Capri', were surely the result of holidays abroad. According to the press, Clarice Cliff's American trip took place in 1934, the year before her European journeyings. That she found the time to visit America that year, with the demands of the Harrods project weighing upon her, in addition to her usual work, is a testament to her inexhaustible energy.

A great deal changed between the very early days of 'Bizarre', when merely a handful of girls worked for Clarice Cliff, and the years of its established success, by which time there was something of a division between the original paintresses and the younger ones in the workshop. Edna Cheetham, who joined the 'Bizarre' shop in 1934, recalled how 'some of the much, much older girls came up together, even though Clarice Cliff was the boss'. She saw less of Clarice Cliff, whom she described as 'a distant, austere, charismatically charming woman . . . one respected her very much indeed'.[30] From time to time, there were glimpses of her other life: a 'dress which spoke of cocktail parties'[31] hung on the back of her office door, and one day Clarice Cliff exchanged her technician's coat for a navy-blue beret and cape on the way to some event. 'She looked so different,' Alice Andrews said, 'I couldn't believe it.'[32]

By the mid-1930s, the few commercial firms employing pottery designers paid salaries of between £300 and £500, with the exception of some six or eight manufacturers who valued their head designer 'so highly' as to pay £600 or £700.[33] Clarice Cliff was probably one of the lucky ones. (In 1935, by comparison, the average salary of a solicitor was £1,238, while a teacher earned £480.) As a family with four adults in employment, and with Clarice one of them, the Cliffs were able to enjoy some of the luxuries of the day – frequent trips to the cinema and local theatre, visits to the opera when the Carla Rosa company toured, a gramophone and a wireless, not forgetting the new delights of the tinned food that was becoming popular, and to which Clarice was partial. In an age of social flux, different economic circumstances could make for pronounced divisions within families. While a grammar school-educated woman of the period and her husband, a school teacher, were able to afford a three-bedroom house and a vacuum cleaner, her sister, who had attended the secondary modern school, and whose husband was a door-to-door salesman, lived without electricity.[34] In an era of such contrasts, the struggle for social position could be tangible.

Clarice Cliff bought her second car in 1935: an Austin Seven Pearl Cabriolet, a model not yet one year old, priced £197. Its blue-grey paintwork was not standard-issue: evidently, she still wished to make her own mark. Even by 1935, cars remained something of a novelty, and not just in Stoke-on-Trent. When a friend of E.M. Delafield's Provincial Lady offers to 'come round at once in her tiny car', the Provincial Lady is 'much impressed . . . at her having a tiny car', a Baby Austin, which draws up 'with terrific *verve* outside the door' shortly thereafter.[35] Clarice Cliff christened her new Austin 'Jenny', only one vowel removed from 'Jinny', the name of her first car, but a greater leap in terms of social class.[36]

That winter, Clarice Cliff dined with aristocracy. At the beginning of November, she and Colley Shorter attended a charity ball in aid of the Paddington Green Children's Hospital, for which they provided 'Clarice Cliff' tableware. Paragon China and Mappin & Webb were also represented, with exhibitions of china and glass. The dinner-dance, held at the Dorchester Hotel – another example of Art Deco splendour – was trailed in the *Daily Mirror* under the headline 'Tablecloths of Black'. 'Traditions of Society will be shattered next Tuesday,' the newspaper reported, 'when . . . several hundred guests will dine at tables covered with black velvet and gold net tablecloths. Modernistic British china, in which all the plates are square instead of round, will be used.'[37] Clarice Cliff's 'Age of Jazz' figures also made an appearance, swooning to the Ambrose Band. The Duke and Duchess of York were present; Lord and Lady Strathcona received the guests. Unusually, for Clarice Cliff, both she and Colley sat on the organising committee – the choice of tablecloths could only have been hers – presumably because he was away for much of that year. The dinner was an opportunity for her to disabuse her fellow diners of the romance of the pottery trade, but she was unlikely to have done any such thing. Her presence was another indicator of how far she and 'Clarice Cliff' had come. A later employee, Norman Smith, spoke of how Clarice Cliff grew in stature during the years in which he knew her. 'She schooled herself,' he said,[38] a process begun early, and polished on occasions such as this.

At another, far less formal, charity event around this time, Clarice Cliff did her best to remain anonymous. This event, a dance at the King Edward Hall, Finchley in aid of the memorial hospital, was co-hosted by Charles England of the Wander Inn, a classy North London tea lounge where ladies sipped their tea from 'Bizarre' tea cups, surrounded by exotically painted murals. An article in *Country Illustrated*, published shortly after the café opened in 1934, described the venue as 'really "new"' in its ideals.[39] Though Clarice Cliff's attendance was reported by a local paper, she 'hid her light under a bushel and preferred to remain unidentified'.[40]

If the overseas press were wooed that year with tales of Clarice Cliff's rise from humble gilder to pottery director, in the eyes of the UK press, at least, she was no longer a 'clever girl artist',[41] but a professional woman. In November 1935, she finally attained professional maturity when she featured in the *Sunday Express* as part of a series, 'Women who make Money'.[42] Clarice Cliff, 'The China Designer', was the last of the five women interviewed. The article is a hymn to ambition: 'Ever since she left school, [she] has had only one idea, and has concentrated every atom of her brains, energy and talent on achieving success in it,' the paper explained. The prose is urgent, its sentences often clipped, with significant details printed in bold: '**Most apprentices refuse to go through more than one department. She went through every one, lapped up in months what others took years to learn** . . . In three months she had twenty assistants. In nine months she had a hundred. She was made art director of her firm.' Women who make money do not have time to waste on extraneous words.

The other women interviewed were Anna Zinkeisen, who was among those decorating the interior of the new Cunard–White Star liner, the *Queen Mary*, and so was currently appearing elsewhere in the press; Mrs Tozer, a beauty expert; the Society photographer Dorothy Wilding; and an independent sales adviser, Gladys Burlton, who ran her own business. An incongruous mix of professionals, suggesting, perhaps, how difficult it was to find suitable women for the theme. What they all shared was not just an ability to earn their own living (and a handsome one at that, in the case of Dorothy Wilding) but – to coin a popular word – drive. 'She went from department to department' (Burlton) . . . '[she] was a girl who knew what she wanted' (Wilding) . . . 'She did everything herself, working till ten-thirty every night' (Wilding again) . . . 'I started with one girl assistant, now I employ thirty' (Tozer) . . . 'how I worked! . . . No theatres, or parties. No holidays' (Zinkeisen). Any one of the above might have applied to Clarice Cliff.

In other ways, she was the exception: Clarice Cliff was the only working-class woman among the interviewees and the only one who was not based in London. The usual contradictions were apparent. Age-conscious as always, she lost more than six years, and her tale of skill and determination shared the page with a recipe for Irish stew, a recommendation for face cream and an article entitled 'Why Girls Break off their Engagements'. ('It's the little things that are the worst,' including the 'habit of constant whistling'.) A poem by Vita Sackville-West struggled to raise the tone. Contradictions apart, the article was a tremendous coup: by 1935, the *Express* was one of the UK's best-selling daily newspapers – 2 million copies by mid-1933 – and the circulation of its Sunday paper almost as high.[43]

Clarice Cliff had little time in which to contemplate her new stature. On 30 November, six days after the article appeared, her sister Dorothy died. She had been admitted to Haywood Hospital, Burslem, for a hysterectomy, and died of acute dilation of the heart, which suggests she developed heart failure after the operation. Clarice was present at her death. She had probably spent that Saturday morning at the factory, as usual, before driving to see Dorothy in the afternoon. Anticipating a typical hospital visit, she was instead confronted with her sister's death, and then required to drive home and break the news. Dorothy was thirty-four, two and a half years younger than Clarice.

Years later, their sister Ethel offered her own explanation for the tragedy: in her estimation, Dorothy died of a broken heart.[44] She was in love with her dancing partner, whom she planned to marry, but discovered he was seeing someone else. Before the relationship ended, Dorothy had been making him a pair of silk pyjamas, black with broad gold stripes. Inevitably, she put them to one side but, after her sister's death, Ethel finished and delivered the pyjamas. She hoped Dorothy's partner would wear them, and regret.

When Dorothy died, the *Evening Sentinel* was advertising Christmas entertainment at Hanley's Grand Hotel and the Burslem Amateur Operatic Society's forthcoming performance of *The Mikado*, in which her brother Frank was due to appear. That day, and for several days thereafter, the newspaper was occupied with the trial of Dr Ruxton for the murder of his wife and nursemaid, a crime which caused considerable speculation, not least in the 'Bizarre' shop, where it became the theme of one of the paintresses' songs. Weeks of gossip and Christmas cheer, but not for Clarice Cliff. She was facing the wholly unexpected loss of a sister, and the one probably closest in temperament.

SIXTEEN

A Life of Her Own

Perhaps Dorothy's death persuaded Clarice Cliff to make changes in her life: 1936 is likely to be the year she moved from Edwards Street to her own flat.[1] Clarice's new home was at 20 Snow Hill, Shelton, a district of Hanley some three miles from Tunstall, and a discreet distance from her family. Even years later, 'visits to Hanley were rare and considered "a treat"' for those who lived in Tunstall. 'Moreover, one had to don one's Sunday garb to go there, such was Hanley's esteem.'[2]

Number 20 Snow Hill stands below a corner of the road that sweeps from Stoke through Hanley, with St Mark's Church a stolid presence nearby. Part of a Victorian terrace, the building housed two flats and a ground-floor hairdressing salon. At last, Clarice Cliff had a room of her own. Four rooms, in fact. The flat comprised a small kitchen with a dining area, sitting-room, bedroom and bathroom. Though it was by no means comparable with the sleek mansion flats that were springing up in London at this time, the very idea of a flat represented the height of modernity. Only a small number existed within Stoke-on-Trent for some years to come.[3]

The move represented the height of daring, too, within the provinces. Unmarried women sharing was one thing, a woman living alone quite another. Perhaps Clarice waited for her father's death before contemplating the move. According to her niece Nancy, her mother was too frail to be overly concerned, although, by 1936, there can have been little Clarice could do that would have surprised her. Perhaps, by now, Ann Cliff had considered the difficulties of her own life and, if she were able to be honest with herself, concluded that the options facing women of her class were few. Her own mother had reared nine children and her husband's mother seven. 'Don't have a load of kids,' one mother of a large family advised her daughter.[4] Many younger women took that advice.[5] In the days before the National Health Service, with broken health, inadequate contraception and large families the outlook for many working-class women, they envisaged similar lives of hardship for their daughters, with little prospect of autonomy before them. If Clarice Cliff resisted the traditional female path and turned propriety on its head, perhaps – if only silently – her mother understood. If the lessons Clarice took from her upbringing were no more unusual than others of her time, her conclusions were always more radical.

Clarice Cliff's decision to live alone may have been unusual within Stoke-on-Trent, but would have been less so within a large city. (Witness the need for hostels run by the YWCA.) The numerous marriage bars in operation between the wars determined that the professional woman was likely to be single. Some remained so by choice; others lacked the opportunity to marry: women exceeded men by some 2 million after the First World War.[6] By 1936, the phenomenon of the single woman was such that the writer Marjorie Hillis found success on both sides of the Atlantic with her light-hearted advice manual, *Live Alone and Like It*. 'We have witnessed, during recent years,' the introduction explained, 'the mustering of an entirely new kind of army, a host of capable and courageous young women, who are not only successfully facing and solving their economic problems, but managing all the while to remain patient, personable and polite about it . . . It was in that way that Business, assisted by its handmaid Emancipation, flooded our towns with a never ebbing tide of working and – frequently – solitary women.'[7] But, Marjorie Hillis insisted, 'This book is no brief in favour of living alone.'[8] She was merely responding to the times.

The Snow Hill flat presented Clarice Cliff with what was surely her most enjoyable design challenge. Hilda Lovatt recalled some of her preparations for the move. The bathroom ceiling was decorated with sheets of black and yellow paper, with a decorative bowl and small 'Elegant' basket, toothbrush-holder and soap dish banded in black and yellow to match, while her dressing-table set was decorated in bands of blue and pink – 'the fashionable colours'[9] of the day – to complement the bedroom furnishings. Unsurprisingly, Clarice Cliff designed the pattern for her own dinner ware, a decoration featuring her initials in black, set off with a band of silver – an interesting choice for someone whose status revolved around her own signature, although not necessarily an entirely vain one, given the status of the monogram at this time. For breakfast, she selected her own tableware in 'Honeydew' – a floral pattern combining warm shades of honey and green. Though she produced small plates for 'slimming modes',[10] she may have been more generous for herself.

Eric Grindley, a Newport employee who did occasional jobs for Clarice Cliff as a young trainee, was one of the few people to see inside the flat. His memories supply the only record of the interior, which he recalled in great detail because its impact was so striking and its appearance unlike anything he had seen: 'The lounge contained a large black and white mottled fireplace with unusual Chinese brass fire-irons. The chimney breast and adjoining wall were decorated with a striking hand-painted mural in orange, red, blue, black and green, which depicted what could only be described as a "Bizarre" forest scene with huge leaves, and lotus flowers and fruits. The wall was papered in a bright-red paper with big scrolled motifs, the doors were painted in vivid red, with panels picked out with black. The walls were adorned with "Picasso-type" pictures. Vases and lamp bases were Clarice Cliff's own shapes, banded in orange and black, colours that matched a Chinese-type carpet. The lounge furniture was of the Regency type, dark wood with upholstery of red and gold brocade. There was an occasional table in mahogany and glass, and an antique cabinet almost the length of one wall.'[11]

The Regency style was finding favour once again. A press photograph showing Clarice Cliff in a dress with raglan sleeves confirms her as a follower of the fashion for historical lines that flourished during this period. A Regency dresser displaying a dinner service decorated with splashes of orange and jade added 'that touch of the incongruous demanded by the modern scheme'.[12] A local antiques dealer and friend of Colley's supplied the furniture.

Had many in Stoke-on-Trent been invited to Snow Hill, the exoticism of its interior would have been a revelation, and its extravagant use of colour a cause for suspicion in itself. In *Miss Pettigrew Lives for a Day*, a 1938 novel, Miss Pettigrew, an old-fashioned 'spinster', visits a similarly decorative flat: 'Brilliant cushions ornamented more brilliant chairs and chesterfield. A deep, velvety carpet of strange, futuristic design decorated the floor. Gorgeous, breath-taking curtains draped the windows . . . Ornaments of every colour and shape adorned mantelpiece, table and stands. Nothing matched anything else. Everything was of an exotic brilliance that took away the breath. "Not the room of a lady," thought Miss Pettigrew,'[13] which may have been the conclusion of those in Stoke-on-Trent who associated the boldly coloured with the brazen.

Women who escaped the confines of conventional living stamped their personalities upon their homes in the brightest of ways. If colour was synonymous with modernity, it also signified new freedoms. The house shared by Olivia and her cousin Hetty in Rosamond Lehmann's 1936 novel, *The Weather in the Streets*, with its 'cherry-coloured curtains' and 'parrot-green and silver cushions',[14] which clash so brilliantly with Hetty's cardinal-red fingernails, is a testament to their desire to live differently. Even Delia, in *The New House*, Lettice Cooper's novel of the same year, who aspires to a flat decorated in 'plain, pale wood', wants 'bowls of jade and orange, or great heaps of cushions, raspberry red, silver-green, and the deep, blue-purple of anemones'.[15] These were bold expressions of individuality and independence, none more so than those of Clarice Cliff who, at the age of thirty-seven, finally attained the privacy enabling her to live her life (more or less) on her own terms. Independence had been a long time coming.

Now that she had her own home, Clarice started smoking, or else finally acquired the freedom to smoke whenever she pleased. Player's were her cigarettes of choice – 'Men may come and Men may go but Player's are constant ever'[16] – which she smoked with that sophisticate's prop, a cigarette-holder, referred to as her 'pipe'.[17] Though telephones were not yet widely used – a photograph in the *Evening Sentinel* the previous year shows a group of schoolgirls learning how to approach this new technology[18] – Clarice Cliff needed one so that

Nancy Craddock

Colley or the factory could reach her. For entertainment, she had a wireless; what pleasure to look about her while the Savoy Orpheans tiptoed across the airwaves. Each room bore her hallmark: plates of her own design, lamps stamped with her signature, bathroom furnishings and a dressing-table set, even her own ashtrays in which to rest her cigarettes. Her satisfaction must have been immense.

With the exception of Ethel, it is debatable whether Clarice's sisters came to Snow Hill. Thursday evenings were reserved for Nancy, who visited her aunt after school, a private day-school in Burslem; Clarice Cliff made a significant contribution to the fees, and was probably responsible for the choice of school: she wanted her niece to have a better education than her own lacklustre one. She also made a gift of a school uniform to a nephew who passed for grammar school – she understood the value of learning. She encouraged Nancy to read and quizzed her on the names of birds and flowers seen on their weekend jaunts. For Nancy, visits to her

aunt must have been something of an adventure – the exoticism of
the flat, the rides in a car, the attention of someone whose life
was so very different from that of her mother and her other aunts.
For Clarice, they offered the chance to enjoy a child's company,
companionship when she would otherwise be alone, and the frank
affection of someone who accepted her for who she was.

Her main visitor was, of course, Colley Shorter. Clarice was
unlikely to have needed Marjorie Hillis's advice on 'How to get rid
of a man friend' from her chapter, 'Etiquette for a Lone Female'.[19]
Even so, appearances had to be kept up. Looking back on the 1930s
in her memoir, *You May Well Ask*, the writer Naomi Mitchison
recalled that more effective methods of contraception helped her
social circle conduct extra-marital affairs.[20] As usual, the intelligentsia
were way ahead. Although middle-class use of birth control was far
more widespread by this time, for the married working-class woman
reliable information about contraception remained exceedingly hard
to find; for the unmarried woman it was pretty much inaccessible.[21]

Whatever your social class, sex was not a topic for discussion.
'You never mentioned sex in those days,' one young woman recalled.
'They didn't even read psalms at school when there were breasts or
pregnant women in them, it was really very hard.'[22] 'I think . . . the
language about sex hadn't been invented,' said novelist and playwright Molly Keane. 'I don't remember the word sex occurring . . .
ever . . . It just wasn't there.'[23] The journalist Mary Stott agreed: '*We*
didn't think about sexual relationships . . . there wasn't such a thing.
My mother never, never, never gave me any explanation of sex or
what would happen, or said to me anything about why I'd started
menstruating. They were *terribly* prudish, our foremothers.'[24]

In 1930, after much opposition, the Ministry of Health permitted
contraceptive advice to be given to married women on medical
grounds, but attempts to make contraceptive knowledge more
widely available, and relieve the burden of large families faced by
so many of the working class, met with strong resistance. The decision to form a North Staffordshire branch of the Birth Control
Association in 1936 was greeted by palpitations and anxious correspondence in the local press.[25] Though the women concerned were
praised for their philanthropy – Dorothy Wedgwood, wife of the

Honourable Josiah Wedgwood V, was the driving force behind the
scheme – the *Evening Sentinel* was adamant: 'Too much is known
already on these matters . . . Let us hope we may hear no more of
the proposal.'[26] Despite protestations (and thanks, no doubt, to the
propelling might of the Wedgwood name), the Mothers' Advice
Clinic opened in Wellesley Street, Shelton, later that year, just
around the corner from Clarice Cliff's flat – not that she would
have been able to make use of it. The Wellesley Street clinic was
the only one of its kind in the district, Manchester and Birmingham
being the nearest other places offering married women contraceptive advice.[27] Even after the clinic opened, the struggle continued
against a hostile press, council opposition and doctors who refused
to co-operate. Clarice's corner of Shelton must have witnessed many
anxious comings and goings. But not among single women: they
did not figure, and certainly not those who were seeing a married
man.

Even if Clarice Cliff's mother preferred not to know, Clarice's
relationship with Colley was thought to be more widely known
within the industry by this time. Milner Gray thought as much when
he met them through 'Modern Art for the Table',[28] although his
connections were not those of the factory floor, nor was he of the
Potteries, so he was not required to note provincial prohibitions.
Though having her own flat undoubtedly gave Clarice Cliff freedom,
she still had her reputation to maintain. For the most part, she was
alone at Snow Hill, alone at the end of the day. With a gin and
tonic to hand and a packet of cigarettes, or a cup of tea and a box
of neapolitans, Clarice travelled to Manderley with Daphne du
Maurier or to Jalna with Mazo de la Roche. She was a fan of Agatha
Christie too, in whose novels identities and intentions are so often
concealed and no one's motives can be trusted. Like much else of
the period, contemporary fiction revealed a preoccupation with questions of belonging and class, and with the 'treacherous and tricky
limits to respectability'.[29] Clarice Cliff would be particularly glad to
retreat to Snow Hill at the end of the year, when mixed reactions
to the abdication of Edward VIII highlighted the consequences for
those who overstepped the bounds of propriety.

*

Clarice Cliff in her studio at the Newport Pottery

By finding her own flat, Clarice Cliff was establishing some privacy for herself, and securing time for her relationship with Colley, but the move was also an affirmation of the shape her life had acquired – of who she was and how she saw her future. With her father dead, her younger sister dying so unexpectedly, and Colley himself recovering from serious illness, Clarice was literally putting her house in order. This was a period for taking stock.

Significant changes were under way at the factory too, with new members of staff being taken on. One of these was Peggy Davies, who would later become known as a ceramic modeller through her long association with Royal Doulton. When she joined the Newport Pottery, however, Davies (then, Gibbons) was sixteen and a senior student at the Burslem School of Art, where Clarice Cliff saw her work and asked her to become an assistant designer. She spent three years working with Clarice Cliff, while continuing to study via evening classes and day-release. Perhaps recollecting her own questing nature years earlier, Clarice Cliff allowed her the 'absolute freedom of the factory',[30] for which Davies was extremely grateful. She modelled some of the later shapes in the, by now, extensive floral range, 'My Garden', and also joined the 'Bizarre Girls' on demonstrations, but is said to have been shocked because the considerable effort required to produce Clarice Cliff's shapes represented the antithesis of the Bauhaus principles of her training.[31] Another apprentice modeller, Betty Silvester,[32] started at the factory around this time, appointed to replace two workshop staff, Harold Walker and John Shaw, who had worked on the 'My Garden' range themselves, but left in 1935, said to be unhappy at having insufficient scope and credit for their designs.[33] The designer Nancy Greatrex was also employed by Clarice Cliff for a short period before the Second World War, as was a decorating manager and modeller, Aubrey Dunn.

It is interesting that the design staff Clarice Cliff appointed at this time were nearly all women. 'It is nothing unusual in these days to hear of women who play a large part on the artistic side of pottery production,' the *Pottery and Glass Record* reported the following year.[34] The existence of a small but growing number of women designers did not mean that the Potteries had now become a haven for the professional woman, however. Although opportunities were opening up in a world that acknowledged the commercial benefit of women designers, gender and class continued to impose limitations. The only other working-class woman to achieve prominence within the industry between the wars, Millicent Taplin,[35] was restricted to the creation of patterns. Clarice Cliff was unusual in giving young women the chance to model and the freedom to explore the factory as she herself had done years before.

New additions to the staff eased the pressure on Clarice Cliff. Though no longer the sole designer, she was still producing material for three factories. But if she was relieving some of the demands upon her time, she was not relinquishing her name, which continued to appear on all work produced by the Newport Pottery.

Professionally, the greatest change during this period was the disappearance of 'Bizarre': in 1936, the name was discontinued. 'Bizarre' featured in trade advertisements as usual that spring but by July had disappeared: only the 'Clarice Cliff' signature remained. The erasure of 'Bizarre' acknowledged a change of climate and of tone, as well as image: connotations of hectic colour and pizzazz had ceased to be appropriate to the decade. Though the word was used to define Clarice Cliff's work as late as 1935 – 'those who do not like the bizarre, will not like these,'[36] a journalist from the *Observer* insisted – as a design label, 'Bizarre' was outmoded.

Any sense that Clarice Cliff was abandoning inventiveness along with the name that represented years of creativity would not have been conveyed by a report of her work in the *Pottery Gazette* in the autumn of 1936, which outlined some of the factors contributing to her success: 'Miss Clarice Cliff seems to be never satisfied unless she is creating something fresh in its impulse . . . she is prolific in her ideas . . . and she is fortunate in having the backing of an organisation which is prepared to take the long view and to embark upon modelling new shapes, almost regardless of initial cost . . . One can never revisit any of the potteries of this concern without being confronted with scores of new creations . . . which cause one to reflect: Why did not someone in the trade think of this before? Perhaps . . . it is not that no one thought about it, but that no one had the confidence and courage to try it out.'[37]

SEVENTEEN

I Know That You Can Be Discreet

When we called upon the firm . . . shortly after the Wakes holidays,' the *Pottery Gazette* reported in 1937, 'we found Mr Colley Shorter, Miss Clarice Cliff and everyone else concerned . . . very much occupied in getting together that stupendous collection of samples for which their special autumn event appears to call.'[1] Although Clarice Cliff remained 'extremely active in the production of new themes',[2] the 'noticeable swinging back to the traditional'[3] that had been observed the previous year continued to inform her work – and that of most other pottery designers – up to the Second World War. A retail sales ledger for 1937 indicates a particular fondness for Clarice Cliff's mushroom glaze,[4] while among the patterns introduced that year was a tea set featuring flowers for each season: 'pale-green clover leaves, rosebuds, soft brown leaves, and the palest blue snowdrops'.[6] The traditional had truly taken hold.

Not all colours were dilute, however. Clarice Cliff's 'My Garden' was said to be selling in even larger quantities, and its range of colourings and shapes constantly extended: embossed bowls, vases, cornucopias, jugs and candlesticks could now be purchased in 'My Garden Verdant', 'Sunrise', 'Sungold', 'Peach', 'Flame', and so on. Though it made commercial sense to expand a successful line, it nevertheless showed Clarice Cliff playing safe. 'Fancies' still answered the call for quirkiness, however, and for one customer, at least, the age of jazz had not quite disappeared: a retailer in Birmingham ordered seven dancing couples and assorted musicians,

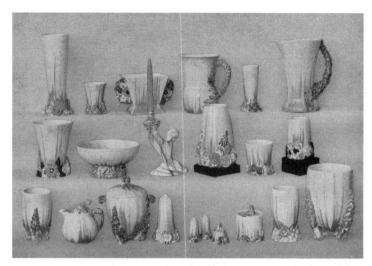

'My Garden'

with a request for a hole to be drilled into each figure.[6] Though the cocktail hour had passed, the craze for wall decorations showed no sign of diminishing. The growing interest in horoscopes would be satisfied with wall plaques too. Elsa Schiaparelli introduced star signs to *haute couture*; Clarice Cliff offered the middle classes zodiacs with which to dress their walls.

By 1937, Colley Shorter's younger daughter, Joan, had joined the factory. In line with her father's hope that she, too, would come to love the pottery industry, she attended the British Industries Fair that year and began learning the ropes. Joan was seventeen, and although she did not work directly for Clarice Cliff, the situation cannot have been easy for either woman. The Paris Bicentennial that summer gave Clarice and Colley the chance to leave the complications of their relationship behind and revisit old haunts, while assessing current trends in pottery design. With a taste for sobriety to the fore, Clarice Cliff's work was not among that shown in the British Pavilion, but appeared in the International Pavilion, together with designs by other manufacturers whose work did not meet the selection criteria of the Council for Art and Industry.[7] A photograph of A.J. Wilkinson's Paris stand shows a somewhat perfunctory display in comparison with previous events.[8]

The Paris exhibition may have been Clarice and Colley's last chance to travel overseas before the outbreak of war. Trade was already looking gloomy, and by the beginning of 1938 was reported to be 'exceptionally quiet'.[9] Annual holidays that year were longer for many potteries than since the First World War, with some closing their doors for nearly three weeks, while at A.J. Wilkinson's annual display that September, shortly before the Munich Crisis, only two buyers called throughout the whole fortnight.[10]

Before the decade – and the pre-war years – came to a close, there was a fresh opportunity for women to see the work of Clarice Cliff. The Woman's Fair at Olympia in November 1938 claimed to be the first-ever event to present 'every possible interest of women',[11] and on a lavish scale. The exhibition covered seven themes: the home, children, food, fashion, beauty, careers and leisure. For Clarice Cliff, it was surely galling, if no surprise, to see careers enter the list at number six. Focus on the home had become increasingly emphatic, and, like some of the designs on offer, had lost the inventiveness of former years. Gone were the invitations to paint patterns on lamp-shades and tables; women were now encouraged to bake cakes and arrange flowers. 'Be Renowned for your Good Coffee,' *Miss Modern* advised.[12]

By now, Clarice Cliff's work featured regularly in Penelope Prim's *Evening News* column, 'At the Housekeeper's Desk', and appeared in the *Daily Herald* in Janet Jay's 'Home-maker's Diary'. *Woman & Home* confirmed the overall tone when a 'Bon Jour' coffee set featured in the same issue as a recipe for a 'Little House Cake', complete with an iced sponge roof.[13] Home planning was a leading feature of the Woman's Fair, where four miles of exhibition stands offered 'everything for the home', from 'natty flats' to household gadgets, and so on. There were items to tempt the dreamer too, one of the chief attractions being the Hollywood Garden section, with its replica of Shirley Temple's Santa Monica beach house.

Despite poor trade and an increasingly desperate outlook, Clarice Cliff continued to develop new ideas. 'Miss Clarice Cliff has evidently been very busy,' the *Pottery Gazette* reported the following autumn, 'and she has caught the right spirit in quite a number of new things which not only unite clever designing with skilful potting, but also sound that note of freshness and novelty which the public is all the while demanding nowadays.'[14] Demands for 'freshness and novelty' were shortlived, however. By the time the article was published, Britain was at war with Germany.

The trade press adopted the appropriate tone immediately, instructing manufacturers to 'Fight for new trade'[15] and advising retailers how to black-out doorways. By December 1939, the decision had been taken to cancel the next British Industries Fair, although this was surely a formality: with bomb shelters a feature of the Ideal Home Exhibition earlier that year, thoughts of home trade were already receding. Some manufacturers were quick to adjust to the new conditions, among them Shorter & Son, which was advertising candle- and night-light holders almost the minute war was declared.

The imposition of a home-trade quota in 1940, and subsequent restrictions applied to the types of pottery that could be produced, abruptly changed the profile of the pottery industry. Until restrictions were lifted in 1952, the decoration of tableware for the home market came to a standstill. The design of shapes was circumscribed, too, with pottery manufacture now geared towards the fulfilment of government contracts and to supplying those whose possessions were destroyed or damaged. With the home market driven by utility, the government pleaded with manufacturers to augment the export trade; Clarice Cliff now focused her efforts in that direction. Among the lines advertised for export that September, in anticipation of the firm's annual display, was her 'Harvest' tableware, an effusively embossed shape with floral handles and harvest motifs, which the *Pottery Gazette* considered 'specially worthy of recommendation',[16] although those with a taste for her earlier work were likely to have disagreed. September 1940 was not a time for showing tableware, however: that month saw the onset of the Blitz.

Some fifty paintresses were employed to decorate 'Clarice Cliff' at the start of the Second World War, but one by one they left. '[T]he army, munitions, mines, etc. claimed all our workers,' Clarice

Cliff recalled, 'except one girl who was a semi-invalid . . . just as they had become *very skilful* and clever.'[17] Some looked to the Land Army; Edna Cheetham volunteered for the WAAF, where she enjoyed 'a glamorous time'[18] as a plotter; many worked long shifts in the munitions factories at nearby Swynnerton and Radway Green, where they exchanged the communal singing of the 'Bizarre' shop for *Music While You Work* and choruses sung in the train on their way home. The building itself was taken over by the Ministry of Supply and became a storage depot; the remaining Girls transferred to A.J. Wilkinson – not quite enemy territory, but almost – where a new, smaller 'Clarice Cliff' workshop was established. With the imposition of decorating restrictions, the effects of a depleted work-force were less devastating than they would otherwise have been, but with the conscription of women in December 1941, the last of Clarice Cliff's paintresses disappeared.

The impact of conscription on the Potteries was dramatic. It was not just the workforce but the landscape of the potbanks that changed. Just as the Newport Pottery was commandeered for the storage of rubber, so the china enamelling department at Wedgwood was turned over to the production of pop rivets for Spitfires and Lancaster Bombers. Years of history dismantled, the 'Bizarre' years dismantled with them. With the closure of her workshop and the disappearance of her workers, the markers of Clarice Cliff's success were gone.

Almost as dramatic were the changes taking place in Clarice Cliff's personal life at this time. On 2 November 1939, at the age of fifty-one, Annie Shorter died. Myocarditis was reported as the primary cause, with a suggestion of further contributory health problems (although nothing to indicate a history of ill-health). Just over one year later, on 21 December 1940, Clarice and Colley married at the register office in Stafford. Some twelve miles from Stoke-on-Trent, the county town afforded anonymity. Clarice Cliff was now forty-one, Colley fifty-eight; they had been together some thirteen years.

Thirteen months had passed since Annie Shorter's death. The formal rules of mourning had been met, although the 'decent interval' between a death and a remarriage – in the days when propriety dictated such an interval – was generally regarded as two years. Perhaps the reason 'decency' was overlooked in this instance was that it would have seemed less 'decent' had Clarice and Colley waited. 'It's about time you married that girl,' a friend is said to have prompted him.[19]

Clarice Cliff's sister Ethel was told of the wedding after the event: 'I was down the factory one time and she said . . . they'd married that morning and that was as much as was said . . . Well, I took it for granted that that's what was coming some day,' she added.[20] As far as Ethel was aware, their mother never met Colley – nor any other member of his family – although Nancy recalled him visiting Ann Cliff prior to the marriage to inform her of his intentions, an old-fashioned gesture, but then Colley was old-fashioned in many ways. He liked to observe the conventions, or to appear to observe them, at least.

Though Clarice Cliff's family learned of her new status, for the most part the marriage remained secret for a year. That it did so offers the most compelling evidence of the impact propriety and fear of scandal had upon her relationship with Colley, even after their marriage, and of how intensely she craved acceptance as his wife. In December 1941, when they had been married nearly a year, Clarice wrote to Ewart Oakes, the salesman who had obtained the very first order for 'Bizarre'. He had seen her career develop; he had doubtless observed much more. 'Dear Ewart,' she confided, 'I have a bit of news for you, which may not come as much of a surprise – Colley and I are married! – this at the moment is not generally known, but I know that you can be discreet.'[21] Even after a year had passed, Clarice was requesting discretion. But she was also amused by the irony of her new situation. 'PS,' she added as an afterthought in the left-hand margin. 'If you write, don't forget it is Shorter not Cliff, or we might get turned out, what a joke.'[22]

Clarice wrote to Ewart Oakes from North Wales, where she and Colley were visiting his mother, who shared her home with his unmarried sisters, Jessie and Louie. Perhaps this was the occasion on which the women were informed that a marriage had taken place (thereby satisfying the 'decent interval' following Annie Shorter's death). That Clarice's letter to Ewart Oakes survived when so much else relating to her life has been lost – or not committed to paper in the first place – is extraordinary. How it came to survive is extraordinary in itself. The letter, marked 'Personal', was sent to Oakes at the Newport Pottery, where it was discovered by a fellow employee and put into a teapot for safekeeping. It stands as an indication of the strength of provincial mores.

After her marriage, Clarice moved to 'Chetwynd', where Colley's younger daughter, Joan, also lived until she joined the WAAF, her presence a further complication in their relationship. Clarice's removal to the house, with its generous proportions and formal hall, let alone extensive garden, represented a significant leap. Her transformation was now complete. And to wake up in clean air, facing the green fields overlooking Hanchurch Woods, intensified the contrast between her past and present circumstances.

In accordance with the Arts and Crafts principles with which 'Chetwynd' was built, great emphasis was placed on the dynamic between the house and its surroundings to create 'as much open-air life within as possible' and to offer 'the greatest possible enjoyment' of the countryside.[23] As part of this intention, a feature of the design was the small central court in the main hallway, surrounded by sliding windows, out of which a tree reached for the sky. At the back of the house, the south-facing elevation presented a multitude of windows to the greenery and light: windows at 360 degrees within the main living-room were designed to maximise light, while the main bedrooms opened on to a veranda (since glassed in).

One of Clarice Cliff's nieces, who occasionally played in the garden as a young girl, described 'Chetwynd' as a 'dream house for a child'.[24] Clarice may not have kept a diary, but she could not have left a stronger indication of the strength of her emotion than the mark she made there after her marriage. One of the kitchen window panes bears a distinctive signature: 'Clarice Shorter' is scratched on to the glass. A tangible statement of possession, exorcising the long, clandestine years. Once again, she proclaimed her achievement with her name.

It must have been extremely strange for Clarice Cliff, working in the factory for nearly a year without announcing how her status had changed, yet, even if she were tempted to confide in someone, it is

'Chetwynd'

difficult to imagine whom she would have trusted. And after so many years of keeping her own counsel, and living a life that was not quite what it seemed, what was one more year, if it brought acceptance and respectability? Of course, marriage did not guarantee acceptance by the Shorters. His mother was a strict Wesleyan; the whole family was now required to acknowledge a woman of whom they disapproved. Marriage formalised the relationship, but did not usher Clarice into the Shorters' circle. The closed world of the Potteries, with its houses and factories side by side, was mirrored by its social relationships: pottery manufacturers socialised with one another, their children played together; second and third generations grew up to replace the first. And the bank manager, solicitor and accountant with whom the family dealt were part of their social circle too. There were also Colley's fox-hunting crowd and his Freemasonry connections to consider. At some point, he was Master of Sutherland Lodge, and a Provincial Grand Superintendent of Works. No doubt friends and associates were grateful that all irregularities had finally been erased and conformity re-established. And if anyone felt otherwise, they knew better than to say as much to Colley Shorter.

EIGHTEEN

A Taste for the Traditional

'The factory is so big a part of one's life, that being away from it, and not knowing what is going on leaves quite a blank,' Clarice Cliff admitted to Ewart Oakes in 1941.[1] Her sense of disconnection can only have grown. With no call for a designer during the war years, the factory had little need of Clarice Cliff. It 'virtually ran itself. The government ran you and 80 per cent of the production of any factory was geared to government contracts.'[2] She was seen there very rarely until the end of the war.

The strict quotas applied to the production of tableware quickly resulted in shortages and, with the bombing of Coventry, Birmingham and Southampton, desperate appeals were made 'for any type of crockery that would hold food'.[3] Soon there was an estimated short-fall of 100 million pieces of crockery a year; jam jars and tooth mugs were pressed into service, with drinkers taking their own to the pub. Austerity hit hard in 1942. Although rationing had been in place for two years by this time, the number of rationed goods was now extended. Soap joined the list, and with fresh fruit and vegetables becoming increasingly hard to find, single onions began to be awarded as raffle prizes. In the Potteries, as elsewhere, there were queues for everything. 'When it got round . . . that oranges or bananas were on sale . . . women left the factory in droves.'[4]

Clarice and Colley responded to the rigours of the times. With petrol now rationed, Colley's beloved Rolls-Royce was put into the garage and he drove to the factory by pony and trap. He joined the

Home Guard and took to wearing a uniform: in interviews with the overseas press shortly after the war he is described as Lieutenant-Colonel Shorter; he must have felt his lack of active service keenly. Alice and Betty, the 'Chetwynd' domestic staff, were less in evidence during the war, but there were the horses to muck out and vegetables to grow – like everyone else, the Shorters were encouraged to turn their substantial flower beds into vegetable plots. All this, and the house itself, now fell to Clarice. If, as a young girl, she had evaded household chores, she certainly acquired her full share now. For someone who had dedicated herself to a profession and enjoyed her independence, the changes wrought by war and marriage were dramatic, and perhaps no less significant than those she had faced at the beginning of her journey through 'Bizarre', but in a period of national upheaval, the upheavals in her own life were merely an insignificant part of the general narrative.[5]

When the Second World War came to a close, restrictions on decorated ware for the home market remained in place, and would do so for a further seven years. Meanwhile, the industry was encouraged to update machinery and plant, and continue with its focus on export. A.J. Wilkinson embarked on an extensive reconstruction, replacing bottle ovens and upgrading methods of production; Clarice Cliff set about reestablishing a small freehand workshop, initially with export in mind. At her request, Hilda Lovatt made contact with some half a dozen Girls – though girls no longer – and Clarice visited Ethel Barrow in person to negotiate a wage that would ensure her return to paint 'Crocus'; the floral pattern 'Rhodanthe' also remained popular, as did the floral shapes 'Water Lily' and 'My Garden', but the mood had changed and could not be recaptured. 'The old world had vanished. A lot of the Girls didn't come back and there were new people coming in – new girls from school.'[6] Other newcomers to the factory included Clarice's sister Hannah, who worked in the office for a period after her husband's death, and Ethel's husband, Arthur Steele, who came to A.J. Wilkinson from Wedgwood; Ethel also rejoined the factory part time and decorating manager, Aubrey Dunn, returned.

Clarice Cliff was now a director of all three Shorter-owned

Colley Shorter and Clarice Cliff, Canada, 1949

companies; significantly, she was also married to the chairman. 'Do
we call you Mrs Shorter, now?' she was asked.[7] But 'Miss Cliff'
would do fine: her name had served her well, and would continue
to be used on designs. In documents she became Clarice Cliff Shorter,
retaining her individuality as well as her professional name.
Socially, she was now Mrs Shorter, a title she was thought to enjoy.
Colley certainly enjoyed her new status: when introducing 'Miss
Clarice Cliff' to an overseas reporter, he could not resist adding,
'Now my wife.'[8]

In 1947, potters regrouped for the first British Industries Fair since
1939. Unlike the 'Britain Can Make It' exhibition held the previous
year, with its emphasis on the contemporary, steered by the newly
formed Council of Industrial Design, the focus here was on the traditional, which the export markets were said to favour. Among the
tableware exhibited by A.J. Wilkinson were a set of vases commissioned from R.Y. Gooden and a series of lithographic patterns
depicting English scenes, whose backstamp announced, 'There'll

Always Be an England!', and illustrated this theme with a drawing of Clarice Cliff's 'Knight Errant', an image from the Depression years resurrected to chime with post-war austerity.[9] Rationing was still in force – and would not be entirely lifted until 1954; clothes were still 'on coupon' too. Only the rich were able to introduce a note of colour to their clothing. Late-1940s Britain was a somewhat colourless place.

The need to extend the wartime spirit into the post-war years was underlined by a Board of Trade initiative the following spring. In 1948, the *Pottery Gazette* introduced the 'auburn-haired and vivacious' 'Potteries Poster Girl', a 25-year-old artist employed by W.T. Copeland & Sons, manufacturer of Spode China. Chosen 'as being typical of the many healthy and good-looking girls engaged in the pottery industry', Jane Dennis was shown on the poster decorating a teapot.[10] Alongside its main message – 'Our work brings in the nation's food' – was a smaller note of encouragement: 'That's how every pottery worker is helping.' Designed to impress upon workers their role in assisting the national recovery – pottery manufacturers were currently being urged to increase export production by 15 per cent – the campaign was supported by a series of lectures in works' canteens (if not at A.J. Wilkinson, where there was no canteen, although Clarice and Colley now had a specially converted lunch room at the back of the Prospect Street shop).

Though full time at the factory once again, Clarice Cliff was working with a seriously depleted workforce, and with little real incentive to develop new designs. Instead, she turned to the company archives for lithograph and print-and-enamel patterns which could be revived with small adjustments to the originals. 'The mid-century look is towards the traditional,' she told a reporter during her first trip to Canada in 1949, 'so we find [its] modernised reproduction . . . most popular.'[11] The taste for the traditional was shared by America, she explained: 'Their mode of living is so different from ours. They like these quick, slick, smart styles for their informal living, but for formal, as they term it, they must have traditional, or, in other words, the elaborate design and quality achieved only by the skilled craftsman, and that is what they look for and expect from us.'[12] Clarice Cliff responded with eighteenth- and nineteenth-century landscape and floral

A.J. Wilkinson dinner plates showing a range of traditional patterns

underglaze prints, such as 'Bristol', based on a design by the French artist Duvivier, circa 1770, and the patterns 'Charlotte' and 'Tonquin'. The latter became extremely popular in the United States, as did 'Rural Scenes' which, with its depiction of an England of pre-revolutionary days, appealed to the Early American revival.

North America now had a further attraction for Colley Shorter: it was the home of his daughter Joan, who settled there following her marriage to a Canadian doctor shortly after the war, and was visited by Colley and Clarice during their 1949 trip and thereafter. While they were away, 'Chetwynd' was updated and an adjacent cottage converted for the use of their two domestic staff. Chief among the renovations were changes to the roof of the central court-yard: this was now glassed over, the tree growing within it replaced with a parquet floor, and a minstrel's gallery built around the first floor for a dance band. Clarice and Colley had parties in mind. Perhaps one of these was the impetus behind a 'Clarice Cliff' design for an ashtray which could hold as many as sixteen cigarettes. They liked to entertain; Colley was a distinguished figure still – 'a tall, imposing man . . . an Errol Flynn',[13] still raising his hat – a fedora, no less – to the ladies.

In 1951, Skylon rose in perpendicular streamlined beauty from London's South Bank as part of the Festival of Britain. Invited to explore Minerals of the Island, Power and Production, the Physical World, Outer Space and more besides, the public was encouraged to reflect upon Britain's past and present achievements and – most importantly – look to the future. The festival opened on 3 May. An A.J. Wilkinson advertisement that month was accompanied by a photograph of the printed floral pattern 'Ophelia' and listed other 'Clarice Cliff' dinner-ware patterns, among them 'Jenny Lind', 'Polly Ann', 'Bristol Spray', 'London Scenes', 'Chelsea Rose' and 'Kew Gardens'.[14] Their names speak volumes of conformity. Clarice Cliff herself was said to have expressed frustration at putting her signature to such conservative designs.[15]

That year, Clarice Cliff took part in a Design Quiz in which she and other 'leading authorit[ies] in the field'[16] answered questions posed by the *Pottery Gazette*; she was the only woman among them. It was here that she commented on the 1930s collaboration between art and industry, when asked to consider 'good' and 'bad' design. She also reflected that, 'Unfortunately for the people who presume to term a thing "bad" design, these designs are invariably found to be amongst the best sellers,' while 'good design', which was 'usually somewhat formal . . . and aesthetic in colour', rarely carried 'the joy of life'.[17] Her statement expressed a long-held view, but perhaps had a particular piquancy: the Council of Industrial Design regarded some of her earlier work as examples of 'Cautionary Ceramics'.[18]

The lifting of restrictions on decorated tableware in 1952 brought into focus almost immediately the juxtaposition of the old and the new. While the Coronation of Elizabeth II the following year prompted manufacturers – A.J. Wilkinson among them – to produce ranges of commemorative pottery, 1953 also saw the launch of 'Stylecraft', 'something entirely new . . . in domestic tableware', produced by the pottery firm Midwinter and created by a young designer, Jessie Tait. The *Pottery Gazette* explained its appeal: 'What

was required . . . was something streamlined, and more in keeping
with a similar trend to be seen in modern schemes of interior
decoration, furniture, motor cars, architecture, and so on . . .
[Midwinter] realised that traditional patterns might be somewhat
out of place in modern homes where habits and furnishings tended
to become more casual and informal.'[19] It was 1928 all over again.
For women, too, the message was little changed: the 1950s woman
was presented as a home-maker – indeed, the name of one of the
most popular tableware patterns of the decade, a black and white
design featuring assorted items of modern furniture, was
'Homemaker'. Even if women could not afford the latest furnishings, they could at least look at them while dining.

Whereas 'Stylecraft' took the lead from America's 'informal living'
– notably with the 'coupe' plate, a softened square whose organic
shape was miles away from Clarice Cliff's own rigid square of years
gone by – A.J. Wilkinson continued to look across the Atlantic to
the 'formal', with its emphasis on quality tableware. A bid to expand
the sale of traditional underglaze patterns and capitalise on American
trade took Shorter to the United States and Canada for four months
during the autumn of 1953. He was joined by Clarice and, later, by
his new export manager, Norman Smith. The following spring an
advertisement in the *Pottery Gazette* announced 'Royal Staffordshire
ceramics by Clarice Cliff' – the first mention of her name in that
journal for two years – in a move designed to unite the commercial
strength of Clarice Cliff's signature with the historic qualities of Royal
Staffordshire. (The deleterious effects of new detergents on on-glaze
patterns were also cited as a reason for A.J. Wilkinson focusing on
the harder-wearing underglaze.)[20] Hilda Lovatt recalled exploring the
mould shop with Clarice Cliff to see what could be found: 'The older
the shape, the better . . . whatever was suggested for the US, she
always found something that would interest them.'[21]

For designers coming fresh to pottery manufacture in the early
1950s, the lifting of restrictions presented an opportunity to redefine
the new. For those like Clarice Cliff, however, who were returning
to design after an extensive fallow period, the situation was very
different. She had lost momentum and, importantly, was not part
of the generation now seeking to make its mark. (Midwinter's young

designer, Jessie Tait, was born in the month 'Bizarre' first shocked the *Pottery Gazette*.) Some pre-war designers – Truda Carter of Poole Pottery, for example – did not return to active designing after the war.

'All over the world, taste in design is changing fast,' Mervyn Jones wrote in the *New Statesman and Nation* in the spring of 1954. 'The style broadly known as contemporary – the clean, simple pattern that is not a picture – is gaining ground.'[22] Design mediums were changing too: printed patterns were coming into their own. This was no longer a means of resurrecting the old; new ways were being sought to develop the technique. The patterns that resulted were far superior to the lithographs of old and are, in tone, identifiably modern. As before, young designers took their lead from fabrics and textiles and, later, from the Space Age motifs that followed in the wake of Sputnik.

Unlike the 1930s, however, when most manufacturers were relatively quick to adopt the latest style, trade advertisements throughout this period show the traditional and the contemporary side by side. Even accounting for the general conservatism of the industry, this suggests a greater reluctance to embrace the new than formerly, driven, perhaps, by the fact that – for now, at least – traditional patterns appealed to an older generation with more spending power, and by the current supremacy of the export markets. With the American and Canadian dollars both strong, some 80 per cent of A.J. Wilkinson's output was now sold for export, an almost complete reversal of the 'Bizarre' years when 75 per cent of 'Clarice Cliff' was sold at home.

By now, Clarice Cliff had appointed a young designer, Eric Eliot, to work with her in producing new designs. Large floral print-and-enamel patterns, especially roses, decorating solid-coloured grounds, featured among his contemporary work, but the fact that A.J. Wilkinson prioritised the traditional in advertisements during this period confirms that this was the market in which it felt most confident of success. There was a twinset-and-pearls quality to much 1950s traditional dinner ware. Though far removed from the tiny, repeating prints of the early 1920s, some post-war evocations of the floral had a delicacy and restraint all of their own. Clarice Cliff's

'Wild Beauty', for example, a finely printed pattern incorporating a buttercup, daisy and clover, made its appeal to formal dining with a group of flowers whose life-sized petals and fine stems enabled the white background to predominate.

The printed patterns that were now in the ascendant were not Clarice Cliff's preferred medium. Her most successful work had achieved its impact through colour, whereas lithographs used colour sparingly and dispensed with the freehand painting that had been so crucial to her earlier popularity. The economics of manufacture were changing too: it was no longer feasible to produce an extensive range of patterns in small quantities to feed the sense of individuality her work had served so well. And yet some 'Clarice Cliff' designs from the 1930s, such as 'Crêpe de Chine' and 'Eating Apples', plus some of her coloured glazes and the 'Eton' teapot shape, could surely have been adapted to satisfy new demands?

A further and important consideration may have weighed as heavily with Clarice Cliff as changing trends: her new role as manufacturer's wife. 'If all we had to do was to sit and turn out designs, what a lovely world it would be!' she commented during the Design Quiz,[23] a reflection in part, perhaps, of her increasingly administrative role. Her new status gave her even greater authority within the factory. 'She would indicate to people in the nicest possible way: I am the senior person here,' said Norman Smith.[24] Margery Higginson recalled that she was 'very much the director's wife': 'She might go up and talk to you, but you wouldn't go up to her.'[25]

Clarice Cliff's marriage did not make her any less guarded; if anything, her formality increased. Part of her new role was ambassadorial, particularly when she was overseas. Colley was still travelling on behalf of A.J. Wilkinson and, although now in his seventies, was 'the youngest man they [knew]', according to an American agent's brochure.[26] When Colley travelled alone, a niece was summoned to 'Chetwynd' to be company for her aunt; increasingly, though, Clarice went with him. Overseas trips were taken in style – first-class cabins on ocean liners every bit as proud as the one Clarice Cliff modelled in clay some twenty years earlier. She and Colley travelled widely: a personalised Christmas card, showing them

Clarice Cliff, 1950

fishing in Bermuda, wished friends 'good health, good fortune and happiness' as their 'catch of the season'. They journeyed within the UK as well as overseas, and liked to search antique shops to further their extensive collection. Visitors to 'Chetwynd' were greeted by a Chinese screen and yellow walls, a Victorian tapestry chair, ivory statuettes, and a heavy malachite and gilt table; elaborate rugs hung from the gallery. It was 'an Aladdin's cave'[27] and an extraordinary sight for a house within easy reach of Stoke-on-Trent. There were cupboards full of pottery and a drawer of pot-pourri lids, plus Colley's collection of Japanese subas and Clarice's rows of foreign dolls. The 'humble little gilder' had come a long way.

In 1957, a change of emphasis took place at A.J. Wilkinson. Having advertised traditional patterns on traditional shapes since the end of the Second World War, the contemporary was now promoted. There had been changes in staffing too: Aubrey Dunn and Eric Eliot had both left the firm and the design focus was entirely Clarice Cliff's. An advertisement for 'Blossom Time' that spring featured the recently introduced 'Devon' shape, with its winged tureen and coupe plates. By the following year 'Devon' was partnered with designs that appealed to the contemporary by mixing solid colour with floral patterns – 'Tit Willow', for example, combined turquoise (or red) tureens with floral coupe plates and tureen lids. One feature of the new design was a palette-shaped saucer or plate which could accommodate a sandwich or some biscuits, in addition to a cup. TV meals were coming into their own. Clarice Cliff was grasping the new mood in the factory, at least, if not at 'Chetwynd', where she resisted the introduction of a television.

Pottery workers themselves were joining the television age. Joan Burnett the jollier* 'beat the panel' in the popular TV series *What's My Line?*, when they failed to guess the occupation she mimed, and the *Pottery Gazette* offered advice on television advertising, but the emergence of a new era sounded the death knell for the old. Several well-known firms went out of business, including Hollinshead & Kirkham, where Clarice Cliff had worked as a lithographer; failure, in most cases, was attributed to an inability to modernise production.

*

Increasingly, Colley's age and chequered health required him and Clarice to spend time away from the factory; Norman Smith was asked to visit them afterhours and report on the day's events. For him, the bond between them was apparent: 'You cannot divide Clarice Cliff from Colley Shorter: they are one.' He describes an occasion when Clarice was ill – she was hospitalised with a stomach ulcer in the early 1950s – and Colley interrupted a meeting to return to her: 'Business was secondary. It was just Clarice . . .'[28]

In 1961, a photograph of three paintresses in A.J. Wilkinson's employ was published by the *Pottery Gazette*[29] in an attempt to refute the notion that hand painting was a thing of the past, yet the image is both depressing and forlorn: the women photographed had been 'Bizarre Girls' some thirty years earlier. The journal was whistling in the dark. Lithography had superseded hand painting and 'girls who might have been good freehand paintresses never got the chance to do it'.[30] Pottery manufacture was continuing to change in numerous ways. 'The difference today in making pots is staggering,' Clarice Cliff explained. 'Cup machines that make thousands of dozens per day, plus dipping them in clay and landing them right to the oven mouth. The same with flat ware, saucers and decorating machines. They say a fortnight to a month is ample time for beginners to gain proficiency.'[31] Industrial methods were not the only developments perplexing Clarice Cliff; she was surprised to see some factory workers driving their own cars. The prize for which she had fought so hard and which had once been such a mark of distinction was now relatively accessible.

The same year also saw the *Pottery Gazette*'s announcement of Colley Shorter's retirement from export – at the age of seventy-nine – after fifty-four years of overseas travel. It was not the end of his journeying, however. In 1962, Colley celebrated his eightieth birthday while holidaying with Clarice in Chicago. To mark the occasion, he received a bouquet from her remaining paintresses and wrote to thank them for their generosity:

My Dear Eight young friends, You really did quite embarrass me with your very nice thought . . . the bouquet was just *lovely*, it added so much to the enjoyment of my birthday with so very many cables, telegrams, letters, cards, from all over the world, that eight nice girls, who had probably known me longer as a group than any, to most of whom, at one time or another, I have been not too polite, with my grumbles or complaints, should have jointly sent me a trophy, a beauty, with such a nice message. Made me wonder if perhaps, hoping of course, there might be something about the 'Old Man' a little nicer than his own opinion . . .

Now I wish you all: may you be as happy as I am, when you arrive at my age, may you have enjoyed the long years behind you as I have, and you know I've had plenty of troubles too, but when overcome, one only remembers the pleasure of having beaten said troubles.

Miss Cliff, who now thoroughly spoils me at home, joins me in sending all of you a very considerable amount of affection, and thanks for many years of very loyal work, and good work too.

At my age I think I may safely finish with My Love, Very Sincerely, Colley A. Shorter.[32]

The letter might have been an epitaph, not just for himself, but for the factory. In December 1963, Colley Shorter died of throat cancer; he had been a heavy smoker for many years. The hypostatic pneumonia recorded on his death certificate as the primary cause of death suggests he had been bedridden for some time; granuloma of the larynx is recorded as a secondary. Colley retained his idio-syncrasy even up to his death. Visiting him in hospital some weeks earlier, his nephew's wife, Charlotte Shorter, found him sitting up in bed, feeling 'bloody' but wearing his hat.

Clarice Cliff and Colley Shorter had been married for more than twenty years and had worked together for almost as long again. After his death, she endeavoured to keep the factory going, but the designs A.J. Wilkinson was now producing could not do enough to satisfy the public mood. Several approaches were made for the company; Clarice Cliff consulted Norman Smith and, at the end of July 1964, wrote again to Ewart Oakes, asking if they could meet: 'My Dear Ewart . . . I do not want to bother you! but, I would like a bit of advice . . .'[33] That year, she sold the factory to Midwinter, the manufacturer whose

'Stylecraft' had introduced a contemporary note to post-war tableware design. If there appears to be a certain symmetry in the company that transformed ceramics after the Second World War purchasing the company that had done so much to revolutionise styles after the First, this was mere coincidence: Midwinter was a thriving manufacturer looking to expand and A.J. Wilkinson needed a buyer. Colley's pony and trap and his Rolls-Royce formed part of the sale.

Clarice Cliff did her best to safeguard the women who had worked so hard for her for so long, and told her remaining paintresses that it was a condition of the sale that they would be kept on. It was an extremely depressing conclusion, nevertheless; the factory which had seen such glory days was closing. Clarice must have felt herself in an impossible position, knowing that the decision she must take was one Colley would have found almost intolerable, but it was the only solution available to her.

Meeting Clarice Cliff in preparation for the transfer, the designer Eve Midwinter recalled how disconsolate and disenchanted she seemed. The A.J. Wilkinson showroom, once the hub of colourful displays, was now a 'heartbreaking' scene of neglect.[34] Laura Knight's 'Circus' ware was pushed into cupboards and corners, its gymnastic clowns tumbled over one another, balancing precariously on shelves, two once-splendid 'Bizookas' leant their fragile ceramic bodies against a wall, while enormous, majestic vases, specially designed for the exhibitions of Clarice Cliff's heyday, blazed like glorious flames. It was as if someone had stepped out of the room thirty years before, without knowing they would not be coming back. Also in disarray was the mould-making shop where the original models for Clarice Cliff's seemingly impossible teapot shapes were stored. This was due for demolition (to make room for a car park) and Eve Midwinter decided to rescue what she could. As she approached the factory in her car, she was confronted by an explosion: the mould shop went up before her eyes.

NINETEEN

After A.J. Wilkinson

If her absence from the factory left a blank in Clarice Cliff's life in 1941, her final departure from it erased much that she had lived for. Within one year she had lost her husband and the place that had defined so much of her life. But Clarice Cliff was not one for giving up – even during the difficult weeks leading to her retirement her strength of will was apparent, as was her ability to intrigue: the Midwinters' teenage son, who visited her during that period, thought he had met no one quite like her.[1]

Clarice Cliff was now aged sixty-five, with nephews, nieces and a great-niece who would visit, even if an overnight stay with Auntie Clarice could be a daunting experience, requiring supervised hairbrushing and the strict observance of table manners. The enforcement of old-fashioned values notwithstanding, Clarice Cliff was fun to be with: she knew how to engage the young and still had her strong sense of humour. She maintained her sense of style as well and, after her retirement, could be seen sporting a turquoise cape with matching turban, or a similar outfit in lemon at her table in a nearby restaurant.[2]

Although her days of travelling had come to an end, Clarice Cliff remained in touch with a wide circle of associates, receiving Christmas letters from some twenty-five people around the world. Her sister Ethel and her husband became regular Saturday-evening visitors, and Hilda Lovatt, who was now living in Wales, began a correspondence with 'Miss Cliff', although whenever her erstwhile employer sat down to reply, something or someone seemed to distract her. When she did find the time to write, Clarice Cliff wrote fondly of the plants in her garden, of the crocuses and pink heather, of her plans for a 'Danse de Feu' climbing rose, and of the geese she and Colley had acquired to keep the grass down. 'Chetwynd' was a large home for one person, and in the years immediately following Colley's death, when memories of their life together were very fresh, Clarice considered exchanging its land and space for a small house in the grounds of Madeley Manor, near Newcastle-under-Lyme. This plan was dropped, however, and her life at 'Chetwynd' continued; she was reported to have kept a loaded shotgun under the bed for protection. She was not entirely isolated, however. Reg Lamb, whom she had known since his days at the clay end, now worked as her gardener, and Alice, her domestic help, still lived in the cottage next door.

For some years after the sale of A.J. Wilkinson, messages from past employees, delivered by her sister Ethel, kept Clarice Cliff up to date with developments at Midwinter, and she spoke frequently with Norman Smith until his departure from the firm. The mergers and takeovers of that period went on; in 1968, Midwinter joined forces with J. & G. Meakin and two years later was absorbed by Wedgwood, as part of that company's ongoing expansion. If Clarice Cliff could not save the factory, she could nevertheless preserve Colley's memory: she approached the museum at Newcastle-under-Lyme, which agreed to display some of his antiques.[3]

Clarice Cliff continued to be creative – she devised a sgraffito-type* finger pattern with which she decorated the 'Chetwynd' stairwell and, with the help of one of her nieces, painted a small table. She craved colour still, cutting out pictures and cartoons from contemporary magazines – anything lively, whimsical or amusing – and pasting them on to the bathroom walls, amassing quite a collection at a time when colour reproductions were less easy to come by than today.

When Clarice Cliff sold A.J. Wilkinson to Midwinter, her work was not considered valuable – far from it. Art Deco, in general, was frowned upon by a design establishment whose tastes inclined towards the rational. Although all surviving A.J. Wilkinson and

Newport Pottery documentation was saved as part of the preservation of industrial history,[4] Clarice Cliff's own work was not considered worthy of the Potteries Museum, nor others at that time. This was 1964: the Beatles were appearing in *A Hard Day's Night* and Terence Conran had just opened the first branch of Habitat.

Shortly thereafter, things began to change. In 1968, Bevis Hillier published *Art Deco of the 20s and 30s*, a pioneering study of the subject and an appraisal which aroused the interest of a younger generation seeking pleasure in the past. The following year the chrome and glass entrance to the Savoy Hotel was rescued from oblivion by the V&A: the 1920s and '30s were beginning to be reconsidered as historical subjects. An exhibition, *The Jazz Age*, opened at the Brighton Art Gallery in the same year, and in 1971 *The World of Art Deco* took place at the Minneapolis Institute of Arts.

A year later, with the help of writer Martin Battersby, the Brighton Art Gallery mounted the first retrospective of Clarice Cliff, much of which came from Battersby's own collection. An advertisement seeking information was placed in *The Times*; Guy Shorter responded, and a very reluctant Clarice Cliff was tracked down. She expressed surprise that her work should be of interest, but agreed to provide notes and loaned some of her own pieces, among them a bowl with a modelled base of fruit, circa 1925; a group of figures, including a banjo player and clown; a 'Conical' tea set and two wall plaques from the mid-1930s. As a record of a life's work, these were hardly adequate, but what need had Clarice Cliff to preserve the past during the years in which the present was so exhilarating? She did not attend the exhibition, nor tell members of her family it was happening, but after it took place she donated some of her work to the museum.

By now, Peter Wentworth-Sheilds and Kay Johnson were preparing a monograph on Clarice Cliff, inspired by their own collecting. During their research, Wentworth-Sheilds managed to contact her by telephone, but was politely told that she had nothing to add. Other collectors who succeeded in reaching Clarice Cliff were thought to have received dusty answers.[5]

*

On 23 October 1972, Clarice Cliff collapsed at the kitchen table, where she was found by Reg Lamb. She was seventy-three. The cause of death was registered as cardiac failure and coronary atheroma (heart failure due to thickening of the arteries), both of which are associated with smoking and excess weight. Her executor, Dick Wenger, the son of the man who had suggested to Colley that it was time he married Clarice Cliff, slept at the house that night to guard its valuables.

Clarice Cliff's death did not make the obituaries of the national press, nor even *Tableware International*, the *Pottery Gazette*'s successor – as a designer she had disappeared from view – but details of her will were published in the *Evening Sentinel*,[6] and the following spring that newspaper recorded 'A Record £6,200 for 8 Chairs' – the auction price achieved for a set of ivory-inlaid Indo-Portuguese walnut chairs – in a day of individual record prices during the sale of the contents of 'Chetwynd'.[7] As if anticipating the success Clarice Cliff's own work would achieve at auction in years to come, the amount bid on the first day was the highest recorded for a one-day sale in the district. Furniture, rugs, pottery, glass, carpets, silver and Martin ware went under the hammer: a 100-year-old embossed-silk Kashan rug, a Louis XVI-style bureau and a French-style Hepplewhite mahogany chest were some of the items noted by the local press. 'Chetwynd' was sold to a developer and bungalows built on part of the land.[8]

When Peter Wentworth-Sheilds and Kay Johnson completed their monograph, they could find no large-scale publisher for their work. That role was taken by Noel Tovey, who had become interested in Art Deco while choreographing the revival of *The Boy Friend* in 1964 and now sold 'Bizarre' through L'Odeon, his London shop, with his partner David Sarel. An exhibition accompanied the book's publication by L'Odeon in 1976 and, although most pieces of 'Clarice Cliff' were loaned for the event, others were for sale: fifteen of them were purchased by the V&A, including a turquoise ceramic telephone cover designed to 'hide your infernal machine'.[9]

By now, the Georgian and Victorian interiors that had been dismantled years before were being lovingly restored and a new generation began to thrill to frocks in crêpe de chine and faded coffee lace and oh, that eye-catching pottery from the late 1920s and '30s, which could generally be picked up for a song. Barbara Hulanicki's Biba, with its seductive reproduction of 1930s glamour, contributed to the revival of the style. In 1985, in recognition of the growing interest in Clarice Cliff and all things Deco, Midwinter issued a limited-edition set of 'Clarice Cliff' reproductions. Its 'Bizarre Collection' featured some of her most popular designs, sugar sifters in 'Pastel Melon' and 'Red Roof Cottage' among them, and a charger showing the fantastical curvaceous trees of 'Summerhouse'. Three years later, a second book was published, written (with Louis K. and Susan Pear Meisel) by the collector Leonard Griffin, who established a collectors' club and has continued to write extensively on Clarice Cliff. And so the revival has rolled. 'Clarice Cliff went wild with her designs,' the *Financial Times* commented. 'Her passion was, and is, reciprocated.'[10]

Auction houses regularly hold dedicated sales of her work, with Christie's sales drawing large audiences and frequently achieving record prices. Interest no longer lies with Clarice Cliff's ceramics alone: her patterns have been reproduced on knitwear, tea towels, fridge magnets and biscuit tins; a Clarice Cliff garden was an entry at a Chelsea Flower Show; there are even 'Clarice' bathroom fittings.[11] Like Midwinter before it, Wedgwood has issued reproductions of some of Clarice Cliff's most popular designs. The woman who drove the Newport and Royal Staffordshire Potteries during the 1930s has now become an industry of her own.

The first 'major reassessment' of Art Deco,[12] staged by the V&A in 2003, broke all records for that museum. In its first five weeks, more than 100,000 visitors passed through the doors. In the four months the exhibition ran, more than a third of a million people delighted in the rescued foyer of the Savoy Palace Hotel, satin and velvet dresses by Chanel, the sensuous dance steps of Josephine Baker, Eileen Gray's exquisite lacquerwork, and even a lift door from 1930s Selfridges. A Clarice Cliff 'Inspiration' vase contributed to this spectacle, as did 'Sunray', an image dating from 1929, in which she paid homage to the New York City skyline with the outline of a skyscraper, a silhouette in black, and fantastic rays of sunlight, moonlight and two glinting stars: a rhapsody in blue and black, orange, mauve and yellow with which Clarice Cliff embraced the future and the new dawn.

Canalside view of A.J. Wilkinson before its demolition in 1997

POSTSCRIPT

I didn't come to Clarice Cliff as a collector of her work, nor am I one today. What drew me in was something different.

I was fifteen or sixteen when Biba came to town, and as this was a northern town, I'm not thinking of the emporium itself, but of the vamp on the Biba poster whose lips and eyes were painted in dramatic shades of mulberry and terracotta, like those in the black and gold pots of Biba make-up I travelled miles to buy. By the mid-1970s, with the secondhand becoming synonymous with chic, beaded purses and diamanté dress clips were once again accessories to crave. I must have mentioned something to my grandmother and great-aunt because that time also introduced me to their magician's trick of conjuring almost anything I requested from within the capacious chests of drawers at their home.

Month after month, I'd discover something 'new' that wasn't in a drawer I'd looked in only weeks before. 'Let's see what we can find,' they'd say, and a French jet necklace or knife-pleat skirt would suddenly appear. Their finds included pottery as well: some brightly coloured tea plates on one occasion, a gilt-edged cup the next. There was nothing of any value. They simply liked nice things and had bought them when they could. Which wasn't often. My grandmother was widowed young, with a daughter to support; my great-aunt never married, was brought up to stay at home and work behind the counter of their mother's corner shop, serving the workers from the nearby mill. Both were spirited women who knew about hard lives. They were great storytellers too, full of tales about their child-hoods. They made the past seem real. Their magic tricks awakened an interest in the 1920s and 30s I've never lost, and in the story behind those decades – and so to Clarice Cliff and her story.

Clarice Cliff 'has always been a phenomenon'. Her work has always aroused strong emotions, either 'deep dislike or passionate desire'.[1] Rarely is there room for half-measures. The dramatic patterns that satisfied the 'long-felt want for colour in the home',[2] and have since established a lively collectors' market, are dismissed by those who speak of 'fairground stuff', fit only for a worthless prize (or smashing with a coconut, perhaps). Clarice Cliff has been described as 'the most important British ceramic designer of the twentieth century';[3] detractors see only a woman who liked bright colours. Colour is what Clarice Cliff is best known for; and it is her colourful work that survives today, her quieter, banded patterns having gone the way of most dinner ware. But if colour was her greatest asset, it is also her greatest offence. Not far along the spectrum from bold and bright comes garish, loud and vulgar, while debates about 'good taste' sidle up to the question of whether or not 'Clarice Cliff' was sold at Woolworth's. Snobbery is often close to hand. That Clarice Cliff's work was popular raises further complications: the aesthetic value of the popular has always been considered debatable.[4]

Inevitably, not all her designs are of a consistent standard: Peter Wentworth-Sheilds and Kay Johnson refer to 'the depths or shallows' of Clarice Cliff's work – and there were shallows, too, especially some of the novelties from the mid- to late-1930s. But seeing the best of her work in the round (and the square and the conical), its sheer presence and vitality is impressive – more impressive than even today's precision photography can suggest. It's no surprise that, unabashed by calls for simplicity and restraint, many women opted for bold design and colour.

Considering reactions to Clarice Cliff, I am struck by the frequent overlap between the personal and the professional, of how often she offends notions of decorum, whether of good design or good behaviour: she is seen as a 'scarlet woman' in every sense. She has been criticised for her 'publicity seeking and self-promotion'[5] and her relationship with Colley Shorter has, in the Potteries at least, coloured past responses to her work. Long after she married, she was regarded as a woman with 'a reputation'. Attitudes change with the times, and one consequence of an intense collectors' market is that, in January 2001, in a local newspaper poll, Clarice Cliff was voted 'Woman of the Century'.

The revival of interest creates its own difficulties. Some, born of a generation which disapproved of her behaviour, if not of Clarice Cliff herself – 'I don't like to think of them like that, even now', one paintress said of the relationship with Shorter[6] – wish to protect her, fearful of sensational interpretations of her life. Inevitably, perhaps, some memories of the woman who painted sunshine on pottery[7] have acquired a sunshine glow: '*Now* all the Girls like her,' another told me.[8]

Just as Clarice Cliff's story attracted elements of romance during the 1930s, some have a romantic perception of her today, although little in her experience warrants that. Colley Shorter was the romantic of the two – he could afford to be: he had not grown up on the factory floor. Some say Clarice Cliff was pushed, and that everything she achieved was down to him, as if talent were somehow passive and she had not been pushing herself for years before they met. She was exceptionally lucky in having Shorter's support, but the handful of women who succeeded in the pottery industry between the two world wars were all encouraged by men. In an industry with few precedents for female achievement, they had to be.

Clarice Cliff's is a story on to which people graft their own interpretations – the racy young designer and It girl, and her extraordinary rise to fame; the scheming minx who set her cap at the boss. The woman I discovered was more substantial, courageous in her refusal to be contained, whether by design orthodoxies, social class or provincial mores, and possessed of a single-mindedness as daunting as it is impressive: she was constantly on the look-out for new ideas. If, as Colley Shorter said, pottery design follows fashion, Clarice Cliff was barely half a step behind. Perhaps that's why memories of her tend to be visually striking – the hat and coat she wore that were the colour of anemones; the cigarette-holder that typified the age. The facts of her life are both complex and elusive: she was a private woman whose work was attention-seeking, and who projected an image of herself that was almost, but not quite, the full story.

Years later again, Clarice Cliff offered another version of events. In her notes for the Brighton exhibition, written shortly before her death, she described passing exams at art school to become a teacher, before deciding to learn pottery decorating at the age of sixteen or seventeen. Perhaps, years after her retirement, she felt the need to establish credentials; perhaps teaching was a private aspiration, hugged to herself when young. Either way, it does not fit the route she followed, nor her working-class beginnings: she needed to earn a wage from early on. Whatever the truth behind the recollection, her words fuel the sense of a woman consciously remaking herself.

The journey Clarice Cliff took from gilder to art director was considerable; her success was of a level few designers hope to achieve. At a time when the world gave women too few choices, she offered them pleasure and the motifs of modernity. It seems fitting for the woman who created colourful narratives for other women's dreams that hers should be a story of reinvention.

NOTES

Abbreviations used in the Notes

PG   *Pottery Gazette and Glass Trade Review*

All newspaper and magazine reviews of Clarice Cliff's work, plus press interviews, are courtesy of the Wilkinson-Newsport Archive, PA/W–N/1, Stoke-on-Trent City Archives, City Central Library, Hanley.

Prologue: The Brilliant Young Girl Artist

1   Advertisement, *Daily Mail*, 4 June 1930
2   'Pleasing Pottery', *Home Chat*, 19 April 1930
3   *Daily Sketch*, 9 June 1931
4   Annette Adams, 'The Newest Colourful Pottery', *Woman's Life* 1 August 1931
5   'Hand Painting on Pottery', *Daily Telegraph*, 4 June 1930
6   'As I See Life: Paintresses of Pottery', *Daily Mirror*, 4 June 1930
7   'Home-Maker Section', *Australian Woman's Weekly*, 29 June 1935
8   Ibid.
9   Susie Cooper (1902–95) was born in Burslem, Staffordshire. The youngest of seven children, she was educated locally, including a period at a private school. The death of her father, a tenant farmer and JP, in 1913 left the family to manage the farm and its associated retail business, and taught Cooper business skills from an early age. At seventeen, she began evening classes at the Burslem School of Art and was awarded a full-time three-year scholarship. In 1922, Susie Cooper joined the pottery manufacturer A.E. Gray on the recommendation of the Superintendent of Art Education,

Gordon Forsyth, and on the understanding that she would become a designer. In 1929, with a family loan of £4,000, she set up in business with her brother-in-law, plus half a dozen paintresses, designing patterns for shapes bought in from other companies. Within weeks, the bankruptcy of her landlord during the Wall Street Crash left Cooper without premises, but by April 1930 she was in business again and, by October 1931, established at the Crown Works where, through an agreement with Wood & Son, she was able to expand and produce her own shapes as well as patterns. In 1940, Susie Cooper became the only woman in the Potteries to be recognised as a Royal Designer for Industry. The purchase of Jason China in 1950 signified a move into china production. At the end of that decade, her company merged with R.H. & S.L. Plant and in 1966 was absorbed by Wedgwood. Susie Cooper married in 1938; a son was born in 1943

10 Some 'Bizarre' patterns were given different names when produced in different colourways; eg. 'Aurea', 'Pink Pearls' and 'Viscaria' are the same floral design as 'Rhodanthe'. When repeat patterns such as these are excluded, Leonard Griffin's 'Bizarre Index', *The Art of Bizarre* (Pavilion, 1999), lists some 270 patterns by name. One of these is the original 'Bizarre', which itself was produced in numerous combinations of diamonds and triangles. This listing mainly covers Clarice Cliff's hand painted designs produced between 1927 and 1936, not her whole output. 'Clarice Cliff', patterns can be identified via contemporary trade and press reports, plus pattern and retail order books in the Wilkinson-Newport Archive. Some original pattern names have been lost, and the patterns renamed by collectors. Where possible, the latter are identified by the phrase 'known as' within the text. The length of time for which a pattern was on sale varied according to its popularity, and during Clarice Cliff's heyday large numbers were on sale at any one time; a retail order book from 1932, for example, lists some 100 patterns by name, as well as patterns identified by numbers

In March 1934, the *Pottery and Glass Record* reported that there were now between 500 and 600 different shapes and sizes to which Clarice Cliff's popular 'Crocus' pattern could be applied. Although some of these shapes predated Clarice Cliff, others had yet to be introduced – the 'My Garden' design, for example, accounted for its own range of shapes from 1934 onwards and there was also a substantial range of novelties

11 The average pottery was said to produce between £500 and £1,000 worth of goods per week; see Gordon Forsyth, 'Pottery Artists and the Manufacturers: Do the Artists Get a Square Deal?', *PG*, May 1933, p605

12 Recollections of sales manager Eric Grindley, *Clarice Cliff's Catalogue and Sources*, Clarice Cliff Collectors Club

13 'Memories of a Staffordshire Londoner', *Gallery*, April–May 1966

Chapter 1: Family, Childhood, Smoke and Flame

1   Family recollection; notes by Peter Wentworth-Sheilds, June 1973
2   In *At the Works* (1906), Florence Bell's study of an ironworkers' community in Middlesbrough, Yorkshire, she described how living near the foundry was considered an advantage and was also an indication of long service
3   Charles Shaw, *When I Was a Child*, Churnet Valley Books, 1998, pp65–6. *When I Was a Child* was written as a series of articles for the *Staffordshire Sentinel* during the 1890s and originally published in book form under the title *An Old Potter* in 1903
4   I am grateful to the Machin Society for the names and ages of Ralph Machin's immediate family
5   In 1831, Chell's population was 535; by 1851 it had risen to 953
6   Shaw, *When I Was a Child*, p57
7   Ibid.
8   Ibid., pp21–2
9   Arnold Bennett, *Hilda Lessways*, Methuen & Co., 1911, p23
10 Arnold Bennett, *The Old Wives' Tale* (1908), Pan Books, 1964, pp28–9
11 By 1841, the population exceeded 68,000. See E.J.D. Warrilow, *A Sociological History of the City of Stoke-on-Trent*, Etruscan Publications, 1960, p235
12 Ibid., p333
13 'Notes from the Potteries', *PG*, December 1933, p1,468
14 Warrilow, *A Sociological History*, p328
15 *Time and Tide*, 22 July 1939, p981
16 W.A. Morland, *Portrait of the Potteries*, Robert Hale, 1978, p9
17 The pottery towns continue to hold fast to their identities. During a BBC Radio 4 broadcast in 2003, an interviewee spoke of the difficulty of encouraging people in Stoke-on-Trent to think collectively in connection with a regeneration project
18 Mervyn Jones, *Potbank: A Social Enquiry into Life in the Potteries*, Secker & Warburg, 1961, p87
19 J.G. Jenkins (ed.), *The Victoria History of the Counties of England: Staffordshire*, Vol. VIII, Institute of Historical Research, Oxford University Press, 1963, p81
20 The 1811 census records a Tunstall population of 1,677; by 1831, that figure had risen to 4,673 and by 1851 was 9,566. J.G. Jenkins (ed.), *The Victoria History of the Counties of England: Staffordshire*, p82
21 Assessing accounts of sexual relationships during the early twentieth century, Ross McKibbin writes of the 'popular inclination' to think that sex with someone you intended to marry did not constitute premarital

sex (*Classes and Cultures: England 1918–1951*, Oxford University Press, 1998, p297). It is, of course, impossible to know the number of women who were pregnant upon marriage during the late nineteenth century, and notional attitudes towards premarital sex are not necessarily borne out by actual experience. In his essay 'Working-Class Women in Britain 1890–1914' (in Martha Vicinius (ed.), *Suffer and Be Still: Women in the Victorian Age*, Indiana University Press, 1973), Peter N. Stearns writes of sexual relationships between factory workers in their early twenties leading to marriage, and in *Women in a Changing Civilisation*, 1936, Winifred Holtby writes of an 'old country custom' practised in North of England villages, of marrying only after pregnancy. In her oral history of working-class women in Lancashire, *A Woman's Place*, however, Elizabeth Roberts concluded that the practice was very limited

22   Edwards Street is sometimes spelled Edward Street in public documents

23   Hannah Cliff's daughter in conversation with the author, 18 January 2001

24   Alison Wright in conversation with the author, 15 February 2001

25   Eve Midwinter in conversation with the author, 22 January 2002

26   Vera Brittain, 'Memories of a Staffordshire Londoner', *Gallery*, April–May 1966, pp3–4

27   Ada Nield Chew, 'All in the Day's Work: Mrs Bolt', *The Englishwoman*, Vol. XV, 1912, reprinted in Juliet Gardiner (ed.), *The New Woman: Women's Voices 1880–1918*, Collins & Brown, 1993, p143

28   Mrs Murray, Derbyshire housewife, interviewed by Carol Adams in *Ordinary Lives: A Hundred Years Ago*, Virago, 1982, p149, 151

29   Nield Chew, 'Mrs Bolt', p142

30   Adams, *Ordinary Lives*, p147

31   Carol Dyehouse, *Girls Growing up in Late Victorian and Edwardian England*, Routledge, 1981, p17. Dyehouse notes that the working-class women who documented their experiences were unusual in doing so, and so may have been more likely to clash with their mothers when young

32   Morland, *Portrait of the Potteries*, p177

33   Margaret Mason in conversation with the author, 6 September 2001

34   Tunstall 1898, *Old Ordnance Survey Maps*, Godfrey Edition

35   Bennett, *Hilda Lessways*, p23

36   In *At the Works* (1906), in a random sample of 200 households from a similar industrial community, Florence Bell found fifty-eight in which husband and wife read only newspapers, fifty in which only novels were read – Mrs Henry Wood and Dickens being among the writers favoured – and only twenty-eight in which neither husband nor wife read at all. Of all the households questioned, seventeen women and eight men were

not able to read; see p230. Set against that, perhaps, is Vera Brittain's recollection of a publisher's salesman telling her father that the Potteries had the lowest record for book buying in England. See *Testament of Youth: An Autobiographical Study of the Years 1900–1925*, Fontana in association with Virago, 1979, p25

Chapter 2: How Pleased I was to Miss Some Lessons

1   'Lilian, 100, Recalls her Artistic School Pal', interview with Lilian Taylor, *Sentinel*, 8 April 1999

2   Diane Baker, *Schools in the Potteries*, Stoke-on-Trent Historic Buildings Survey, City Museum and Art Gallery, Stoke-on-Trent, 1984, p5

3   In his Report on the Infants' Department, 2 December 1902, His Majesty's Inspector, W.P. Beach, 'found the noises in the street very distracting' and 'a serious disadvantage in the working of the school'; High Street Elementary School Log Book 1902 –, SA-ED-LOG 142, Stoke-on-Trent City Archives, City Central Library

4   W.P. Beach on his return to the Infants' Department, November 1904

5   Reports by the School Medical Officer to meetings of the School Management and School Attendance Sub-Committee, for the three months ending 31 March 1909, the three months ending June 1909, and the Annual Report for 1909 for all schools within the jurisdiction; Tunstall Education Committee Minutes, April 1907–July 1909, SA-ED 103, and August 1909–October 1910, SA-ED 104

6   J.H. Yoxhall, Ernest Gray and T.A. Organ, *The New Code (1904): Board of Education Code of Regulations for Public Elementary Schools, with Schedules*, NUT, 1904, p6

7   Ibid.

8   Mrs M1P, b.1913, interviewed by Elizabeth Roberts, *A Woman's Place: An Oral History of Working-Class Women 1890–1940*, Basil Blackwell, Oxford, 1984, pp26–7

9   Yoxhall, Gray and Organ, *The New Code*, p8

10   Alison Wright in conversation with the author, 29 March 2001

11   1904 Scheme of Work, Standard I, High Street Council School Log Book, May 1896–July 1938, SA-ED-LOG 142

12   Ibid.

13   Reports by His Majesty's Inspectors for the Infants' Department, 1902 and 1904, SA-ED-LOG 142

14   Carol Dyhouse, *Girls Growing Up in Late Victorian and Edwardian England*, Routledge, 1981, p89

15   Report by Her Majesty's Inspector, Mr Maudsley, following a visit to the High Street Council School, 16, 17 and 18 October 1907, Meeting of

the School Management and School Attendance Sub-Committee, 22 January 1908; Tunstall Education Committee Minutes April 1907–July 1909, SA-ED 103

16   Carol Adams, *Ordinary Lives: A Hundred Years Ago*, Virago, 1982, p48

17   Scheme of Work for the 1st Class, 1903, High Street Council School Log Book, May 1896–July 1938, SA-ED-LOG 142

18   Report by the Art Director at a meeting of the Higher Education Sub-Committee, 22 January 1906, Tunstall Education Committee Minutes, April 1905–April 1907, SA-ED 102

19   Stanley Thorogood, *Free Brush Drawing Applied to Pattern in Seven Stages*, c.1903

20   'Lilian, 100, Recalls her Artistic School Pal'

21   Notes by Clarice Cliff for the retrospective of her work, *Clarice Cliff* exhibition catalogue, Brighton Art Gallery, 15 January–20 February 1972

22   Yoxhall, Gray and Organ, *The New Code*, p6

23   Kath Gosling, 'Revival of the Art Deco Era', *Evening Sentinel*, 24 May 1976. Gosling was speaking to Ethel Cliff, who had earlier told Peter Wentworth-Sheilds that her sister attended the High Street Elementary School

24   Vera Brittain, *Testament of Youth: An Autobiographical Study of the Years 1900–1925* (1933), Fontana in association with Virago, 1979, p28

25   Ibid., p32

Chapter 3: A Humble Little Gilder

1   J.S. Hurt, *Elementary Schooling and the Working Classes 1860–1918*, Routledge & Kegan Paul, 1979, p211

2   'Bringing Brightness to the Table', *Reynolds Illustrated News*, 27 September 1931

3   Samuel Smiles, 1843, quoted by Carol Dyehouse, *Girls Growing up in Late Victorian and Edwardian England*, Routledge, 1981, p79

4   'Women in Pottery Works', *PG*, October 1915, p1,106. Changes in methods of production, with semi-skilled female machine operatives replacing skilled men in certain areas of the industry, together with women's willingness to accept lower wages, were largely responsible for the increase

5   See Cheryl Buckley, 'A Woman Potter's Lot', *Potters and Paintresses: Women Designers in the Pottery Industry 1870–1955*, Women's Press, 1990, and Jacqueline Sarsby, 'The Forgotten Missuses: Myth-Making', *Missuses and Mouldrunners: An Oral History of Women Pottery Workers at Work and at Home*, Open University Press, 1988, for further information about the nature of women's work in the Potteries

6   Richard Pankhurst, *Sylvia Pankhurst: Artist and Crusader, An Intimate Portrait*, Paddington Press, 1979, p80

7   See Iris Edwards, figure painter, Royal Doulton, talking to John Abberley, 'The Way We Were' No. 41, *Sentinel*, 29 March 1997

8   For example, an A.J. Wilkinson employee, Gerald Pearson, who joined the factory as a young man, was shocked by the language and behaviour of women at the clay end; Gerald Pearson in conversation with the author, 28 February 2001

9   1913 Photograph Album, Wedgwood Museum Archives, courtesy Wedgwood Museum Trust, Barlaston, Staffordshire

10   *Pottery Ladies: Miss Cooper, Miss Cliff, Miss Rhead and all the Forgotten Girls*, No. 3, a four-part film series by Jenny Wilkes, a Metropolis/Arts Council of Great Britain production for Channel 4, 1985

11   15 October 1910, Boys' Department, Summerbank Council School Log Book 1909–1924, Tunstall, CEL/84/1, Staffordshire Record Office

12   'Bringing Brightness to the Table'

13   Notes produced by Ethel Steele (née Cliff) for Peter Wentworth-Sheilds and Kay Johnson, 1973

14   Brenda Fredericks in conversation with the author, 10 May 2002

15   On a visit to the Wedgwood factory in 1888, H.G. Wells wrote, 'Considering the great reputation of the firm, I was rather surprised at the ramshackle state of the works'; Rodney Hampson, 'H.G. Wells and the Staffordshire Potteries', 1978, quoted by Sharon Gater and David Vincent, *The Factory in a Garden: Wedgwood from Etruria to Barlaston – the transitional years*, Keele Life Histories Centre, University of Keele, 1988, p25. Maurice Rena, visiting the Potteries on behalf of *The Studio* in 1936, described factories 'of every shape and size thrown together in haphazard fashion'; 'The English Pottery Industry', *The Studio*, Vol. 112, November 1936, p267

16   Nikolaus Pevsner, *An Enquiry into Industrial Art in England*, Cambridge University Press, 1937, p83

17   'Bringing Brightness to the Table'. The rates quoted by Clarice Cliff were contemporaneous with her newspaper interview

18   *Pottery Ladies*, No. 3

19   'The British Industries Fair', *PG*, June 1915, p657

20   Edmund Shenton, 'The Production of Earthenware from the Biscuit State, including the Various Stages of Decorating', lecture to the Royal Society of Arts, November 1923, reproduced in *PG*, December 1923, p1,953

21   1913 Wedgwood Photograph Album

22   Dorothy Shemilt, gilder, liner and colour bander, Newhall Pottery, Hanley, 'The Way We Were' No. 28, *Sentinel*, 25 October 1997

23   'Notes from the Potteries', *PG*, January 1912, p79

24 'Editorial Notes: The Coal Strike and After', *PG*, April 1912, p373, describing conditions the previous month

25 'The Potteries and the Coal Strike' by a Pottery Gazette Special Correspondent, *PG*, April 1912, p408

26 'Trade Reviews for 1912', *PG*, February 1913, p155

27 Summerbank Council School Log Book, 1909–1924, CEL/84/1

28 'Notes from the Potteries', *PG*, June 1912, p664

29 'Notes from the Potteries', *PG*, May 1913, p503

30 I have been told that pottery workers did not strike. Perhaps, more accurately, strikes were short-lived and a strong sense of community has erased their memory

31 'Today's Royal Visit', *Sentinel*, 23 April 1913

32 'The Street Decoration of Tunstall', *Sentinel*, 24 April 1913

33 'Fragments', *PG*, May 1913, p582

34 See Jill Liddington and Jill Norris, *One Hand Tied Behind Us: The Rise of the Women's Suffrage Movement*, Virago, 1978

35 Crest Book, Wedgwood, courtesy Wedgwood Museum Trust, Barlaston, Staffordshire

36 'Buyers' Notes', *PG*, 1 February 1916, p158

37 'Buyers' Notes', *PG*, August 1913, p903

38 Arnold Bennett, *Anna of the Five Towns*, Methuen, 1902; Penguin, 1976, p121

39 Mrs Farrier, b.1902, interviewed by Jacqueline Sarsby, *Missuses and Mouldrunners*, p13

40 Edna Barker, paintress, Wiltshaw and Robinson and Spode Copeland, 'The Way We Were' No. 31, *Sentinel*, 24 January 1998

41 'Bizarre' Girl Mollie Browne, in conversation with the author, 24 February 2001. As the women who worked for Clarice Cliff did so as young girls, they are identified by their maiden names throughout

42 In notes for the retrospective of her work at Brighton Art Gallery, 1972, Clarice Cliff wrote of winning scholarships to attend both the Tunstall and Burslem Schools of Art. This information cannot be verified, however. The register for the Burslem School of Art, 1921–7, SA-ED-115, Stoke-on-Trent City Archives, shows Clarice Cliff as a fee-paying student 1924–5. Although students sometimes paid to continue with their studies when their scholarships came to an end, these studies tended to be consecutive. There is no record of Clarice Cliff's attendance at Burslem before or after 1924–5. Although registers for the Tunstall School of Art no longer exist, she is known to have attended classes there and someone with her precocious talent was likely to have been awarded a scholarship to do so. Years later, the two may have merged in her memory

43 'Notes from the Potteries,' *PG*, October 1912, p1,113

44 Notes by Clarice Cliff for the retrospective of her work, *Clarice Cliff*

exhibition catalogue, Brighton Art Gallery, 15 January–20 February 1972

45   'Report by the Board of Education upon the Art School for the Sessions 1906–7', Tunstall Education Committee Minutes, April 1907–July 1909, SA-ED-103, Stoke-on-Trent City Archives

46   'Buyers' Notes', *PG*, May 1915, p529

47   'Buyers' Notes', *PG*, June 1914, p687

48   Bennett, *Anna of the Five Towns*, p121

49   Alfred Powell, 'New Wedgwood Pottery', *Studio*, Vol. 98, July–December 1929, p880

50   See 'Buyers' Notes', *PG*, August 1913, p903

Chapter 4: Women Workers in the Firing Line

1   Vera Brittain, *Testament of Youth: An Autobiographical Study of the Years 1900–1925* (1933), Fontana in association with Virago, 1979, p97

2   Vera Brittain refers to the German raid on Scarborough, Hartlepool and Whitby, on the morning of 15 December 1914, in *Testament of Youth*, p112; Winifred Holtby, who was in Scarborough at the time, dramatised the incident in Chapter 18 of her novel *The Crowded Street* (1924)

3   *Staffordshire Advertiser*, 16 January 1915, quoted by N.W. Rodgers in 'The Effects of the Great War on the Potteries 1914–18', Dissertation for BA Hons, Keele University, May 1987, Stoke-on-Trent City Archives

4   Notes by Ethel Steele (née Cliff) for Peter Wentworth-Sheilds and Kay Johnson, 1973

5   Ibid.

6   This photograph was published in 'The Way We Were', *Sentinel*, December 2003, captioned as 'The first known picture of Clarice Cliff, fourth left, back row, with fellow paintresses.' No evidence has come to light to suggest this is a group of paintresses and several factors militate against it, this being a studio rather than a factory shot, plus the formality, sobriety and quality of the women's clothing, and the apparent social mix of the occasion. Several period photographs feature young women with large bows in their hair, others indicate that high necklines and floor-length gowns were worn by some women up to the First World War and beyond.

     The girl with the black bow shows a resemblance to Clarice Cliff and other family members, and Clarice Cliff's great-niece, Alison Wright, believes the woman seated, centre, to be a Cliff. To add still further to the speculation, the woman between 'Clarice Cliff' and 'Clarice Cliff's mother' bears a resemblance to Sarah Cliff, which reinforces the possibility that the girl with the bow could be her sister, Clarice. If the date of the photograph is even earlier, however, that possibility recedes.

7   Notes by Ethel Cliff, 1973.

8   Early twentieth-century attitudes to pottery designers were mixed. Some manufacturers maintained that good craftsmen were, by default, good designers – a view much disputed by outsiders – and resisted the cost of employing someone in that specific capacity; other, more forward-thinking manufacturers, plus those engaged in the production of porcelain and prestige wares, employed artists and designers, even if only on an occasional basis. Openings for designers in general were few, however

9   'The British Industries' Fair', *PG*, June 1915, p657

10   In the years immediately before the First World War, lithography looked set to supersede hand-painting; Dr Gordon Elliott in conversation with the author, 22 November 2001

11   'Women Who Make Money – 5: The China Designer', *Sunday Express*, 24 November 1935

12   It is impossible to be exact about the date Clarice Cliff moved to A.J. Wilkinson. In 1935, the *Sunday Express* reported, 'At sixteen she was apprenticed to pottery decorating', and in notes for the exhibition of her work at the Brighton Art Gallery in 1972, Clarice Cliff wrote that she decided she 'would most like to learn the various branches of pottery decorating' at 'the ages of sixteen or seventeen'. Family recollections and her own background make this an unlikely starting point, but Clarice Cliff may have been recalling her decision to learn more about pottery decorating by moving to A.J. Wilkinson. Minnie Rowley, who worked in the lithography department with Clarice Cliff, joined the firm in December 1918 and when salesman Ewart Oakes joined in May 1919, Clarice Cliff was working there as a decorator (Rowley and Oakes information courtesy of Peter Wentworth-Sheilds and Kay Johnson)

13   'Editorial Notes: Women Workers in Potteries', *PG*, June 1916, p599

14   'Fragments', *PG*, June 1916, p650

15   Advertisement, *PG*, February 1918, p124

16   'Pottery Girls in the Firing Line', *PG*, April 1918, p302

17   'Buyers' Notes', *PG*, April 1914, p441

18   'Buyers' Notes', *PG*, February 1931, p231, reflecting on A.J. Wilkinson's achievements during the past twenty years

19   A.J. Wilkinson sales brochure, Stoke-on-Trent City Archives

20   'Buyers' Notes', *PG*, February 1931, p231

21   'Buyers' Notes', *PG*, April 1917, p351

22   'Buyers' Notes', *PG*, April 1917, p353

23   Brittain, *Testament of Youth*, p114

24   Letter from Vera Brittain to Roland Leighton, 8 November 1915; Alan Bishop and Mark Bostridge (eds.), *Letters from a Lost Generation: The First World War Letters of Vera Brittain and Four Friends: Roland Leighton, Edward Brittain, Victor Richardson, Geoffrey Thurlow*, Little, Brown, a division of Time Warner Book Group UK, 1998, pp185–6

25   Lyn Macdonald, *The Roses of No Man's Land* (1980), Penguin, 1993, p70

26   Ibid., p171; also letter from Vera Brittain to Edith Brittain, 21 July 1916, Bishop and Bostridge, *Letters from a Lost Generation*, p267

27   I am grateful to Beryl Storey for the information about her father, Arthur Cliff

28   Potteries Postcard Society, *Potteries Picture Postcards II: A Second Portrait of the Six Towns*, Brampton Publications 1987, p10

29   'Pottery Girls in the Firing Line'

30   'Female Labour in the Pottery Industry', *PG*, May 1919, p479

Chapter 5: A Talented Lady Modeller

1   'Women and the New Year', *Daily Mail*, 1 January 1920

2   Women over thirty, with a household qualification

3   'Dancing to the Gramophone', *Ladies' Field*, 24 January 1920

4   'The Tickle-Toe and Twinkles', *My Weekly*, 10 January 1920

5   Annie Beresford in conversation with the author, April 2001

6   Ethel Steele (née Cliff) interviewed by Kath Gosling, 'Woman's World: Revival of the Art Deco Era', *Evening Sentinel*, 24 May 1976

7   Unfinished letter from Clarice Cliff to Hilda Lovatt, 27 June 1971, courtesy of Peter Wentworth-Sheilds and Kay Johnson

8   Former Lord Mayor, Tom Brennan, recalling his childhood, 'The Way We Were' No. 35, *Sentinel*, 23 May 1998

9   Winnie Haywood, tower, A.J. Wilkinson, 'The Way We Were' No. 40, *Sentinel*, 24 October 1998

10   Dates given for the early history of A.J. Wilkinson vary from one account to another – see *Pottery and Glass Record*, March 1923, p375; *PG*, October 1926, p1,571; and *British Bulletin of Commerce, City of Stoke-on-Trent Potteries Survey*, Parts 1–3, 1955. I have judged the *Pottery and Glass Record* the most reliable in this instance

11   Notes by Ethel Cliff for Peter Wentworth-Sheilds and Kay Johnson, 1973. The story also appears in contemporary press reports

12   'I Love Designing Modern Pottery', *Bristol Times*, 11 September 1931

13   Notes by Clarice Cliff for the retrospective of her work, *Clarice Cliff* exhibition catalogue, Brighton Art Gallery, 15 January–20 February 1972

14   'The British Industries Fair, A.J. Wilkinson Ltd', *Pottery and Glass Record*, March 1920, p187

15   'New British Pottery: Representative Examples', *Pottery and Glass Record*, September 1920, p380

16   Pattern numbers 7,858 and 7,499, Description Book October 1921–1925, PA/W-N/41, Stoke-on-Trent City Archives

17 Property of private collector; see 'Frenzied bids put Clarice Cliff relic on line for US', *Sentinel*, 21 March 1996

18 In 1906, the average weekly wage of women in the pottery industry was eleven shillings and one penny compared with thirty-two shillings and fourpence paid to men. By 1926, women received twenty-two shillings and sixpence in comparison with a male wage of fifty-five shillings and sixpence. Most work was piecework, with rates substantially lower for women than for men throughout the industry. See 'Women in the Pottery Industry', *Pottery and Glass Record*, April 1930, p130

19 Among commercial manufacturers, the exceptions were Hannah Barlow, who worked for Royal Doulton during the nineteenth century, and was allowed to design some shapes as well as patterns, and the husband-and-wife team Alfred and Louise Powell, who established a decorating shop at Wedgwood during the 1920s and designed some fifty shapes in addition to patterns. See Cheryl Buckley, *Potters and Paintresses: Women Designers in the Pottery Industry 1870–1955*, Women's Press, 1990

20 'Royal Staffordshire Potteries Showroom', *Pottery and Glass Record*, March 1925, p154

21 Notes by Clarice Cliff, *Clarice Cliff* exhibition catalogue

22 Pattern number 7,309, Description Book October 1921–1925, PA/W-N/41. Individual patterns are not dated within this pattern book

23 'Buyers' Notes', *PG*, October 1923, p1,621. I am grateful to Andrew Casey who kindly sent me a copy of this and several other trade press articles at the outset of my research

24 Old Dutch Man (7,482) and Dutch Woman (7,483), PA/W-N/41

25 'Buyers' Notes', p1,621

26 'Wembley Exhibits', *Pottery and Glass Record*, June 1924, p208 and 'Buyers' Notes', *PG*, September 1942, p1,507. See Leonard Griffin, *The Art of Bizarre*, Pavilion, 1999, p27, re Clarice Cliff's embossed signature

28 Opening speech, King George V, 23 April 1924, *Illustrated London News*, 26 April 1924

29 Ibid.

30 'Pottery and Glass at the British Empire Exhibition', *PG*, July 1924, p1,198

31 'Buyers' Notes', *PG*, September 1924, p1,507

32 Burslem School of Art Register, 1921–27, SA-ED-115, Stoke-on-Trent City Archives. Information about Clarice Cliff and Susie Cooper is reproduced with permission

33 Helen Appleton Read, 'The Exposition in Paris', *International Studio*, Vol. 82, Part 1, November 1925, p96

34 Ibid.

35 Ibid., p94

36 Gordon Forsyth, 'Pottery', *Reports on the Present Position and*

Tendencies of the Industrial Arts as Indicated at the International Exhibition of Modern Decorative and Industrial Arts, Paris 1925, Department of Overseas Trade, 1925

37 Sir Hubert Llewellyn Smith, quoted in the *Pottery and Glass Record*, May 1931, p170

38 'Editorial Notes', *PG*, August 1913, p889

39 Forsyth, 'Pottery', p129

40 Gordon Forsyth, 'Art: its Effects upon the Pottery Industry'; address at a meeting of the National Pottery Council, July 1921, reported in *PG*, August 1921, p1,219

41 H.J. Plant reacting to Gordon Forsyth's 'Pottery Design from the Manufacturers' Point of View', a paper given to the Ceramic Society and reported in *PG*, quoted by Judy Spours, *Art Deco Tableware: British Domestic Ceramics 1925–39*, Ward Lock, 1988, p17

42 'A Correspondent', 'Art and Pottery', *PG*, September 1921, p1,355

43 Marjorie Howard, 'Fashions', *Good Housekeeping*, September 1925

44 'A Frock of Many Moods Comes as a Stand-by of the Limited Wardrobe', *Good Housekeeping*, November 1925

45 Sonia Delaunay, *La Rencontre Sonia Delaunay–Tristan Tzara*, exhibition catalogue, Musée d'Art Moderne de la Ville de Paris, 1977, quoted by Isabelle Anscombe, *A Woman's Touch: Women in Design from 1860 to the Present Day*, Virago, 1984, p120

46 'Introduction', *The Studio Yearbook of Decorative Art*, 1925, p2

47 Rosamond Lehmann, *Dusty Answer* (1927), Penguin, 1936, p140. Colourful transformations continued: visiting her old college room, the narrator later discovers that its once 'blue, purple and rose' walls now have 'black and orange stripes everywhere', the ubiquitous colours of the late 1920s (p298). See also Nicola Humble, 'Imagining the Home', *The Feminine Middlebrow Novel, 1920s to 1950s: class, domesticity and bohemianism*, Oxford University Press, 2001, for an exploration of the home in fiction by women writers during this period

48 *Homes and Gardens*, 1924, *Our Homes and Gardens 1919–1989, Celebration Supplement*, 1989

49 'Modern Developments in Pottery Design', lecture by Gordon Forsyth at a meeting of the Art Section of the Ceramic Society, 2 November 1925, reported in *PG*, December 1925, p1,861

50 'British Institute of Industrial Art: Conference on Pottery', *PG*, January 1924, p117

51 See Ann Eatwell, 'Gordon Mitchell Forsyth (1879–1952) – Artist, Designer and Father of Art Education in the Potteries', *Journal of the Decorative Arts Society*, No. 13, 1989, and Reginald Haggar, 'Gordon Mitchell Forsyth', 'Staffordshire Artists Past & Present, No. 6', *Staffordshire Life*, 1954–5, p20, for assessments of Forsyth's achievements

52   Reginald Haggar, *Staffordshire Life*
53   Rose Cumberbatch, 'The Way We Were' No. 35, *Sentinel*, 23 May 1998.
      Cumberbatch went on to become a tube liner for Charlotte Rhead at the
      Gordon Pottery, Tunstall

Chapter 6: A Strange New Creature Called Woman

1   'Woman as News', *Guardian*, 13 November 1925
2   Number 8,022, Decoration Description Book May 1925–December 1928,
      PA/W-N/34, Stoke-on-Trent City Archives. I am grateful to Andrew Casey,
      Maureen and Harold Woodworth and Chris Latimer, archivist, for infor-
      mation about this figure, which is also known as 'The Turquoise Ring'
3   'Royal Staffordshire Potteries Showrooms', *Pottery and Glass Record*,
      March 1925, p154
4   'The British Empire Exhibition', *PG*, July 1924, p1,198
5   Notes by Clarice Cliff for the retrospective of her work, *Clarice Cliff*
      exhibition catalogue, Brighton Art Gallery, 15 January–20 February 1972
6   Harold Hales called his life story *Autobiography of 'The Card'*. In her
      biography of Arnold Bennett, Margaret Drabble notes that although
      Hales, a schoolfriend of Bennett's, no doubt furnished him with ideas,
      'The Card' was 'clearly a fictitious character, a kind of dream hero'. See
      Arnold Bennett, Weidenfeld & Nicolson, 1974, p159
7   'Royal Staffordshire Pottery', *British Bulletin of Commerce*, City of Stoke-
      on-Trent Potteries Survey, Parts 1–3, 1955, Stoke-on-Trent City Archives
8   Letter from Colley Shorter to his sister Jessie, 24 March 1910. I am
      grateful to Charlotte Shorter for copies of this and other letters by Colley
      Shorter
9   Ibid.
10   Letter from Colley Shorter to his mother, Henrietta Shorter, 8 January
      1922
11   Ibid.
12   Notes by Clarice Cliff, *Clarice Cliff* exhibition catalogue
13   'Trade Reports', *PG*, July 1926, p1,108
14   Ibid.
15   Clarice Cliff's bust of Arthur Shorter has not survived
16   'New China: Woman Designer of Modern Staffordshire', *Sydney Morning
      Herald Women's Supplement*, 13 June 1935

Chapter 7: A New World at Every Turn

1   'Bringing Brightness to the Table', *Reynolds Illustrated News*, 27
      September 1931

2 'Preliminary Report of the Industrial Art Committee of the Federation of British Industries', *PG*, June 1921, p912

3 'Short Refresher Courses for Design Students', Royal College of Art, ED 23/943, Public Record Office

4 'Girl Artist's Success: From Gilder to Art Director', *Yorkshire Evening News*, 1 September 1931

5 Registration details, Registry, Royal College of Art

6 Leonard Griffin, *The Art of Bizarre: A Definitive Centenary Celebration*, Pavilion, 1999, p32

7 Prospectus 1926–27, Royal College of Art, p7

8 Griffin, *The Art of Bizarre*, p32

9 Letter from Gilbert Ledward to Colley Shorter, quoted in Richard Green and Des Jones, *The Rich Designs of Clarice Cliff*, Rich Designs Ltd, 1995, p24

10 Christopher Frayling, *The Royal College of Art: 150 Years of Art and Design*, Barrie & Jenkins, 1987, p107

11 Interview with Edna Ginesi, *Henry Moore: Carving a Reputation*, Part 1, 1898–1945, BBC 2, 18 July 1998, executive producer Keith Alexander

12 *The Studio*, Vol. 112, July–December 1936, p334

13 *Winnipeg Tribune*, 7 November 1949

14 *Modern French and Russian Designs for Costume and Scenery*, March–June 1927, Victoria & Albert Museum, National Art Library

15 Alexandra Benois, *Reminiscences of the Russian Ballet*, translated by Mary Britnieva, Putnam, 1941, p363, quoted by Richard Buckle, *Diaghilev*, Weidenfeld & Nicolson, 1979, p275

16 Osbert Lancaster, *Home Sweet Homes*, John Murray, 1939, p58

17 Cyril W. Beaumont, *The Diaghilev Ballet in London: A Personal Record*, Putnam, 1940, p93

18 Ibid., p94

19 Dr Gordon Elliott in conversation with the author, 22 November 2001. The pottery is now held by the City of Stoke-on-Trent Museum and Art Gallery

20 Alice Gostick, Castleford School

21 Quoted by John Russell, *Henry Moore*, Allen Lane, 1968, p7

22 H.W. Maxwell, curator of the City of Stoke-on-Trent Museum and Art Gallery, 'Modern Tendencies in the Staffordshire Potteries', *The Studio*, Vol. 98, July–December 1929, p568

23 'The World of Women', *Illustrated London News*, 7 May 1927

24 An unnamed critic quoted by the *Illustrated London News*, 7 May 1927, in its assessment of 'one of the most-talked-of' pictures at the Royal Academy that spring

25 Notes by Ethel Steele (née Cliff) for Peter Wentworth-Sheilds and Kay Johnson, 1973

26 Ibid.

27 See Irene and Gordon Hopwood, *The Shorter Connection: A Family Pottery 1874–1974*, Richard Dennis, 1992

28 Vera Brittain, *Testament of Youth: An Autobiographical Study of the Years 1900–1925* (1933), Fontana in association with Virago, 1979, p73

29 In 1932, the number of YWCA hostels in London numbered thirty and accommodated some 984 beds; the figure may have been slightly lower in 1927; *Enquiry into Lodging Accommodation for Girls and Women in London 1932*, Central Council for the Social Welfare of Girls and Women in London. I am grateful to Eileen Hawkins, volunteer archivist, Women's Link, for this and other information regarding the YWCA

30 Russell, *Henry Moore*, p7

31 William Packer and Gemma Levine, *Henry Moore: An Illustrated Biography*, Weidenfeld & Nicolson, 1985, p49

32 Barbara Hepworth writing to her old school magazine from the Royal College of Art, quoted by Sally Festing, *Barbara Hepworth: A Life of Forms*, Viking, 1995, p36

33 Peter Walsh in Virginia Woolf's novel *Mrs Dalloway* (1925), seeing London, as if for the first time, following a long absence from the city; Penguin, 1992, p179.

34 The Royal College of Art was open only to the School of Engraving on Saturdays during 1927; Prospectus 1926–27, Royal College of Art

35 Picture caption, *Illustrated London News*, 12 March 1927

36 Roy Porter, *London: A Social History*, Hamish Hamilton, 1994, p325

37 'Women Who Make Money – 5: The China Designer', *Sunday Express*, 24 November 1935

38 'Bringing Brightness to the Table'

39 'Pleasing Pottery', *Home Chat*, April 1930

40 'Fashions and Fancies', *Illustrated London News*, 26 March 1927

41 'Fashions and Fancies', *Illustrated London News*, 30 April 1927

42 'Fashions and Fancies', *Illustrated London News*, 23 April 1927

43 1927 advertisement from *Good Housekeeping*, B. Braithwaite and N. Walsh, *Things My Mother Should Have Told Me: The Best of Good Housekeeping 1920–1940*, Ebury Press, 1991, p72

44 Christopher Frayling, *Art and Design: 100 Years at the Royal College of Art*, Richard Dennis, 1999, p115. Capey was speaking to one of his students, the textile designer Astrid Sampe

45 Letter from Gilbert Ledward to Colley Shorter, quoted by Griffin, *The Art of Bizarre*, p32–3

46 'Women Who Make Money – 5: The China Designer'

47 Nikolaus Pevsner, *An Enquiry into Industrial Art in England*, Cambridge University Press, 1937, p146

48 There were 1,003 male students to 788 women at the Central School of

Art in 1926–7, and 1,023 men to 769 women in 1927–8, 'LCC Central
School of Arts and Craft, Report of the Advisory Council on the Work
of the Session 1927–8', ED 83/70, Public Record Office

49   Governing body, LCC Central School of Arts and Crafts, ED 83/70,
Public Record Office

Chapter 8: Bizarre

1   'Pleasing Pottery', *Home Chat*, 19 April 1930
2   'Little Girl as Pottery Painter', *Daily Mirror*, 12 September 1930
3   'Bringing Brightness to the Table', *Reynolds Illustrated News*, 27
September 1931
4   'The Newest Colourful Pottery', *Woman's Life*, 1 August 1931
5   'Bringing Brightness to the Table'
6   'The Newest Colourful Pottery'
7   Ibid.
8   Notes by Ethel Steele (née Cliff) for Peter Wentworth-Sheilds and Kay
Johnson, 1973
9   Ethel Cliff interviewed, *Pottery Ladies: Miss Cooper, Miss Cliff, Miss
Rhead and all the Forgotten Girls*, No. 2, a four-part film series by Jenny
Wilkes, a Metropolis/Arts Council of Great Britain production for
Channel 4, 1985
10   Ibid.
11   Notes by Ethel Cliff, 1973
12   'Buyers' Notes', *PG*, September 1927, p1,415
13   Although the striped pattern is not attributed to any designer in the
Pottery Gazette review, the banded decoration corresponds with a pattern
Clarice Cliff later used to decorate an 'Elegant' basket for her own flat
14   Leonard Griffin, *The Art of Bizarre: A Definitive Centenary Celebration*,
Pavilion, 1999, p39
15   Alice Andrews in conversation with the author, 19 January 2001
16   Notes by Clarice Cliff for the retrospective of her work, *Clarice Cliff*,
exhibition catalogue, Brighton Art Gallery, 15 January–20 February 1972
17   Ibid.
18   'Pleasing Pottery'
19   Letter to Peter Wentworth-Sheilds, November 1973
20   Colley Shorter, 'What the Manufacturer Expects from the Designer',
Colley Shorter address, North Staffordshire branch of the Society of
Industrial Artists, *PG*, 1 April 1933, p499
21   Letter from Ewart Oakes to Peter Wentworth-Sheilds, November 1973
22   Notes by Clarice Cliff, *Clarice Cliff* exhibition catalogue
23   In years to come, it was not unusual for new designs by Clarice Cliff

to be on sale in advance of their first appearance at the British
Industries Fair and consequent appraisal by the trade press, but the
advertisement was probably referring to orders taken in 1927, rather
than deliveries

24 Advertisement, *PG*, March 1928, p353

25 'Pleasing Pottery'. The term 'bizarre' had been applied to pottery before.
According to *PG*, patterns produced by A.J. Wilkinson in 1917 were
thought likely to 'appeal strongly to a more extreme taste without
approaching the "bizarre"', while Wedgwood's 'Fairyland Lustre'
patterns of that time were said to belong to 'the modern bizarre school,
connected with the names of Rackham and Du Lac'. The fact that Clarice
Cliff described her painted bedroom as 'bizarre' confirms that the word
was currently in vogue: for example, *Good Housekeeping* featured a pair
of gloves with 'a bizarre cuff of peacock feathers' in 1925

26 'Buyers' Notes', *PG*, March 1928, p445

27 For example, see 'Buyers' Notes', *PG*, February 1918, p123: 'A
commendatory note must be added here as to the exceptional quality of
the colour employed by A.J. Wilkinson'; and 'Buyers' Notes', September
1926, p1,355: 'There are few firms in the Potteries who have done more
to bring into vogue brilliant colours in pottery'

28 L.L. Grimwade, 'Exhibition of Modern Pottery at Stoke', *PG*, 1 March
1920, p347

29 Osbert Lancaster, *Home Sweet Homes*, John Murray, 1939, p72

30 'Exhibition of Modern Pottery', *PG*, March 1920, p347

31 A new toilet shape, the 'Isis', 'modelled on the lines of [an] Egyptian pot',
was seen at the 1920 British Industries Fair (*Pottery and Glass Record*,
March 1920, p187), and described as a 'striking new effect in pink, lined-
out black with Isis motif on white', when photographed the following
month (April 1920, p200). It was not the only design to be perceived as
'striking', however: a rival manufacturer's yellow ewer, with a fringed
effect of small black diamonds dripping from its rim, and Edwardian in
tone, was described in the same way (November 1920). A.J. Wilkinson's
'Isis' shape and motif formed part of an illustration for an 'Oriflamme'
brochure issued in 1920 and reproduced as an advertisement for the
company in November 1922–May 1923; the 'Isis' shape was also reviewed
by *PG* (April 1922). It is now also known as 'Lotus'

32 'Buyers' Notes', *PG*, February 1931, p231, reflecting on the earlier
achievements of A.J. Wilkinson

33 'Editorial Notes: Colour', *PG*, September 1928, p1,405

34 'Around the London Showrooms', *Pottery and Glass Record*, October
1928, p294

35 'Little Girl as Pottery Painter'

36 'Buyers' Notes', *PG*, June 1930, p941, recalling initial reactions to 'Bizarre'

37 See 'Pottery Section', *Furnishing Trades Organiser*, August 1928

38 Dr Gordon Elliott in conversation with the author, 22 November 2001

39 'From a Child to a Child' or 'Kiddies Ware', as it was also known, is an extraordinary example of Colley Shorter's marketing panache. Joan Shorter (b. June 1920) was eight when the first pieces were produced, but the bulk of their promotion followed her ninth birthday, and although each piece of tableware was signed with her name and she was interviewed about her drawings in 1929 and 1935, the childlike images which decorate the nursery ware were unlikely to have been all her own creation. Clarice Cliff conceived some, if not all, the shapes that appeared in the series, and probably the majority of the patterns. If eight-year-old Joan Shorter's drawings gave Colley Shorter the initial idea for the scheme, its development thereafter seems to have been Clarice Cliff's. See press reviews PA/W–N1 and PA/W–N3; also Chris Purkis in conversation with the author, 31 March 2004

40 Josiah Wedgwood, quoted by Sharon Gater, 'Women and Wedgwood', Amanda Devonshire and Barbara Woods (eds.), *Women in Industry and Technology from Pre-History to the Present Day: Current Research and the Museum Experience*, The Museum of London, 1966, p172

41 'Buyers' Notes', *PG*, November 1928, p1,751

42 Barbara Tilson, 'The Modern Art Department Waring & Gillow, 1928–1931', *Journal of Decorative Arts Society, 1890–1940*, Vol. 8, 1983

43 Recollection of Eric Grindley, *Clarice Cliff Collectors Club Review*, Edition 3, 1989, p7

44 Advertisement, *PG*, October 1928, p1,513

45 It has been suggested that the inspiration behind 'Bizooka' may have been a set of prints by the Italian artist Giovanni Batista Bracelli, donated to the British Museum in August 1927 by Campbell Dodgson, which depicted a series of figures made from everyday objects. See Griffin, *The Art of Bizarre*, p34. However, figures created from vegetables, household implements etc. also appeared in children's literature of the time and may have provided Clarice Cliff with the idea

46 Information re Clarice Cliff's first car is courtesy of Leonard Griffin, *The Art of Bizarre*, p54. Thanks also to Bob Cross of the Austin Seven Owners' Club, London.

47 Arthur Marwick, *Britain in our Century: Images and Controversies*, Thames & Hudson, 1984, p82

48 Mervyn Jones, *Potbank: A Social Enquiry into Life in the Potteries*, Secker & Warburg, 1961, p106

49 *Lady*, 23 August 1928

50 Ibid.

51 Advertisement for Star Motor Company from *Good Housekeeping*, B. Braithwaite and N. Walsh, *Things My Mother Should Have Told Me:*

The Best of Good Housekeeping 1920–40, Ebury Press, 1991, p82

52   Advertisement for Vauxhall Cadet from *Good Housekeeping*, Braithwaite and Walsh, *Things My Mother Should Have Told Me*, p116

53   Jones, *Potbank*, p107

54   Nancy Craddock quoted by Griffin, *The Art of Bizarre*, p55

55   Leonard Griffin in conversation with the author, 26 September 2000

56   Letter from Norman Smith to Peter Wentworth-Sheilds, 23 November 1973

57   Notes by Nancy Craddock for Leonard Griffin, courtesy of Alison Wright, 15 February 2001

58   *Pottery Ladies*, No. 3

59   Rough Decoration Book, January 1928–June 1930, PA/W-N/35

60   Ibid.

61   Ibid.

62   Rene Dale in conversation with the author, 17 January 2001

63   Backstamps changed over time, with slight alterations in wording designating different years of production

64   Letter from Susie Cooper to Peter Wentworth-Sheilds, 13 September 1973

65   See Griffin, *The Art of Bizarre*, p44

Chapter 9: Cup and Saucer Cubism

1   'Buyers' Notes', *PG*, February 1929, p251

2   Bevis Hillier, *Art Deco of the 20s and 30s*, Studio Vista/Dutton Pictureback, 1968, p13. Hillier's pioneering study defined Art Deco as: 'an assertively modern style, developing in the 1920s and reaching its high point in the 1930s; it drew inspiration from various sources, including the more austere side of Art Nouveau, Cubism, the Russian Ballet, American-Indian art and the Bauhaus; it was a classical style in that, like neo-classicism but unlike Rococo or Art Nouveau, it ran to symmetry rather than asymmetry, and to the rectilinear rather than the curvilinear; it responded to the demands of the machine and of new materials such as plastics, ferro-concrete and vita-glass; and its ultimate aim was to end the old conflict between art and industry, the old snobbish distinction between artist and artisan, partly by making artists adept at crafts, but still more by adapting design to the demands of mass production.' See also Charlotte Benton, Tim Benton and Ghislaine Wood (eds.), 'Introduction: The Style and the Age', *Art Deco 1910–39*, V&A Publications, 2003, pp12–27, for a discussion of further interpretations of the style

3   'Poem for the Dress of the Future', *Oeuvres Complètes de Joseph Delteil*,

Éditions Bernard Grasset, 1962, See also Jacques Damase, *Sonia Delaunay: Rhythms and Colours*, Thames and Hudson, 1972, pp177–8

4   See Richard Green and Des Jones, *The Rich Designs of Clarice Cliff*, Rich Designs, 1995, pp66, 144. The pattern name 'Mondrian' was not coined by Clarice Cliff but, more recently, by collectors of her work

5   See 'Cubism in a Tea Set', *Daily Express*, 14 November 1929

6   Influenced by Eugène Chevreul, Sonia Delaunay and her husband Robert developed the theory of 'simultaneity', whereby contrasting colours and tones could be used to create visual harmonies and dissonances. The Decorative Arts Group exhibition catalogue (1990) raised the possibility of an affinity between the Clarice Cliff pattern 'Sliced Circle' and Sonia Delaunay's work; more recently, Dr P.J. Woodward has attributed 'Circle Tree' and other patterns to her influence. See *An Exhibition of Ugly Ware*, Chi Publishing, 1999

7   Sonia Delaunay, *Designs for Fashion in an Interior*, 1924

8   Advertising Literature 1910–c1929, PA/W-N/3, Stoke-on-Trent City Archives

9   See Christopher Frayling, 'Egyptomania', *Art Deco 1910–1939*, V&A Publications, 2002, pp40–9

10   Pattern number S.524, Rough Decoration Book January 1928–June 1930, PA/W-N/35

11   'Fantasque' was 'supposed to be a little different', to allow more shops to sell 'Clarice Cliff', as 'Bizarre' was usually sold through one retailer per town. Notes by Clarice Cliff for the retrospective of her work, *Clarice Cliff* exhibition catalogue, Brighton Art Gallery, 15 January–20 February 1972

12   'Delecia' was created by dribbling different-coloured enamel paints down a ceramic surface and fanning the resultant streams with card to set them before firing

13   Notes by Clarice Cliff, *Clarice Cliff* exhibition catalogue

14   'The British Industries Fair', *Pottery and Glass Record*, March 1929, p77

15   'English Pottery in the Modern Mode', *British Stationer*, June 1929

16   'Modern Colour and Design are Altering the Homes of Today', *Evening News*, 14 November 1929

17   'The British Industries' Fair', *PG*, April 1930, p619, quoting from an A.J. Wilkinson advertisement

18   'Women's Day at the Polls', *Daily Mail*, 31 May 1929

19   Notes by Clarice Cliff, *Clarice Cliff* exhibition catalogue

20   Silver designed by Ilonka Karasz, made by Paye and Baker, *The Studio*, Vol. 96, December 1928, p452. Born in Hungary in 1896, Ilonka Karasz moved to New York's Greenwich Village in 1913, where she was quickly established as a designer working in textiles, furniture, wallpaper and ceramics, as well as silver, and was one of the few women to design

textiles for planes and cars. Her work was seen at exhibitions organised by the American Designers' Gallery where, in 1928, she was the only woman given the responsibility of designing full rooms. See Wendy Kaplan, 'The Filter of American Taste: Design in the USA in the 1920s', including figure 31.6, p340; Benton, Benton and Wood (eds.), *Art Deco 1910–39*, and Ashley Brown, 'llonka Karasz: Rediscovering a Modernist Pioneer', *Studies in the Decorative Arts*, Vol. VIII, No.1, Fall–Winter 2000–2001

21   Undecorated white pottery by L.J. Muller, who had exhibited at Haarlem, Amsterdam, The Hague, Utrecht, Paris and Rotterdam, and was currently employed as a designer by the firm Zuid-Holland at Gouda, *The Studio*, Vol. XCV, February 1928, p142

22   Fruit bowl in brass, designed by D. Peche, Vienna, executed by Wiener Werkstätte, *The Studio Decorative Yearbook* 1929, p179. The *Yearbook* was published at the beginning of each year

23   'Design Quiz 3', *PG*, May 1951, p749

24   'What the Pottery Manufacturer Expects from the Designer', meeting of the North Staffordshire branch of the Society of Industrial Artists, 8 March 1933, reported in *PG*, April 1933, p499

25   *Mobilier et Décoration, Revue Mensuelles Des Arts Décoratifs et de l'Architecture Moderne* was published by Edition Edmond Honoré, 66 rue de Ville-d'Array, Sèvres. The Wilkinson–Newport Archive contains issues of this magazine for 1929 and 1930, originally presented in six-monthly volumes. See PA/W-N/72 and PA/W-N/73

26   'Bringing Brightness to the Table', *Reynolds Illustrated News*, 27 September 1931

27   Ibid.

28   A press report from 1935 referred to Clarice Cliff visiting Paris (see Chapter 15) as well as other European cities; a niece also recalled that her aunt had visited the French capital, and a tourist trinket belonging to Clarice Cliff showed Parisian scenes. However, none of these helps to confirm how early she visited the city

29   See Barbara Tilson, 'The Modern Art Department Waring & Gillow, 1928–1931', *Journal of Decorative Arts Society*, No. 8, 1983

30   Marcel Valotaire, 'The Paris Salons', *The Studio*, Vol. 96, July–December 1928, p200

31   *Clarice Cliff's Catalogue and Sources*, Clarice Cliff Collectors Club, p57

32   See 'English Pottery in the Modern Mode'

33   Globe-shaped vases featured in several illustrations in *Mobilier et Décoration* during 1929

34   A Clarice Cliff lamp base, on sale in Lawley's, Regent Street, and photographed by the *London Illustrated News* (12 April 1930), appears to have been suggested by a vase designed by Robert Lallement, whose

work also appeared in *Mobilier et Décoration*; see René Chavance, 'A Propos de Quelques Céramiques Nouvelles de Robert Lallement', Juillet à Décembre 1929, Tome II, pp130–9, PA/W-N/72. Lallement has also been suggested as the source for a rare Clarice Cliff vase (shape 511), which echoes his use of raised forms

35 'More Cheerful Pottery: Women's Demand for the Bizarre', *Birmingham Gazette*, 26 September 1929

36 'British Pottery and Glass: Exhibition in London', *PG*, December 1929, p1,926

37 'More Cheerful Pottery'

38 'Bizarre Potter: Girl Artist's Novel Work at a British Show', *Daily Mail*, 14 November 1929

39 'Cubism in a Tea Set'

40 Mary Marlowe, 'Modern Pottery', *Evening World*, 2 December 1929

41 'Cubism in a Tea Set'

42 Ibid.

43 Notes by Clarice Cliff, *Clarice Cliff* exhibition catalogue

44 Ibid.

45 'Pleasing Pottery', *Home Chat*, 19 April 1930

46 'Cubism in a Tea Set'

47 'London Sees the Staffordshire Potter' *Birmingham Gazette*, 14 November 1929

48 'Modern Colour and Design are Altering the Homes of Today'

49 Virginia Woolf, *A Room of One's Own*, Hogarth Press, 1929, p109

50 'New Ideas in China and Earthenware', *Farm, Field and Fireside*, 11 October 1929

51 'Child as Designer: Amusing Studies on Nursery China at Pottery Exhibition', *Daily Sketch*, 13 November 1929

52 'Modern Pottery', *Evening World*, 2 December 1929

53 'London Sees the Staffordshire Potter'

54 Griffin, *The Art of Bizarre*, p32

55 Gladys Scarlett, *Pottery Ladies: Miss Cooper, Miss Cliff, Miss Rhead and all the Forgotten Girls*, No. 2 in a four-part series by Jenny Wilkes, a Metropolis/Arts Council of Great Britain production for Channel 4, 1985

56 Rene Dale in conversation with the author, 17 January 2001, and Mollie Browne in conversation with the author, 24 February 2001

57 Alice Wilson (née Andrews), Millennium Memory Bank, National Sound Archive, 25 March 1999

58 Mollie Browne in conversation with the author, 24 February 2001

59 Sidney H. Dodd, British Pottery Manufacturers Federation, 16 March 1927, Miscellaneous Correspondence 1927–1972, PA/W-N/58/2

60 Between 1890 and 1928, the percentage of women employed in the

pottery industry rose from 37.68 per cent to 50 per cent, with relatively low wages thought to be a chief factor in the increase. See 'Women in the Pottery Industry', *Pottery and Glass Record*, April 1930, p130. By 1931, of 5,762 'young persons' placed in the industry since 1925, no fewer than 4,375 were female

61 Doris Johnson in conversation with the author, 2 March 2001

62 Annie Clowes (née Beresford) talks to Virginia Heath, 'The Way We Were', *Sentinel*, 27 February 1999

63 Advertisement, *PG*, August 1929, p1,173

64 Rene Dale in conversation with the author, 17 January 2001

65 Pattern number S410, Rough Decoration Book January 1928–June 1930, PA/W-N/35

66 Alice Andrews in conversation with the author, 19 January 2001

67 Irene Burton (née Dale), Millennium Memory Bank

68 Alice Andrews in conversation with the author, 25 January 2001

69 Alice Wilson (née Andrews), Millennium Memory Bank

70 Doris Johnson in conversation with the author, 2 March 2001

71 Alice Andrews, 'Clarice's girls – still so "bizarre"', *Sentinel*, 22 January 1999

72 Annie Beresford in conversation with the author, April 2001

73 Sadie Maskrey interviewed by Leonard Griffin, *Clarice Cliff Collectors Club Review*, January 1989, p9

Chapter 10: A Woman Knows Best

1 'Pleasing Pottery', *Home Chat*, 19 April 1930

2 'Fashions and Fancies', *Illustrated London News*, 28 May 1927

3 Editress of Home Page, 'Colour Directs Fashion in Modern Pottery', *Evening News*, 4 September 1930

4 'The 1931 Catalogue Part 1', *Clarice Cliff Collectors Club Review*, June 2001, p6

5 The naming of patterns was not new to pottery manufacture, although pattern names proliferated during this period. Despite the increased use of names, patterns continued to be numbered – the Clarice Cliff pattern 'Secrets', for example, was number 6,070 – and most banded patterns were known by numbers alone

6 'As I See Life: Paintresses of Pottery', *Daily Mirror*, 4 June 1930

7 'Bringing Brightness to the Table', *Reynolds Illustrated News*, 27 September 1931

8 'Modern Colour and Design are Altering the Homes of Today', *Evening News*, 14 November 1929

9 'Bringing Brightness to the Table'

10 'Pleasing Pottery'

11 'Colour Directs Fashion in Modern Pottery'

12 *Winnipeg Tribune*, 7 November 1949

13 Doris Johnson in conversation with the author, 2 March 2001

14 Letter from Hilda Lovatt to Peter Wentworth-Sheilds, 1973

15 'Conical or Circular Pottery: Some New Designs by a Clever Girl Expert', *Evening News*, 22 May 1930

16 'Modern Pottery Exhibition', *PG*, June 1930, p1,135

17 Advertisement, 'Come to Lawley's and Meet Miss Clarice Cliff', *Daily Mail*, 4 June 1930

18 Annie Beresford in conversation with the author, 16 January 2001

19 Ibid.

20 'Amongst the China and Glass Shops', *PG*, October 1929, p1,605

21 Ibid., p1,606

22 'Modern Pottery Beauties: Girls' Creations', *Star*, 10 June 1930

23 Ibid.

24 'Hand Painting on Pottery', *Daily Telegraph*, 4 June 1930

25 Ibid.

26 'Pleasing Pottery'

27 'Fragments', *PG,* December 1929, p1,958

28 'Factories and Art Designers', *PG*, October 1929, quoting the *Evening Sentinel*, September 1929, p1,291

29 'Trade Reports', *PG*, January 1929, p124

30 Ross McKibbin, *Classes and Cultures: England 1918–1951*, Oxford University Press, 1998, p111

31 Ibid., p82

32 'Keeping House for Him', unnamed popular magazine, quoted (despairingly) by Vera Brittain in 'Keeping his Love', *Manchester Guardian*, 29 November 1929, reproduced by Paul Berry and Alan Bishop (eds.), *Testament of a Generation: The Journalism of Vera Brittain and Winifred Holtby*, Virago, 1985, p127

33 Rose Macaulay, *Crewe Train*, Collins, 1926, Methuen, 1985, p254–5; also cited in Nicola Humble, *The Feminine Middlebrow Novel, 1920s to 1950s: class, domesticity and bohemianism*, Oxford University Press, 2001, p129

34 Robert Graves and Alan Hodge, *The Long Weekend: A Social History of Great Britain 1918–39*, Faber & Faber, 1940, pp41–2

35 'Now That We Are Feminine Again', *Home Chat*, 8 February 1930

36 'Women Want Cheerful China', *Modern Home*, November 1930

37 Some 4 million-plus houses were built between 1919 and 1939: A.H. Halsey (ed.), *Trends in British Society Since 1900*, Macmillan, 1972, p89, quoted by Diana Gittins, *Fair Sex: Family Size and Structure 1900–39*, Hutchinson, 1982, p40

38 J.C. Bailey, director and general manager, Royal Doulton, *PG*, August 1929, p1,291

39 'Little Girl as Pottery Painter', *Daily Mirror*, 12 September 1930

40 With its solid, square shape, 'concealed spout, sunken lid and built-in handle', the 'Cube' teapot was described as 'revolutionary'. See 'Buyers' Notes', *PG*, October 1925, p1,559

41 G. Rémon, 'Orfèvrerie d'Argent, Les Dernières Créations de Tétard Frères', *Mobilier et Décoration, Revue Mensuelle, Des Arts Décoratifs et de l'Architecture Moderne*, Edition Edmond Honoré, Janvier à Juin 1930, pp197–208

42 'Modern Pottery Art', *PG*, April 1930, p666

43 *Mobilier et Décoration*, Juillet à Décembre 1930, Tome II, p201

44 Margaret Stuart, 'Colour Schemes for Hospitality' re Ideal Home Exhibition, *Ideal Home*, April 1930

45 Elizabeth Berry, 'To Whet Your Appetite', *Morning Post*, 28 November 1931

46 Isabelle Anscombe, *A Woman's Touch: Women in Design from 1860 to the Present Day*, Virago, 1984, p168

47 *Punch*, Vol. 176, 12 June 1929

48 Royal Doulton advertisement, *PG*, April 1932, p452

49 Advertisement, *PG*, February 1932, p196

50 Sharon Gater and David Vincent, *The Factory in a Garden: Wedgwood from Etruria to Barlaston – the transitional years*, Keele Life Histories Centre, University of Keele, 1988, p13

51 'Modern Colour and Design are Altering the Homes of Today', *Evening News*, 14 November 1929

52 Margaret Benn, 'Daily Maids in the Small Town House', 1923, B. Braithwaite, N. Walsh and G. Davies (eds.), *From Ragtime to Wartime: The Best of Good Housekeeping 1922–1939*, Ebury Press, 1986, p15

53 'Colour Directs Fashion in Modern Pottery'

54 Letter from Hilda Lovatt to Peter Wentworth-Sheilds, 1973

55 'Colour Directs Fashion in Modern Pottery'

56 Ibid. 'Subway Sadie' was also marketed as nursery ware

57 Carolyn Hall, *The Thirties in Vogue*, Octopus Books, 1984, p116

58 'Young Art Genius', *Daily Sketch*, 25 September 1930

59 Leonard Griffin, *The Art of Bizarre: A Definitive Centenary Celebration*, Pavilion, 1999, pp10–13. Although presented as fiction, the incident had a factual basis

60 John Montgomery, *The Twenties: An Informal Social History*, Allen & Unwin, 1957, p278. By 1930, the number of people who owned a radio licence was not much above 2 million. Radio ownership 'must at this time be regarded as a middle-class rather than a national phenomenon': Arthur Marwick, *Britain in our Century: Images and Controversies*,

Thames & Hudson, 1984, p83

61   René Chavance, 'A Propos de Quelques Céramiques Nouvelles de Robert
      Lallement', *Mobilier et Décoration*, Juillet à Décembre 1929, Tome II,
      p138

62   See Alastair Duncan, *Art Deco*, World of Art Series, Thames & Hudson,
      1988, p112, for Robj's 'Jazz Musicians'. Robj also produced a later set
      of figures, 'Jazz Argentin', which featured in the November issue of
      Mobilier et Décoration, Juillet à Décembre 1930, p208, after Clarice
      Cliff's own figures were on sale

63   'Women Want Cheerful China', *Modern Home*, November 1930

64   Marwick, *Britain in Our Century*, p92

65   'Gay Modernistic Tableware', *Christian Science Monitor*, 14 October 1930

66   Editress of Home Page, 'Flower-Like Pottery for Everyday Use', *Evening
      News*, 4 September 1931. By 1935, the twenty-four patterns had been
      produced in a matter of five hours, according to a further press report:
      when Colley Shorter explained that he was 'not quite satisfied that the
      designs submitted by Miss Cliff had reached the high standard of previous
      years', she returned five hours later with 'twenty-four entirely new designs
      sketched out, not one of which he could conscientiously reject, so good,
      so original, so different from anything else previously exhibited were
      they' (*Sydney Morning Herald Women's Supplement*, 13 June 1935). See
      Daily Sketch, 9 June 1931, re Clarice Cliff speaking of creating twelve
      new designs in one particular week

67   Advertisement for 'Bizarre', *PG*, April–September 1931

68   Others included the 'Odilon' dinner service and a banded pattern, both
      patented 1929, and the 'Stamford' and 'Conical' teapots, patented 1931

69   Notes by Clarice Cliff for the retrospective of her work, *Clarice Cliff*
      exhibition catalogue, Brighton Art Gallery, 15 January–20 February 1972

70   'Designs and their Ownership', 'specially contributed by a designer', *PG*,
      January 1914, p66

71   'Buyers' Notes', *PG*, September 1932, p1,121

72   'The Newest Colourful Pottery', *Woman's Life*, 1 August 1931

73   'Buyers' Notes', *PG*, March 1932, p339

74   The first appearance of Barker Brothers' modern designs appears to be
      July 1928; see 'Buyers' Notes', *PG*, p1,091. A review of their work in
      the *Pottery and Glass Record* in February of that year does not suggest
      their patterns were modern at that point

75   'Women Want Cheerful China'

Chapter 11: The Art Director of a Famous Firm

1   *Time and Tide*, 7 March 1936, quoted by Betty Vernon, *Ellen Wilkinson*,

Croom Helm, 1982, p128. This statement, in a review of Winifred Holtby's novel *South Riding*, was probably the closest Ellen Wilkinson came to commenting on her own life

2   *The Provincial Lady Goes Further* (1932), Virago omnibus edition, 1984, p242.

3   Eric Grindley speaking to Nicole Swengley, 'A Bizarre Passion', *You* magazine, *Daily Mail*, 10 December 1995

4   Annie Beresford in conversation with the author, 16 February 2002

5   Winnie Pound in conversation with the author, 25 January 2001

6   Alice Andrews in conversation with the author, 19 January 2001

7   Jim Hall speaking to Nicole Swengley, 'A Bizarre Passion'

8   Norman Smith, *After Bizarre*, Clarice Cliff Collectors Club, p6

9   Joy Couper in conversation with the author, 10 April 2001

10 Mary Stott (b.1907), *Forgetting's No Excuse* Faber & Faber, 1973, quoted by Melissa Benn, 'Divorce – Right or Privilege?', BBC Radio 4, 19 July 2000, producer Sally Flatman

11 Figures remained substantially unchanged until 1937 when further amendments to the Matrimonial Causes Act eased proceedings. Some 4,900 divorces were granted that year; by 1939 the figure had risen to 8,200. See Lawrence Stone, *Road to Divorce: England 1530–1987*, Oxford University Press, 1990, p401

12 Somerset Maugham, Act One, *The Constant Wife*, Methuen, 1927

13 Chris Purkis in conversation with the author, June 2001

14 'Court' column, *The Times*, 26–9 January 1938

15 'Ask Mrs Jim!', *Home Chat*, 8 March 1930

16 'Ask Mrs Jim!', *Home Chat*, 19 April 1930

17 'Buyers' Notes', *PG*, February 1931, p231

18 A letter from Colley Shorter to Ewart Oakes, 20 January 1931, recorded his sales for the first week of January at £618 as against £404 for the first week of the previous year. See Leonard Griffin, *The Art of Bizarre: A Definitive Centenary Celebration*, Pavilion, 1999, p55

19 'Notes from the Potteries', *PG*, February 1931, p275

20 'Notes from the Potteries', *PG*, June 1931, p865

21 Ian Jeffrey, 'Year by Year', *Thirties: Art and Design in Britain Before the War*, Arts Council, 1980, p12

22 *Daily Sketch*, 9 June 1931

23 Arthur Marwick, *Britain in our Century: Images and Controversies*, Thames & Hudson, 1984, p94

24 'Pottery Tone Poems', *Sheffield Mail*, 4 June 1931

25 Millicent Hardman, 'I Love Designing Modern Pottery', *Bristol Times*, 11 September 1931

26 Isabelle Anscombe, *A Woman's Touch: Women in Design from 1860 to the Present Day*, Virago, 1984, p170

27 René Cutforth, *Later Than We Thought*, David & Charles, 1976, p37

28 'Appliqué Idyll' has been attributed to 1931 and sold into 1932; 'Idyll' was also produced in quieter 'Fantasque' colourings

29 Advertisement, *PG*, November 1931, p1,455

30 'Knight Errant' was based on a drawing John Butler added to a decorative panel on the inglenook fireplace at Colley Shorter's home, 'Chetwynd', where the living-room contains a triptych image of a castle atop high cliffs. Butler introduced a procession of questing knights to its central panel and signed his work circa 1926

31 'An Educative Trade Display by Pottery Manufacturers', *PG*, October 1931, pp1,395–7

32 Osbert Lancaster, *Home Sweet Homes*, John Murray, 1939, p72

33 *Punch*, 2 July 1930

34 A 1932 order book refers to 'Bathing Belle' ashtrays; see PA/W-N/15, Stoke-on-Trent City Archives. Royal Doulton also produced a 'Lido Lady' at this time

35 'Echoes of the Town', *Daily Sketch*, 5 September 1930

36 Ibid.

37 Bevis Hillier, *Art Deco of the 20s and 30s*, Studio Vista/Dutton Pictureback, 1968, p61: 'The iridescent bubble about to burst is almost the official symbol of the twenties'

38 'Some Actresses Choose Pottery', *Daily Mirror*, 1 September 1932

39 'England's Amusing Pottery Horse', *Pasadena Post*, 20 May 1932

40 Noël Coward, *Design for Living*, Methuen, 1933; cited in Alison Light, *Forever England: Femininity, Literature and Conservatism between the Wars*, Routledge, 1991, p96

41 Christopher Dee, 'People: Factory Girl Wins Fame', *Sunday Chronicle*, 14 October 1934

42 Advertisement, *Modern Home*, March 1930

43 Ambrose Heath, *Good Food: Month by Month Recipes* (1932), cited in Nicola Humble, *The Feminine Middlebrow Novel, 1920s to 1950s: class, domesticity and bohemianism*, Oxford University Press, 2001, p126

44 Clarice Cliff's directorship has sometimes been ascribed to 1930, although newspaper reports of that year refer to her as 'chief woman designer'. Her promotion was not reported in the press until 1931 and was not likely to have passed unremarked had it occurred earlier

45 'Girl Artist's Success: From Gilder to Art Director', *Yorkshire Evening News*, 1 September 1931

46 'How Famous Bizarre Ware is Made at Stoke', *Daily Sketch*, 4 December 1931

47 See Notes, Prologue

48 Cutforth, *Later Than We Thought*, p34

49 Griffin, *The Art of Bizarre*, p45

50   'The Man Colleague', *Manchester Guardian*, 24 May 1929, Paul Berry and Alan Bishop (eds.), *Testament of a Generation: The Journalism of Vera Brittain and Winifred Holtby*, Virago, 1985, p62

51   'Five Women MPs See it Through', *Daily Mail*, 14 November 1929

52   Griffin, *The Art of Bizarre*, p45

53   Richard Green and Des Jones, *The Rich Designs of Clarice Cliff*, Rich Design Ltd, 1985, p58

54   'I Love Designing Modern Pottery'

55   Ibid.

56   See Anscombe, *A Woman's Touch*, pp168–9

57   'An Educative Trade Display by Pottery Manufacturers', *PG*, October 1931, p1,395

58   Ibid.

59   Cynthia White, *Women's Magazines 1693–1968*, Michael Joseph, 1970, pp95–6

60   'To Our Readers', *Modern Home*, October 1928

61   Ibid.

62   Ibid.

63   'New Veneers and Space-Saving China at the British Industries Fair', *Daily Mail*, 20 February 1931

64   For an assessment of designs produced by Clarice Cliff for Shorter & Son, see Irene and Gordon Hopwood, *The Shorter Connection: A Family Pottery, 1874–1974*, Richard Dennis, 1992, plus trade reviews in *PG* and the *Pottery and Glass Record*

65   'I Love Designing Modern Pottery'

66   Ron Birks, the son of a pottery manufacturer, studied modelling and hand-painting under Clarice Cliff as part of his A.J. Wilkinson apprenticeship, but was not part of the 'Bizarre' workshop. See Griffin, *The Art of Bizarre*, p142

67   See Greg Slater, 'Fred Salmon', www.theagora.com. Salmon left the factory in 1932 because 'he wanted to do more traditional hand painting' (Griffin, *The Art of Bizarre*, p89)

68   Pattern number 6,140, Decoration Description Book Newport No.1 c193–, /PA/W-N/45. Leonard Griffin cites a further example of a Harold Walker design, incorporating a skyscraper and car, which is thought to have been produced as a sample only. See Leonard Griffin with Louis K. and Susan Pear Meisel, *The Bizarre Affair*, Thames & Hudson, 1988, p42

69   Alice Wilson (née Andrews) and Irene Burton (née Dale), Millennium Memory Bank, National Sound Archive, 25 March 1999. Some paintresses are associated with particular patterns, nevertheless. Ethel Barrow was the original paintress of 'Crocus' and taught other Girls how to apply it. Ellen Browne was the principal outliner of 'House and Bridge'; many examples of this pattern are identified as her work

70   Green and Jones, *The Rich Designs of Clarice Cliff*, p126

71   'Pleasing Pottery', *Home Chat*, 19 April 1930
72   'Bringing Brightness to the Table', *Reynolds Illustrated News*, 27 September 1931
73   'Pleasing Pottery'
74   'Bringing Brightness to the Table'
75   Annette Adams, 'The Newest Colourful Pottery', *Woman's Life*, 1 August 1931
76   'As I See Life: Paintresses of Pottery', *Daily Mirror*, 4 June 1930
77   'China in Autumn Colours', *Daily Telegraph*, 25 October 1932
78   Picture caption, *Daily Mirror*, 24 April 1931
79   Home-Maker Section, *Australian Woman's Weekly*, 29 June 1935
80   'The Slimming Craze', *Punch*, 11 January 1933; Christina Walkley, *The Way to Wear 'Em: 150 Years of Punch Fashion*, Peter Owen, 1985, Fig. 59
81   'Fashions and Feminism', Mary Stott (ed.), *Women Talking: An Anthology from the Guardian Women's Page, 1922–35 and 1957–71*, Pandora, 1987
82   E.M. Delafield, *Diary of a Provincial Lady* (1930), Virago omnibus edition, 1984, p50
83   *The Provincial Lady Goes Further* (1932), Virago omnibus edition, p220.
84   'She Bought a Liberty Scarf (An Improving Tale)', *c*1935, City of Westminster Archives Centre, 788/55/4. I am grateful to Alison Kenney, archivist, for directing me to this delightful advertising brochure
85   Edna Cheetham in conversation with the author, 10 February 2001
86   Margery Higginson speaking to Nicole Swengley, 'A Bizarre Passion'
87   'Bringing Brightness to the Table'
88   'Women Who Make Money – 5: The China Designer', *Sunday Express*, 24 November 1935
89   'The Newest Colourful Pottery'
90   'I Love Designing Modern Pottery'
91   'A Potter Looks Back: Old Designs Inspire the New', *Sydney Morning Herald Women's Supplement*, 12 December 1935
92   A calculation based on the actual employment dates recollected by the 'Bizarre Girls' puts their numbers into the seventies for several of the 'Bizarre' years, if their memories were correct. See 'Clarice's Bizarre Team', Griffin, *The Art of Bizarre*, pp217–18
93   'Girl Artist's Success: From Gilder to Art Director'
94   'The Newest Colourful Pottery'

Chapter 12: A Furore of Colouring

1   'The Pottery Designer: What the Industry Needs – Women Designers', *PG*, April 1932, p514

2 Gwladys Rogers, whose work featured in *The Studio* during this period, was employed by the Pilkington Tile Works at Clifton Junction, of which Gordon Forsyth was a director; Truda Carter designed for Poole Pottery

3 The tradition of anonymity within the industry contributed to the invisibility of women designers. Daisy Makeig-Jones designed and signed her 'Fairyland Lustre' for Wedgwood before the First World War; Louise Powell designed for Wedgwood during the early 1920s (see Notes, Chapter 5); and Hannah Barlow designed for Royal Doulton (see Chapter 8). See also Cheryl Buckley, *Potters and Paintresses: Women Designers in the Pottery Industry 1870–1955*, Women's Press, 1990 and Andrew Casey, *20th Century Ceramic Designers in Britain*, Antique Collectors Club, 2001, for information about these and other women designers

4 'The Pottery Designer: What the Industry Needs – Women Designers', p514

5 'What the Pottery Manufacturer Expects from the Designer', meeting of the North Staffordshire Society of Industrial Artists, *PG*, April 1933, pp499–503

6 Ibid.

7 The first order, marked 'letter', is dated 4/7/32, although the earliest date within the order book is 9/6/32. The last date given is 31/10/32, on the penultimate page; Order Book 1932, PA/W-N/15, Stoke-on-Trent City Archives

8 'Buyers' Notes', *PG*, September 1932, p1,121

9 Woolworth's achieved its pricing policy by dividing items into their component parts: if the body of a teapot cost sixpence, so did the teapot lid. The notion that 'Clarice Cliff' was sold at Woolworth's has sometimes been used to denigrate her work, although that arbiter of 'good taste', *The Studio*, featured pottery and glass sold there

10 'London Delights for Visitors and Residents in Summer-Time', *Illustrated London News*, 20 August 1932

11 28 June 1932; from *The Diary of Virginia Woolf*, Vol. 4, 1931–5, edited by Anne Olivier Bell, published by Hogarth Press

12 'London Delights for Visitors and Residents in Summer-Time'

13 Contemporary advertisement, Press Cuttings, PA/W-N/1

14 Sharon Gater and David Vincent, *The Factory in a Garden: Wedgwood from Etruria to Barlaston – the transitional years*, Keele Life Histories Centre, University of Keele, 1988, pp33–4

15 Elsie Wardle, cup-handler, Wedgwood, 'The Way We Were' No. 18, *Sentinel*, 28 December 1996

16 Kitty Ratcliffe, transferrer, Minton, 'The Way We Were' No. 36, *Sentinel*, July 1998

17 Alice Andrews in conversation with the author, 19 January 2001

18   Susie Cooper interviewed by Madeline Marsh, *Independent on Sunday*, 8 November 1992. Isabelle Anscombe suggests that Susie Cooper's move was 'well timed . . . following the boost to "designer tableware" given by Clarice Cliff's work'. (*A Woman's Touch: Women in Design from 1860 to the Present Day*, Virago, 1984, p181)

19   Gater and Vincent, *The Factory in a Garden*, p35

20   James H. Cope, 'Buyers' Notes', *PG*, March 1930, p431

21   'Buyers' Notes', *PG*, September 1932, p1,121

22   In her introduction to *Forever England: femininity, literature and conservatism between the wars*, Routledge, p9, Alison Light comments that the 'slough of feminine despond' which so often characterises this period fails to take into account women's expanding social horizons. Ross McKibbin also refers to the paradox whereby women's cultural horizons expanded as their relative status within the workforce deteriorated; see *Classes and Cultures: England 1918–1951*, Oxford University Press, p107

23   Sheila Rowbotham, *A Century of Women: The History of Women in Britain and the United States*, Viking, 1997, p192

24   Vera Brittain, 'I Denounce Domesticity!', *Quiver*, August 1932, Paul Berry and Alan Bishop (eds.), *Testament of a Generation: The Journalism of Vera Brittain and Winifred Holtby*, Virago, 1985, p141

25   'Some Problems of a Woman's Life', August 1923, B. Braithwaite and N. Walsh, *Things My Mother Should Have Told Me: The Best of Good Housekeeping 1920–1940*, Ebury Press, 1991, p15

26   'Financial Independence for Wives', February 1933, Ibid., p128

27   *Daily Sketch*, 9 June 1931

28   'Royal Staffordshire Pottery', *British Bulletin of Commerce, City of Stoke-on-Trent Potteries Survey*, Parts 1–3, 1955

29   'Being at work every day meant I never had a social sort of life,' fellow designer Susie Cooper explained in an interview with Angela Levin. *You* magazine, *Daily Mail*, 26 June 1983

30   'No one begrudges the pottery workers their annual breathing space, but there is nothing exhilarating in being domiciled in an abandoned city.' 'Trade Reports', *PG*, September 1929, p1,468

31   'A Small House in the North', *Town and Country Homes*, July 1932, pp32–3

32   J.B. Priestley, *English Journey* (1934), Folio Society, 1997 edition, p180

33   Notes prepared by Nancy Craddock for Leonard Griffin, courtesy of Alison Wright, 15 January 2001

34   'Autumn Sample Displays in London', *PG*, October 1935, p1,275, recollecting the 1932 Throne Room display

35   'Some Actresses Choose Pottery', *Daily Mirror*, 1 September 1932

36   'Trees Inspire New Art', *Daily Sketch*, 31 August 1932

37 'The Ideal China', *Woman's Life*, 28 November 1931

38 Photographs, PA/W-N/54

39 'Ladies in Restaurants', *Manchester Guardian*, 28 March 1930; Berry and Bishop, *Testament of a Generation*, pp67–70

40 René Cutforth, *Later Than We Thought*, David & Charles, 1976, p89

41 Debut of the recently formed North Staffordshire branch of the Society of Industrial Artists, *PG*, October 1932, p1,263

Chapter 13: Thoroughly Individualistic

1 'The Trend of Decorative Art 1931–2', *The Studio Decorative Yearbook 1932*, p9

2 'Latest Trend in English China' by 'Venetia', *Morning Post*, 10 September 1932

3 The British Industries Fair, *Pottery and Glass Record*, March 1933, p74

4 'Buyers' Notes', *PG*, September 1932, p1,121

5 'Pottery from Logs', *Star*, 2 September 1932

6 'Trees Inspire New Art', *Daily Sketch*, 31 August 1932

7 'Buyers' Notes', *PG*, September 1932, p1,122

8 Clarice Cliff's rectangular plates, an original and novel idea, were originally introduced in 1929; see *Daily Mail*, 13 November 1929. The origin of the flat-sided, semi-circular tureen which accompanied the 'Biarritz' dinner service has been attributed to Josef Hoffmann, founder of the Vienna Secession and co-founder of the Wiener Werkstätte. See Richard Green and Des Jones, *The Rich Designs of Clarice Cliff*, Rich Designs, 1995, p155; a cigarette and ashtray set has also been attributed to Hoffmann

9 Notes by Clarice Cliff for the retrospective of her work, *Clarice Cliff* exhibition catalogue, Brighton Art Gallery, 15 January–20 February 1972

10 A 'Bon Jour' teapot is listed in a 1932 order that corresponds with the display at Barker's, South Kensington, that autumn; see PA/W-N/15, Stoke-on-Trent City Archives. An A.J. Wilkinson employee, Eric Grindley, witnessed a meeting at which the copyright fee for 'Bon Jour' was negotiated; see Green and Jones, *The Rich Designs of Clarice Cliff*, p150

11 Picture caption, *Homes Notes*, January 1935

12 Irene Burton (née Dale), Millennium Memory Bank, National Sound Archive, 25 March 1999

13 J.B. Priestley, *English Journey* (1934), Folio Society, 1997 edition, p185

14 Ibid., pp176–181

15 'Come to the Potteries! No. 3, Burslem and Tunstall', *PG*, March 1930, p453

16 Colonel Josiah Wedgwood, 'Spotlight on the Provinces', *Time and Tide*, 22 July 1939

17   'Vera Brittain Peers Back Through Mists of the Past', *Evening Sentinel*, 26 July 1965

18   Edna Cheetham in conversation with the author, 21 June 2004

19   Nancy Craddock quoted by Leonard Griffin, *The Fantastic Flowers of Clarice Cliff*, Pavilion, 1998, p23

20   Notes prepared by Nancy Craddock for Leonard Griffin, courtesy of Alison Wright, 15 February 2001

21   Decoration Description Book Newport No. 1 c.193-, PA/W-N/45

22   Pattern number 9062, Decoration Description Book December 1928–September 1932, PA/W-N/37

23   'Bringing Brightness to the Table', *Reynolds Illustrated News*, 27 September 1931

24   'Report on British Industries Fair', *PG*, April 1933, p479

25   'Buyers' Notes', *PG*, September 1933, p1,071

26   Rene Dale in conversation with the author, 17 January 2001

27   Alice Andrews in conversation with the author, 19 January 2001

28   Rene Dale in conversation with the author, 17 January 2001

29   'Potting to Music', *Daily Sketch*, 26 November 1931

30   Mollie Browne in conversation with the author, 24 February 2001

31   Doris Johnson in conversation with the author, 2 March 2001

32   Edna Cheetham in conversation with the author, 7 April 2001

33   Alice Wilson (née Andrews), Millennium Memory Bank, National Sound Archive, 25 March 1999

34   Mollie Browne in conversation with the author, 24 February 2001

35   Annie Clowes (née Beresford) talking to Virginia Heath, 'The Way We Were', No. 44, *Sentinel*, 27 February 1999

36   'Among the China and Glass Shops', *PG*, August 1932, p1,007

37   'Snapshots from the Shops by a Woman Correspondent', *Evening Standard*, 24 October 1932

38   Rene Dale in conversation with the author, 27 March 2001

39   Edna Cheetham in conversation with the author, 7 April 2001

40   Ethel Barrow in conversation with the author, 28 March 2001

41   Annie Beresford in conversation with the author, April 2001

42   Rene Dale in conversation with the author, 27 March 2001

43   Edna Cheetham in conversation with the author, 7 April 2001. The incident was indicative of Clarice Cliff's management style: although she watched the young woman applying make-up during factory hours, she did not call attention to this, but waited until the paintress was leaving the workshop

44   Mary Stocks, quoted by Elizabeth Owen, *Fashion in Photographs: 1920–1940*, B.T. Batsford Ltd in association with the National Portrait Gallery, 1993, p10. This view is contradicted by René Cutforth in his recollection of the period and also by the historian Arthur Marwick, but

was shared by Colonel Wedgwood, when writing about Stoke-on-Trent in 1939. Perhaps the views expressed by Stocks and Colonel Wedgwood reflected the anxieties of those who feared the blurring of social boundaries. 'Bizarre Girl' Edna Cheetham's own experiences lent support to Colonel Wedgwood's remarks: she had a new dress made for every day of a one-week holiday during the late 1930s

45   Sally Alexander, 'Becoming a Woman in London in the 1920s and 30s', *Becoming a Woman and Other Essays in 19th- and 20th-Century Feminist History*, Virago, 1994, p221

46   Diana Gittins, *Fair Sex: Family Size and Structure: 1900–1939*, Hutchinson, 1982, p42

47   An advertisement for Gorringes, in *Modern Home*, December 1933, featured a 'Bon Jour' afternoon tea set in 'Cowslip' for fourteen shillings and sixpence; an 'Eight O' Clock' 'Bon Jour' morning set – involving less decoration – retailed for ten shillings. Information courtesy of Harold and Maureen Woodworth, Clarice Cliff Collectors' Club, October 1996

Chapter 14: Art *Out* of Industry

1   Fiona MacCarthy, *All Things Bright and Beautiful: Design in Britain 1830 to Today*, George Allen & Unwin, 1972, p105

2   Ibid., p104

3   Ibid.

4   Peter Wentworth-Sheilds, notes on conversation with Milner Gray, 20 March 1973

5   Paul Nash, one of the founders of Unit One, quoted by Herbert Read, 'Unit One', *Architectural Review*, October 1933, p125

6   Letter from T.A. Fennemore to the Private Secretary to the President of the Board of Trade, 27 September 1934; Council for Art and Industry Pottery Committee Memos and Minutes 1934–36, Public Record Office, BT 57/3

7   'The Steel Age', *The Times*, 24 June 1933

8   Ibid.

9   'An Exhibition of British Industrial Art in Relation to the Home', *PG*, July 1933, p844

10   Letter from Milner Gray to Peter Wentworth-Sheilds, 7 November 1973

11   'An Exhibition of British Industrial Art in Relation to the Home', p844

12   'The Steel Age'

13   Mr Ciceri of Waring & Gillow, quoted in a review of 'Modern Pottery: An Exhibition at Waring & Gillow's', *PG*, May 1934, p604

14   'The New Idea in Tableware', *PG*, 1934, p604

15   'Special Exhibition of Bizarre Ware and Foley China', *Pottery and Glass Record*, September 1934, p226

16   'Some Autumn Sample Displays', *PG*, October 1934

17   Letter from T.A. Fennemore to the Private Secretary of the President of the Board of Trade, 27 September 1934, BT 57/3

18   Ibid.

19   See Anne Eatwell, 'A Bold Experiment in Tableware Design', *Antique Collecting*, November 1984, pp32–5, for a full list of contributors and an assessment of the project

20   'Exhibition of Glass and Painted Pottery', *Journal of the Royal Society of Arts*, 2 November 1934

21   Letter from Gordon Forsyth to T.A. Fennemore, 13 August 1934, courtesy of Peter Wentworth-Sheilds and Kay Johnson

22   Notes by Clarice Cliff for the retrospective of her work, *Clarice Cliff* exhibition catalogue, Brighton Art Gallery, 15 January–20 February 1972

23   Alice Andrews in conversation with the author, 19 January 2001

24   Letter from T.A. Fennemore, BT 57/3

25   Freda Beardmore found that 'several [designs] . . . were adapted only with difficulty to Brain's shapes'. See Cheryl Buckley, *Potters and Paintresses: Women Designers in the Pottery Industry 1870–1955*, Women's Press, 1990, p114

26   'Modern China and Glass', *Observer*, 21 October 1934

27   Milner Gray to Peter Wentworth-Sheilds

28   The President of the Board of Trade, Frank Pick, was invited to open 'Modern Art for the Table', but declined. He visited the exhibition, however, and wrote to T.A. Fennemore on 29 October 1934. Although he criticised the treatment of some designs, he congratulated Fennemore on 'a brave venture' and hoped the experiment would continue 'year by year effectively' (letter courtesy of Peter Wentworth-Sheilds and Kay Johnson). Thereafter, Colley Shorter and T.A. Fennemore were invited to an informal discussion with members of the Pottery Committee of the Council for Art and Industry. The Public Record Office file referring to that invitation contains an intriguing reference: a hand-written note at the bottom of a letter to F.V. Burridge, 10 November 1934, the day after Shorter met the committee, reads: 'PS: I heard over the phone: Fancy pouncing* a Picasso through paper for a paintress ['paintress' crossed out and replaced with something illegible] to paint and so pretending that Picasso is on pottery.' Given the timing of this reference, it is tempting to assume the comment referred to Clarice Cliff. See Council for Art and Industry Pottery Committee Memos and Minutes, 1934–36, BT 57/3

29   'Safety first! – In Women's Fashions', *Sunday Chronicle*, 14 October 1934. Laura Knight was reported to have met a male director, presumably Colley Shorter, but in a later press account the chance meeting was said to have been with Clarice Cliff

30   Milner Gray and Graham Sutherland would have liked to produce shapes

for the experiment, had they been asked; Peter Wentworth-Sheilds, notes on conversation with Milner Gray, 20 March 1973

31 Details from hand-written label by Clarice Cliff, *Clarice Cliff* exhibition catalogue, p88

32 Leonard Griffin, *The Art of Bizarre: A Definitive Centenary Celebration.* Pavilion, 1999, p162

33 Helen Persis, 'Artists in the China Cupboard', *Everyman*, 2 November 1934

34 'Round the Shops: Artists' Designs in China and Glass', *The Times*, 22 October 1934

35 'From Easel to Cups: Artists Among the Crockery', *Observer*, 28 October 1934

36 'Modern Artists Have New Ideas in China Design', *Evening Standard*, 24 October 1934

37 Letter from T.A. Fennemore to the Board of Trade

38 Raymond Mortimer, 'Saucers and Socialism', *New Statesman and Nation*, 27 October 1934

39 'The Crafts Delivered', *Spectator*, 26 October 1934

40 'Gracie Fields's Philosophy', *Bristol Times and Mirror*, 8 September 1931

41 'The Artist in Industry', *PG*, January 1935, p85

42 Reginald Haggar quoted by Garth Clark, 'Art Deco Ceramics: England', *Ceramics Monthly*, September 1979

43 'Design Quiz 2', *PG*, April 1951, p572

44 Letter from Gordon Forsyth to T.A. Fennemore, 13 August 1934, courtesy of Peter Wentworth-Sheilds and Kay Johnson

45 Letter from Kearley, Board of Trade, to Sir Hubert Llewellyn Smith, quoting G. Forsyth, 30 November 1934, Council for Art and Industry Pottery Committee Memos and Minutes, 1934–36, Public Record Office, BT 57/3

46 Jennifer Hawkins, 'Industrial Ceramics and Glass', *Thirties: Art and Design in Britain before the War*, Arts Council, 1980, p93

47 'Buyers' Notes', *PG*, April 1936, p517

48 Betty Joel, 'A House and a Home', John de la Valette (ed.), *The Conquest of Ugliness: A Collection of Contemporary Views on the Place of Art in Industry*, Methuen & Co. Ltd, 1935, p94. In an editor's note prefacing Joel's essay, de la Valette disassociated himself from her enthusiams

49 'Editorial Notes: Then and Now', *PG*, January 1935, p51

50 'British Art in Industry', *The Studio*, Vol. 109, January–June 1935, p55

51 'Entertainment: British Art in Industry', *The Times*, 11 January 1935

52 W.A. Thorpe, 'A Personal Impression of the Pottery', *PG*, February 1935, p223

53 'Decorative Art', *New Statesman and Nation*, 12 January 1935

54 'A Triumph of Ugliness', *New Statesman and Nation*, 26 January 1935

55   'Editorial Notes', *PG*, February 1935, p191
56   'Design Quiz 2', *PG*, April 1951, p573

Chapter 15: Women Who Make Money

1   'Introduction', *Decorative Art: The Studio Yearbook*, 1935, p10
2   'Trade Notes', *PG*, March 1935, p393. Shorter returned to the UK in time for the September display
3   'Royal Staffordshire Pottery', *British Bulletin of Commerce*, City of Stoke-on-Trent Potteries Survey, Parts 1–3, 1955
4   Norman Smith in conversation with the author, 27 June 2001
5   'Royal Staffordshire Pottery', *British Bulletin of Commerce, City of Stoke-on-Trent Potteries Survey*, Parts 1–3, 1955
6   'Home-Maker Section', *Australian Woman's Weekly*, 29 June 1935
7   Ibid.
8   'Royal Academy Exhibition: From the Pottery and Glass Sections', *Furnishing Trade Organiser*, January 1935
9   Judith Day, '"Best" China for Everyday Tables', *Manchester Evening News*, 16 May 1935
10   'From Portraits to Plates: Modern China *by* Famous Artists', *Manchester City News*, 19 October 1935
11   Ross McKibbin, *Classes and Cultures: England 1918–1951*, Oxford University Press, 1988, p419
12   'Opening of Jaeger House, Regent Street, 2 April 1935', City of Westminster Archives Centre, 1327/535. I am grateful to Alison Kenny, archivist, for directing me to this material
13   'Dainty Pottery in Lovely Colours', PA/W–N/1, Stoke-on-Trent City Archives
14   'Autumn Sample Displays in London', *PG*, 1 October 1935, p1,276
15   Gladys Mann, 'Coffee and Cakes', *Miss Modern*, November 1935
16   E.M.V., 'Sea Jade Walls and Crystal Chains in Modern Rooms', *Evening News*, 23 October 1935
17   'Autumn Sample Displays in London', *PG*, 1 October 1935, p1,275
18   Dorothy Critchlow, 'Six Weeks to Make a Cup', *Manchester Evening News*, 13 May 1935
19   Joan Bailey, figure-paintress, Royal Doulton, 'The Way We Were' No. 30, *Sentinel*, 29 December 1997
20   Alice Wilson (née Andrews), Millennium Memory Bank, National Sound Archive, 25 March 1999
21   Iris Edwards, figure-paintress, Royal Doulton, talking to John Abberley, 'The Way We Were' No. 21, *Sentinel*, 29 March 1997
22   Mollie Browne in conversation with the author, 24 February 2001

23   Alice Andrews in conversation with the author, 12 March 2002

24   Alice Wilson (née Andrews), Millennium Memory Bank, National Sound
      Archive, 25 March 1999

25   Mollie Browne in conversation with the author, 24 February 2001

26   'Accessories to the Dining Table', *Sydney Mail*, 27 November 1935

27   'New China: Woman Designer of Modern Staffordshire', *Sydney Morning
      Herald Women's Supplement*, 13 June 1935

28   'A Potter Looks Back: Old Designs Inspire the New', *Sydney Morning
      Herald Women's Supplement*, 12 December 1935

29   Ibid.

30   Edna Cheetham in conversation with the author, 10 February 2001

31   Ibid.

32   Alice Andrews in conversation with the author, 19 January 2001

33   Nikolaus Pevsner, *An Enquiry into Industrial Art in England*, Cambridge
      University Press, 1937, p78. Pevsner began his enquiry in 1934

34   'The Carpenter Family', *Family Century*, Channel 4, August 2000

35   E.M. Delafield, *The Provincial Lady in America* (1934), Virago, 1984, p271.

36   Leonard Griffin, *The Fantastic Flowers of Clarice Cliff*, Pavilion, 1998,
      p54

37   'Tablecloths of Black', *Daily Mirror*, 30 October 1935

38   Norman Smith in conversation with the author, 27 June 2001

39   'A Place to be Visited', *Country Illustrated*, April 1934

40   Unsourced review, PA/W-N/1

41   'Pleasing Pottery', *Home Chat*, 19 April 1930

42   'Women Who Make Money – 5: The China Designer', *Sunday Express*,
      24 November 1935

43   Some 1,949,873 copies of the *Sunday Express* were purchased in
      November 1935; *Sunday Express* Research Department

44   Ethel Cliff's views were recalled by her niece, Alison Wright, in conver-
      sation with the author, 15 February 2001

Chapter 16: A Life of Her Own

1   Although Clarice Cliff's name appeared on the electoral role for Edwards
      Street up to the Second World War, she was living at Snow Hill by the
      time of her fortieth birthday in 1939. Several factors point to 1936 as
      a probable date for her move: Eric Grindley, who did odd jobs at Snow
      Hill as a young trainee, joined the Forces in 1939; Clarice Cliff was still
      living at the family home when her sister Dorothy died in November
      1935; and Nancy Craddock, who visited her aunt at her flat after school,
      left school in 1936; the style and patterns with which Clarice Cliff dec-
      orated her flat also suggest this period. The 'Bizarre' paintress Rene Dale

(b.1917), who was related to the Cliffs through marriage, stayed overnight at Edwards Street when she was 'about eighteen', and Clarice Cliff had already left home

2 Bill Ridgway, 'Memories of the 1950s', 'The Way We Were', *Sentinel*, April 2001

3 Mervyn Jones, *Potbank: A Social Enquiry into Life in the Potteries*, Secker & Warburg, 1961, p85

4 Jean Moremont, in Jean McCrindle and Sheila Rowbotham (eds.), *Dutiful Daughters*, Penguin, 1974, 1977, quoted by Sally Alexander, 'Becoming a Woman in London in the 1920s and 30s', *Becoming a Woman and Other Essays in 19th- and 20th-Century Feminist History*, Virago, 1994, p221

5 The birth rate in Stoke-on-Trent declined steadily through the 1920s and 1930s. See Jacqueline Sarsby, *Missuses and Mouldrunners: An Oral History of Women Pottery Workers at Work and at Home*, Oxford University Press, 1988, p47

6 'Excess Females' UK Population 1920–1995, Office of National Statistics, courtesy of Dr E. Heyderman

7 Marjorie Hillis, *Live Alone and Like It: A Guide for the Extra Woman*, Duckworth, 1936, p8

8 Ibid., p13

9 'P.P.', 'Flower Pottery', *Evening News*, 12 September 1935

10 'At the Shops: China in Autumn Colours', *Daily Telegraph*, 25 October 1932

11 Eric Grindley, quoted by Griffin, *Taking Tea with Clarice Cliff*, p28

12 Storm Jameson, *Company Parade*, Virago, 1982, p47

13 Winifred Watson, *Miss Pettigrew Lives for a Day* (1938), Persephone Books, 2000, p4

14 Rosamond Lehmann, *The Weather in the Streets* (1936), Virago, 1981, p5.

15 Lettice Cooper, *The New House* (1936), Virago, 1987, p11

16 Advertisement, *Illustrated London News*, 5 March 1927

17 Ethel Steele (née Cliff), notes for Peter Wentworth-Sheilds and Kay Johnson, 1973

18 Picture caption, *Evening Sentinel*, 3 December 1935

19 Hillis, *Live Alone and Like It*, Chapter 4

20 See Naomi Mitchison, 'Patterns of Loving', *You May Well Ask: A Memoir 1920–1940*, Victor Gollancz, 1979

21 In *Working-Class Wives* (1939), Virago, 1981, p44, Margery Spring-Rice concluded from her data on the health of 1,250 women that 'contraceptive advice seems practically non-existent', while in *Missuses and Mouldrunners*, p49, Jacqueline Sarsby concluded there was 'talk but little knowledge about contraception' in the potbanks

22 Maud Wood (b.1914), interviewed by Steve Humphries and Pamela Gordon, *Forbidden Britain: Our Secret Past 1900–1960*, BBC Books, 1994, p166

23 Molly Keane (b.1904) talking with Polly Devlin; Mary Chamberlain (ed.), *Writing Lives: Conversations between Women Writers*, Virago, 1988, p127

24 Mary Stott (b.1907) talking with Liz Heron; Chamberlain (ed.), *Writing Lives*, p238

25 Florence Hawthorne, 'Pioneer of the Family Planning Clinic in the Potteries and Worker for the Disabled: Dorothy Winser Wedgwood OBE, 1893–1924', unpublished paper, Wedgwood Museum, courtesy of the Wedgwood Museum Trust, Barlaston, Staffordshire

26 'Crocks and Crazes', *Evening Sentinel*, 29 February 1936. Impassioned correspondence continued into the following month; see 'Our Readers' Views', 5, 7, 9 and 10 March 1936

27 Florence Hawthorne, 'Pioneer of the Family Planning Clinic'

28 Milner Gray in conversation with Peter Wentworth-Sheilds, 20 March 1973

29 Alison Light, *Forever England: femininity, literature and conservatism between the wars*, Routledge, 1991, p13; plus, see Light's detailed analysis of Agatha Christie's and Daphne du Maurier's fiction in this volume

30 Letter from Peggy Davies to Peter Wentworth-Sheilds, 26 October 1973

31 See Cheryl Buckley, *Potters and Paintresses: Women Designers in the Pottery Industry 1870–1955*, Women's Press, 1990, p148

32 Scrapbook of Miscellaneous Patterns c193-, PA/W-N/79, contains examples of Betty Silvester's work

33 Richard Green and Des Jones, *The Rich Designs of Clarice Cliff*, Rich Designs, 1995, p193

34 'Miss Charlotte Rhead: Pottery Artist and Designer', *Pottery and Glass Record*, 1937, Vol. 19, p220

35 Millicent Taplin was three years younger than Clarice Cliff. Born in 1902, she left school at the age of thirteen and, with the aid of a scholarship, attended evening art classes. Like Clarice Cliff, Taplin's first job was as a gilder, of which she quickly tired. Training as a paintress at Minton thereafter enabled her to secure work at Wedgwood, where she came to the attention of the husband-and-wife design team Alfred and Louise Powell (see Notes, Chapter 5). She was put in charge of the freehand decorating shop they established there in 1928 and later promoted to the role of designer. One of several designers employed by Wedgwood between the wars, Taplin worked under the direction of the company's art director, Victor Skellern, often collaborating with him on patterns

36 H. Pearl Adams, 'Woman and her World', 'Fashions in Table Pottery: Mass Production and Artistic Design', *Observer Sunday Supplement*, 15 September 1935

37 'Buyers' Notes', *PG*, September 1936, p1,199

Chapter 17: I Know That You Can Be Discreet

1   'Buyers' Notes', *PG*, September 1937, p1,199
2   'Report on the British Industries Fair', *PG*, January 1938, p250
3   'Buyers' Notes', *PG*, September 1936, p1,201
4   'Retail Sales 1937', Wilkinson-Newport Archive, PA/W-N/11, Stoke-on-Trent City Archives
5   *Good Housekeeping*, March 1937
6   'Retail Sales 1937', PA/W-N/11
7   The Council for Art and Industry's selection for the British Pavilion drew criticism within the Potteries because it was thought to be unrepresentative of the industry as a whole. However, companies with whom A.J. Wilkinson would previously have been grouped – Brain & Co., Susie Cooper, A.E. Gray, Moorcroft and Wedgwood, for example – who were better able to satisfy the tendency towards rational design, were included. Giving an indication of the stringent criteria applied, William Moorcroft wrote to *The Times*: 'The Council of Art [for] Industry . . . not only made an inadequate selection of pottery . . . but tried to advise me . . . how to make it . . . I feel that unless there are found . . . men less influenced by the fashions which are now known as ultra-modern,* there will be little hope for better things. At previous International Exhibitions, including the British Empire Exhibition, I was always allowed to make my own selection.' See *PG*, August 1937, p1,069. (*The 'ultra-modern' of the late 1930s spoke to the severe, not the zany.)
8   *PG*, November 1937, p1,495
9   'Notes from the Potteries', *PG*, January 1938, p104
10   Gerald Pearson in conversation with the author, 28 February 2001
11   'The Seven Interests of Women', *Illustrated London News*, 12 November 1938
12   Gladys Mann, 'Coffee and Cakes', *Miss Modern*, November 1935
13   *Woman & Home*, June 1938
14   'Buyers' Notes', *PG*, October 1939, p1,249
15   'Editorial Notes', *PG*, October 1939, p1,243
16   'Britain Can Export – Buy British Ware', *PG*, September 1940, p845
17   Notes by Clarice Cliff for the retrospective of her work, *Clarice Cliff* exhibition catalogue, Brighton Art Gallery and Museum, 15 January–20 February 1972
18   Edna Cheetham in conversation with the author, 10 February 2001
19   Eric Wenger quoted by Leonard Griffin, *The Art of Bizarre: A Definitive Centenary Celebration*, Pavilion, 1999, p174
20   *Pottery Ladies: Miss Cooper, Miss Cliff, Miss Rhead and all the Forgotten Girls*, No. 2, a four-part film series by Jenny Wilkes, a Metropolis/Arts Council of Great Britain production for Channel 4, 1985

21   Letter from Clarice Cliff to Ewart Oakes, 10 December 1941; property
      of a private collector; copy of the letter courtesy of Paul Gibbs, curator,
      Conwy Teapot Museum

22   Ibid.

23   Barry Parker and Raymond Unwin, 'The Art of Designing Small Houses
      and Cottages', *The Art of Building a Home: A Collection of Lectures
      and Illustrations*, Longmans, Green & Co., 1901, p116 and p111.
      'Chetwynd' features as 'A house at Northwood, Staffordshire'.
      'Chetwynd' is now called Chetwynd House

24   Hannah Cliff's daughter in conversation with the author, 18 January
      2001

Chapter 18: A Taste for the Traditional

1   Letter from Clarice Cliff to Ewart Oakes, 10 December 1941; property
      of a private collector; copy of the letter courtesy of Paul Gibbs, curator,
      Conwy Teapot Museum

2   Norman Smith in conversation with the author, 27 June 2001

3   'Notes from the Potteries', *PG*, January 1941, p70

4   Joan Wilks, decorating manageress, Sadlers, 'The Way We Were' No. 26,
      Sentinel, 25 August 1997

5   Wartime life was not all privation. Like Clarice Cliff before them, a
      younger generation of women discovered its opportunities: with the men
      away at war, the paintresses at Royal Doulton were finally allowed to
      paint the faces of figurines. (Opportunity had its limits, however. When
      the original figure-painters returned, the women working alongside them
      received only two-thirds of the male wage.)

6   Rene Dale in conversation with the author, 17 January 2001

7   Margery Higginson quoted by Leonard Griffin, *The Art of Bizarre: A
      Definitive Centenary Celebration*, Pavilion, 1999, p174

8   *Winnipeg Tribune*, 7 November 1949

9   Andrew Casey, *20th Century Ceramic Designers in Britain*, Antique
      Collectors' Club, 2001, p86

10   'Potteries Poster Girl', *PG*, May 1948, p421

11   *Winnipeg Free Press*, 5 November 1949

12   'Design Quiz 5', *PG*, September 1951, p1,382

13   Norman Smith in conversation with the author, 27 June 2001

14   Advertisement, *PG*, May 1951, p643

15   Peter Wentworth-Sheilds and Kay Johnson, *Clarice Cliff*, L'Odeon, 1976,
      p28

16   'Design Quiz 1', *PG*, March 1951, p412

17   'Design Quiz 2', *PG*, April 1951, p572

18   The Council of Industrial Design's Cautionary Ceramics initiative was
      one of several intended to promote 'good design', primarily by educating
      schoolchildren. A photograph of a 'Bizarre' lemonade set bore the caption:
      'Described as "futuristic" design. Now fortunately outmoded, but still
      to be seen, and avoided. The unfunctional [triangular] handle and the
      decoration ["Ravel"] provide a cautionary study. A design by another
      manufacturer was deemed 'worthy of the juke box and the pin-table
      saloon, but all too common in some places' ('Cautionary Ceramics',
      Design Council Archive Collection; I am grateful to Catherine Moriarty,
      curator, for her help in locating this material). See also *Times Educational
      Supplement*, 28 March 1952, and Dr P. J. Woodward, *An Exhibition of
      Ugly Ware*, Chi Publishing, 1999, pp23–4. When asked her opinion of
      the Council of Industrial Design's general objectives in 'Design Quiz 4',
      July 1951, Clarice Cliff described them as 'bureaucratic fancies'.

19   'Welcome to British Coupe Ware', *PG*, February 1953, pp250–2

20   'Royal Staffordshire Pottery', *British Bulletin of Commerce*, City of Stoke-
      on-Trent Potteries Survey, Parts 1–3, 1955

21   Letter to Peter Wentworth-Sheilds, 1973

22   'Design for Selling', *New Statesman and Nation*, 27 March 1954

23   'Design Quiz 4', *PG*, July 1951, p1,075

24   Norman Smith in conversation with the author, 27 June 2001

25   Margery Higginson, *Clarice Cliff Collectors Club Review*, Edition 1,
      1990

26   'Royal Staffordshire Ware', Crownford China, Stoke-on-Trent City
      Archives

27   Richard Midwinter in conversation with the author, 16 November 2001

28   Norman Smith in conversation with the author, 27 June 2001

29   'Potteries Misinterpreted', *PG*, December 1961, p1,442

30   Joan Wilks, decorating manageress, Sadlers, 'The Way We Were' No. 26,
      Sentinel, 25 August 1997

31   Wentworth-Sheilds and Johnson, *Clarice Cliff*, p31

32   Letter from Colley Shorter to the 'Bizarre Girls', 4 April 1962, courtesy
      of Peter Wentworth-Sheilds and Kay Johnson

33   Letter from Clarice Cliff to Ewart Oakes, 30 July 1964, courtesy of Paul
      Gibbs, curator, Conwy Teapot Museum

34   Eve Midwinter in conversation with the author, 22 January 2002

Chapter 19: After A.J. Wilkinson

1   Richard Midwinter in conversation with the author, 16 November 2001

2   Alison Wright in conversation with the author, 15 February 2001

3   The bequest included numerous pearlware figures, late eighteenth- and

nineteenth-century earthenware and porcelain. A gallery within the museum was called 'The Shorter Room' for a period

4   The Wilkinson-Newport Archive is not comprehensive. Although all available documentation was saved, inevitably some records had not survived; others were water-damaged and were destroyed

5   Conversation with Alison Wright, 15 February 2001

6   *Evening Sentinel*, 12 December 1972

7   *Evening Sentinel*, 2 March 1973

8   The house has since been purchased by an admirer of the Arts and Crafts movement and its original features preserved and/or restored

9   'Commentary: Dappled things', *Times Literary Supplement*, 21 May 1976. The V&A had purchased its first piece of Clarice Cliff, an 'Inspiration' vase, in 1970

10 Holly Finn, *Financial Times*, 24 April 1999

11 Information courtesy of the Clarice Cliff Collectors Club

12 Fiona MacCarthy, *Guardian*, 3 April 2003. *Art Deco 1910–1939*, V&A, March–July 2003, was curated by Ghislaine Wood

Postscript

1   Paul Atterbury, 'Collecting Clarice', *Homes and Gardens*, July 1985

2   Annette Adams, 'The Newest Colourful Pottery, *Woman's Life*, 1 August 1931

3   John Sandon, 'Deco Delights of Clarice Cliff', *Antique Dealer and Collectors' Guide*, November 1999

4   In his *Enquiry into Industrial Art in England*, begun in 1934 and published three years later, Nikolaus Pevsner analysed current trends in tableware, based on a discussion with a sample of leading stores. In one, the buyer disliked 'Modern Floral' (as it was then categorised) to such a degree he could barely bring himself to stock it; in another, its sales almost doubled during the course of Pevsner's enquiry; while a third found that the banded ware that was actually cheaper to produce attracted a more monied clientele and had to be stocked among the more expensive ranges, with 'Modern Floral' consigned to the cheaper ones. As always, it was all a matter of taste. In his own description of the 'meretricious modernistic decoration' that had 'forced its way into the British market', Pevsner's Modernist aesthetic was as plain as the tableware he approved.

Those who share his tastes today see in Clarice Cliff's 'Bizarre' the worst excesses of 1930s style. However, other accounts of the period took a different view. 'Although her designs are modern, they have none of that eccentricity that many of us find so trying nowadays,' *Woman's*

Life noted in November 1932. 'I am not usually an admirer of the extremely modern,' a reviewer for the *Morning Post* confessed, 'but I was so captivated by this fascinating work that I promptly ordered some of it myself.' Within the Potteries, a manufacturer described Clarice Cliff as someone 'who could popularise modern art on pottery in a legitimate way, combining good forms with designs that were exceptional without being extravagant.' (See Bernard Rhead, 'Modern Pottery Art', *PG*, December 1936, p 1,622). Women's magazines and fellow manufacturers might be expected to support Clarice Cliff, but the fact that her banding was commended by the assistant keeper of ceramics at the V&A is a reminder that her work always catered for a variety of tastes.

5   Cheryl Buckley, *Potters and Paintresses: Women Designers in the Pottery Industry 1870–1955*, Women's Press, 1990, p127, quoting responses to Clarice Cliff's work

6   An unidentified 'Bizarre Girl' speaking on *Woman's Hour*, BBC Radio 4, December 2000

7   A visitor to the A.J. Wilkinson stand at the Ideal Home Exhibition in 1935 was heard to describe Clarice Cliff's work as 'sunshine captured in pottery'; *PG*, May 1935, p640

8   Alice Andrews in conversation with the author, 19 January 2001

GLOSSARY

Biscuit oven – the first stage of firing. This took three days and produced pottery with a porous, biscuit-like texture

Cartouche – a framed image. Clarice Cliff used cartouches for restrained decoration; the pattern 'Stroud', for instance, consists of a small framed image of a house and tree at the rim of an otherwise undecorated plate

Casting – tableware shapes such as teapots and jugs were cast in a mould, using liquid clay (slip). With 'Clarice Cliff' teapots such as 'Conical', 'Stamford' and 'Bon Jour', the difficulty of casting their shapes in one piece initially presented a challenge. When creating copies for reproduction some sixty years later, Wedgwood had to resolve that problem anew

China – a term generally taken to refer to bone china, but which applies to all soft porcelains. It is also sometimes used as a generic term for tableware

Dipping – after the initial or biscuit stage of firing, tableware is dipped into a liquid glaze

Earthenware – pottery made from poorer-grade clays, generally porous

Enamel (or muffle) kiln – the last stage of the firing process for decorative tableware; the application of 'Bizarre' patterns immediately preceded this firing. As some parts of the kiln are hotter than others, the placing of an enamel kiln required care and experience. 'Bizarre' ware was placed in the centre of the kiln and surrounded by vitrified whiteware, the production of the mundane assisting in the creation of the fanciful

Engine-room – the powerhouse of the pottery, housing the steam engine

Fettle – tableware is fettled to remove extrusions and other imperfections when the ware is cheese-hard prior to firing in the biscuit oven

Glost – the second firing, which took two days

Jasperware – unglazed vitreous stoneware, developed by Wedgwood

Jolley – the jolley machine, introduced into pottery manufacture in the late nineteenth century, was used to make bowls via a mould held within a revolving head; a similar machine, a jigger, was used in the production of plates. Both made it easier for women to take more significant roles in the 'making' of pottery

Majolica – glazed earthenware with coloured decoration in relief

Marl – rough clay

On-glaze patterns are applied at the penultimate stage of pottery production and fired in the enamel kiln. Metal oxides are painted on to the fired tableware using fat oil and turpentine, and fired in a low-temperature oven (700–800C) to fix their colours, the lower temperature allowing for a much wider range of colours to be used than **underglaze** patterns. 'Bizarre' patterns were created in this way. On-glaze patterns will eventually fade with use

Placers stacked saggars of tableware in the kilns of bottle ovens prior to firing. A full saggar could weigh half a hundredweight.

Pochoir – a printing method, usually involving hand-coloured stencils

Potbank – the name given to factories within the pottery industry

Pounce – the name given to the article, usually tissue paper, used in the tracing of patterns. A pounce was placed over the pattern to be copied and the pattern's features delineated with pinpricks. The pattern was then transferred to the object with charcoal

Saggar – a fireclay box in which tableware was placed to protect it during firing. Approximately 2,000 saggars could be accommodated per bottle oven, in columns some thirty-two saggars high known as bungs

Sgraffito – a decorative technique whereby patterns are scratched on to a ceramic surface or on-glaze to reveal an earlier, contrasting colour beneath

Shords – discarded pieces of broken and/or rejected pottery (also known as shards or sherds). Over time, these formed a waste heap known as a shord ruck. For years after the manufacture of 'Bizarre', brilliantly coloured shords could be dug up outside the Newport Pottery; some pieces of mispainted 'Bizarre' met a different fate, being pitched into the canal by paintresses hoping to avoid detection

Shoulder motif – an image to the top right- or left-hand rim of a plate or saucer

Slip – a smooth blend of water and clay, used for casting and sometimes applied as pottery decoration. The clay itself is a mixture of clay and stone – plus bone in the making of bone china – with different proportions of each used to make different kinds of pottery. Each potbank had its own, closely guarded recipe for the mix produced in its slip-house

Throwing – tableware shapes such as cups were thrown on the potter's wheel and their shapes finished by turning

Towing – the name given to the process whereby the rims of plates were smoothed after their initial firing

Underglaze patterns are applied prior to the glost firing, which fixes the glaze, making such patterns impossible to erase

SELECT BIBLIOGRAPHY

Periodicals

Pottery Gazette and Glass Trade Review, *Pottery and Glass Record*, *Sentinel*, *The Studio*, *The Studio Yearbook*, *Good Housekeeping*, *Illustrated London News*, *Modern Home*, *Punch*

Publications

Harold Acton, *Memoirs of an Aesthete*, Methuen, 1948

Sally Alexander, *Becoming a Woman and Other Essays in 19th- and 20th-Century Feminist History*, Virago, 1994

Isabelle Anscombe, *A Woman's Touch: Women in Design from 1860 to the Present Day*, Virago, 1984

Arts Council of Great Britain, *Thirties: Art and Design in Britain before the War*, Arts Council, 1980

Stanley Baron, *Sonia Delaunay: The Life of an Artist*, Thames & Hudson, 1995

Maureen Batkin, *Gifts for Good Children: The History of Children's China Part II, 1890–1900s*, Richard Dennis, 1996

Martin Battersby, *The Decorative Twenties*, revised and edited by Philippe Garner, Herbert Press, 1988

Nicola Beauman, *A Very Great Profession: The Woman's Novel 1914–39*, Virago, 1983

Deirdre Beddoe, *Back to Home and Duty: Women Between the Wars 1918–1939*, Pandora, 1989

Florence Bell, *At the Works* (1906), Virago, 1985

Arnold Bennett, *Anna of the Five Towns*, Methuen, 1902; Penguin, 1936
    Clayhanger, Methuen, 1910; Penguin, 1954

Hilda Lessways, Methuen, 1911

The Grim Smile of the Five Towns, 1907; Penguin, 1946

The Matador of the Five Towns, 1912; Alan Sutton, 1990

The Old Wives' Tale, Chapman & Hall, 1908; Pan, 1964

Charlotte Benton, Tim Benton and Ghislaine Wood (eds.), *Art Deco 1910–1939*, V&A Publications, 2003

Paul Berry and Alan Bishop (eds.), *Testament of a Generation: The Journalism of Vera Brittain and Winifred Holtby*, Virago, 1985

Paul Berry and Mark Bostridge, *Vera Brittain: A Life*, Chatto & Windus, 1995

Stella Bowen, *Drawn from Life*, Collins, 1941; Virago 1984

B. Braithwaite and N. Walsh, *Things My Mother Should Have Told Me: The Best of Good Housekeeping 1920–1940*, Ebury Press, 1991

B. Braithwaite, N. Walsh and G. Davies, *From Ragtime to Wartime: The Best of Good Housekeeping 1922–1937*, Ebury Press, 1986

Vera Brittain, *Testament of Youth: An Autobiographical Study of the Years 1900–1925*, Victor Gollancz, 1933; Fontana in association with Virago, 1979

Cheryl Buckley, *Potters and Paintresses: Women Designers in the Pottery Industry 1870–1955*, Women's Press, 1990

Bernard Bumpus, *Charlotte Rhead: Potter and Designer*, Kevin Francis Publishing, 1987

Andrew Casey, *20th Century Ceramic Designers in Britain*, Antique Collectors' Club, 2001

Lettice Cooper, *National Provincial* (1938); Gollancz, 1987

The New House (1936); Virago, 1987

René Cutforth, *Later Than We Thought*, David & Charles, 1976

Jacques Damase, *Sonia Delaunay: Rhythms and Colours*, Thames & Hudson, 1972

Margaret Llewellyn Davies (ed.), *Life As We Have Known It*, Hogarth Press, 1931; Virago, 1977

E. M. Delafield, *The Diary of a Provincial Lady* (1930), *The Provincial Lady Goes Further* (1932), *The Provincial Lady in America* (1934), *The Provincial Lady in Wartime* (1940); collected edition, Macmillan, 1947; Virago, 1984

Margaret Drabble, *Arnold Bennett*, Weidenfeld & Nicolson, 1974

Janet Dunbar, *Laura Knight*, William Collins & Sons, 1975

Alistair Duncan, *Art Deco*, World of Art Series, Thames & Hudson, 1988

Carol Dyhouse: *Girls Growing up in Late Victorian and Edwardian England*, Routledge, 1981

Anne Eatwell, 'A Bold Experiment in Tableware Design', *Antique Collecting*, 1984 *Susie Cooper Productions*, Victoria and Albert Museum, 1987;

Margaret Leonora Eyles, *The Woman in the Little House*, Grant Richards, 1922

Sally Festing, *Barbara Hepworth: A Life of Forms*, Viking, 1995

Margaret Forster, *Hidden Lives: A Family Memoir*, Viking, 1995; Penguin, 1996

Gordon Forsyth, *The Art and Craft of the Potter*, Chapman & Hall, 1934

Twentieth-Century Ceramics: An International Survey of the Best Work, Studio, 1936

Christopher Frayling, *Art and Design: 100 Years at the Royal College of Art*, Richard Dennis, 1999
The Royal College of Art: One hundred and fifty years of art and design, Barrie & Jenkins, 1987

Sharon Gater and David Vincent, *The Factory in a Garden: Wedgwood from Etruria to Barlaston – the transitional years*, Keele Life Histories Centre, University of Keele, 1988

Diane Gittins, *Fair Sex: Family Size and Structure: 1900–39*, Hutchinson, 1982

Robert Graves and Alan Hodge, *The Long Weekend: A Social History of Britain 1918–1939*, Faber & Faber, 1940; Penguin, 1971

Oliver Green, *Underground Art: London Transport Posters 1908 to Present*, Studio Vista, 1990

Richard Green and Des Jones, *The Rich Designs of Clarice Cliff*, Rich Designs Ltd, 1995

M.W. Greenslade and J.G. Jenkins (eds.), *A History of the County of Staffordshire*, Volumes II (1967), III (1970) and VIII (1963), *Victoria History of the Counties of England*, published for the Institute of Historical Research by Oxford University Press, 1963

Leonard Griffin, *The Art of Bizarre: A Definitive Centenary Celebration*, Pavilion, 1999
The Fantastic Flowers of Clarice Cliff: A Celebration of her Floral Designs, Pavilion, 1998
Taking Tea with Clarice Cliff, Pavilion, 1996

Leonard Griffin with Louis K. and Susan Pear Meisel, *The Bizarre Affair*, Thames & Hudson, 1988

Teresa Grimes, Judith Collins and Oriana Baddelay, *Five Women Painters*, Channel 4 in association with the Arts Council of Great Britain, 1984

Reginald Haggar, *A Century of Art Education in the Potteries*, pamphlet, Stoke-on-Trent, 1953

Carolyn Hall, *The Thirties in Vogue*, Octopus Books, 1984

Nina Hamnett, *Is She a Lady? A Problem in Autobiography*, Alan Wingate, 1955
Laughing Torso, Constable, 1932; Virago, 1984

Cate Haste, *Rules of Desire: Sex in Britain World War 1 to the Present*, Chatto & Windus, 1992

Bevis Hillier, *Art Deco of the 20s and 30s*, Studio Vista/Dutton Pictureback, 1968
The World of Art Deco, Minneapolis Institute of Arts, Studio Vista, 1971

Bevis Hillier and Stephen Escritt, *Art Deco Style*, Phaidon, 1997

Marjorie Hillis, *Live Alone and Like It: A Guide for the Extra Woman*, Duckworth, 1936

Winifred Holtby, *Women in a Changing Civilisation*, John Lane, Bodley Head, 1936

Irene and Gordon Hopwood, *The Shorter Connection: A Family Pottery 1874–1974*, Richard Dennis, 1992

Nicola Humble, *The Feminine Middlebrow Novel, 1920s to 1950s: class, domesticity and bohemianism*, Oxford University Press, 2001

Steve Humphries and Pamela Gordon, *Forbidden Britain: Our Secret Past 1900–1960*, BBC Books, 1994

Owen James, *The Grammar of Ornament*, Day, 1856

David Joel, *Furniture Design Set Free*, Dent, 1963

Mervyn Jones, *Potbank: A Social Enquiry into Life in the Potteries*, Secker & Warburg, 1961

Osbert Lancaster, *Home Sweet Homes*, John Murray, 1939

Rosamond Lehmann, *Dusty Answer* (1927), Penguin, 1981
The Weather in the Streets (1936), Virago, 1891

Jane Lewis, *Women in England 1870–1950*, Wheatsheaf, 1984

Alison Light, *Forever England: femininity, literature and conservatism between the wars*, Routledge, 1991

John G. Llewellyn, *The Story of Christ Church, Tunstall, 1832–1982*, pamphlet, Stoke-on-Trent, 1982

Rose Macaulay, *Crewe Train* (1926), Methuen, 1985

Fiona MacCarthy, *All Things Bright and Beautiful: Design in Britain 1830 to Today*, Allen & Unwin, 1972
British Design Since 1880, Lund Humphries, 1982

Norman and Jeanne MacKenzie, *The Diaries of Beatrice Webb*, Virago in association with the London School of Economics, 1982–1985

Ross McKibbin, *Classes and Cultures: England 1918–1951*, Oxford University Press, 1998

Arthur Marwick, *Britain in our Century: Images and Controversies*, Thames & Hudson, 1984

Colin Mawston, *British Art Deco Ceramics: A Schiffer Book for Collectors*, Schiffer, 2000

Naomi Mitchison, *You May Well Ask: A Memoir 1920–1940*, Victor Gollancz, 1979

John Montgomery, *The Twenties: An Informal Social History*, Allen & Unwin, 1957

Elizabeth Morano (ed.), *Sonia Delaunay: Art into Fashion*, Braziler, 1989

W.A. Morland, *Portrait of the Potteries*, Robert Hale, 1978

Paul Overy, *De Stijl*, Studio Vista, 1969

Elizabeth Owen, *Fashion in Photographs: 1920–1940*, B.T. Batsford Ltd in association with the National Portrait Gallery, 1993

Nikolaus Pevsner, *An Enquiry into Industrial Art in England*, Cambridge University Press, 1937

Roy Porter, *London: A Social History*, Hamish Hamilton, 1994

J.B. Priestley, *English Journey*, 1934; Folio Society, 1997

Maud Pember Reeves, *Round About a Pound a Week*, G. Bell & Sons, 1913; Virago, 1979

Elizabeth Roberts, *A Woman's Place: An Oral History of Working-Class Women 1890–1940*, Basil Blackwell, 1984

Katrina Rolley and Caroline Aish, *Fashion in Photographs 1900–1920*, B.T. Batsford Ltd, in association with the National Portrait Gallery, 1992

June Rose, *Marie Stopes and the Sexual Revolution*, Faber & Faber, 1992

Cathy Ross, *Twenties London: A City in the Jazz Age*, Museum of London, Philip Wilson Publishers, 2003

Sheila Rowbotham, *A Century of Women: The History of Women in Britain and the United States*, Viking, 1997

John Russell, *Henry Moore*, Allen Lane, 1968

Jacqueline Sarsby, *Missuses and Mouldrunners: An Oral History of Women Pottery Workers at Work and at Home*, Open University Press, 1988

Charles Shaw, *When I Was a Child*, Churnet Valley Books, 1998

Frances Spalding, *Vanessa Bell*, Weidenfeld & Nicolson, 1983

Judy Spours, *Art Deco Tableware: British Domestic Ceramics 1925–39*, Ward Lock, 1988

Margery Spring-Rice, *Working-Class Wives: Their Health and Conditions*, Penguin, 1939; Virago, 1981

Peter N. Stearns, 'Working-Class Women in Britain, 1890–1914', in Martha Vicinius (ed.), *Suffer and Be Still: Women in the Victorian Age*, Indiana University Press, 1973

Greg Stevenson, *Art Deco Ceramics*, Shire Publications, 1998

Lawrence Stone, *Road to Divorce: England 1530–1987*, Oxford University Press, 1990

Mary Stott (ed.), *Women Talking: An Anthology from the Guardian Women's Page 1922–35 and 1957–71*, Pandora, 1987

E.J.D. Warrilow, *A Sociological History of the City of Stoke-on-Trent*, Etruscan Publications, 1960

Chris Watkins, William Harvey and Robert Senft, *Shelley Potteries: The History and Production of a Staffordshire Family of Potters*, Barrie & Jenkins, 1980

Winifred Watson, *Miss Pettigrew Lives for a Day*, Methuen, 1938; Persephone, 2000

Peter Wentworth-Sheilds and Kay Johnson, *Clarice Cliff*, L'Odeon, 1976

Cynthia White, *Women's Magazines 1693–1968*, Michael Joseph, 1970

Dr P.J. Woodward, *An Exhibition of Ugly Ware*, Chi Publishing, 1999

Adrian Woodhouse, *Susie Cooper*, Trilby Books, 1992

Virginia Woolf, *Mrs Dalloway*, Hogarth Press, 1925; Penguin, 1992
   A Room of One's Own, Hogarth Press, 1929; Penguin, 1945
   Three Guineas, Hogarth Press, 1938; Penguin, 1977

Bryn Youds, *Susie Cooper: An Elegant Affair*, Thames & Hudson, 1996

ACKNOWLEDGMENTS

Particular thanks are due to Kay and Peter Wentworth-Sheilds for their generosity in making their research material available to me and for the patience and kindness with which they answered my questions; to Alexandra Pringle for making it possible for me to write this book; to Victoria Millar for her skills in seeing the text through press, and to Aamer Hussein, Kate Kellaway and Gordon Willis for their editorial comments and encouragement.

I am grateful to the Paul Mellon Centre for Studies in British Art for a Research Support Grant which contributed to the cost of research travel.

My thanks are due to the numerous people who invited me into their homes and shared their recollections of Clarice Cliff and their knowledge of the pottery industry, and to all those whose help and information have assisted my research. My indebtedness to many sources is reflected in the notes, but I would like to express additional gratitude to Terry Abbotts, Winnie Banks, Irene Burton, Andrew Casey, Laura Chadwick, Dr Lynette Challands, Annie Clowes and Julie Johnson, Jessie Clews, Joy Couper, Ann Eatwell, Marcia Elliott, Dr Gordon Elliott, Mollie Ferneyhough, Brenda Fredericks, Angelica Garnett, Leonard Griffin, Jim Hall, the late Doris Hammond, Kathleen Hancox, Ann and Martin Harris, Eileen Hawkins, Florence Hawthorne, Don Henshall, Edna Hirth, G.A. Jackson, Ray Johnson, Brenda Jones, May Martin, Margaret Mason, Eve Midwinter, Richard Midwinter, Gerald Pearson, Chris Purkis, Bill Ridgway, the late Ethel Robinson, Chris Rushton, Sylvia Rushton, Charlotte Shorter, Norman Smith, Beryl Storey, Professor Flavia Swann, Phyllis Norris, Jane Walker, the late Dave Wallett, the late Alice Wilson, Alison and Michael Wright.

Special thanks are due to Sharon Gater of the Wedgwood Museum, Barlaston, Staffordshire, for her help and for manuscript advice regarding the pottery industry; also to Gaye Blake-Roberts and Lynn Miller of the Wedgwood

Museum Trust; and to Margaret Beard and Chris Latimer at the Stoke-on-Trent City Archives, City Central Library, Hanley. I am also grateful to the following archivists, curators, librarians and libraries for their assistance: Steven Bateman at the Central Saint Martins College of Art & Design; Stella Beddoe at the Brighton Museum and Art Gallery; Christine and Paul Gibbs, Conwy Teapot Museum and Teapot World, Conwy, North Wales; the Gladstone Pottery Museum, Longton, Stoke-on-Trent; Miranda Goodby and Alan Taylor at the Potteries Museum and Art Gallery, Hanley, Stoke-on-Trent; Charlotte Grant at Christie's Images; Alison Kenney at the City of Westminster Archive Centre; the London Library; Teresa Mason at the Borough Museum & Art Gallery, Newcastle-under-Lyme; Darlene Maxwell at the Royal College of Art; Catherine Moriarty, Design History Research Centre Archive, University of Brighton; the National Art Library; Emma Neave at the V&A; the Public Record Office; Stuart Robinson at the *Sentinel,* Etruria, Stoke-on-Trent. Thanks are also due to Michael Jeffery of Woolley & Wallis, Salisbury.

I am grateful to John Abberley for permission to quote from 'The Way We Were', the *Sentinel,* Staffordshire Sentinel Newspapers Ltd, Etruria, Stoke-on-Trent, and to Leonard Griffin for permission to quote from the *Clarice Cliff Collectors Club Review.* The strap line for a 1927 advertisement for Player's cigarettes is reproduced with the permission of the Imperial Tobacco Group plc. Quotations from the *Pottery Gazette and Glass Trade Review* and the *Pottery and Glass Record* are reproduced with the permission of *Tableware International.* Thanks are due to the Staffordshire Record Office, Stafford; the Stoke-on-Trent City Archives, City Central Library, Hanley; and the Wedgwood Museum Trust, Barlaston, Staffordshire, for permission to quote from archive material. The author and publishers would also like to acknowledge permission to quote passages from the following works:

Vera Brittain, *Testament of Youth: An Autobiographical Study of the Years 1900–1925* (1933). Reprinted with permission of Victor Gollancz, a division of the Orion Publishing Group. Alan Bishop and Mark Bostridge (eds), *Letters from a Lost Generation: First World War Letters of Vera Brittain and Four Friends,* published by Little Brown, a division of Time Warner Book Group UK, 1988; 'Memories of a Staffordshire Londoner', *Gallery,* 1966; and 'I Denounce Domesticity!', *Quiver,* 1932. All quotations from the work of Vera Brittain are included with the permission of Mark Bostridge and Rebecca Williams, her literary executors.

Lettice Cooper, *The New House* (1936). Reproduced by permission of A.P. Watt on behalf of Leo Cooper.

Noël Coward, *Design for Living,* Methuen, 1933. Copyright © The Estate of Noël Coward.

E.M. Delafield, *Diary of a Provincial Lady* (1930), Copyright © The Estate of E.M. Delafield, 1930; *The Provincial Lady Goes Further* (1932), Copyright © The Estate of E.M. Delafield, 1932; *The Provincial Lady in America* (1934), Copyright © The Estate of E.M. Delafield, 1934. Reproduced by permission of PFD (www.pfd.co.uk) on behalf of The Estate of E.M. Delafield.

Joseph Delteil, 'Poem for the Dress of the Future', *Oeuvres Complètes*, 1962, reprinted by permission of Éditions Bernard Grasset

Storm Jameson, *Company Parade* (1934). Copyright © The Estate of Storm Jameson, 1934. Reproduced by permission of PFD (www.pfd.co.uk) on behalf of The Estate of Storm Jameson.

Rosamond Lehmann, *Dusty Answer* (1927); *The Weather in the Streets* (1936). Reprinted by permission of The Society of Authors as the Literary Representative of The Estate of Rosamond Lehmann.

Rose Macaulay, *Crewe Train*, Collins, 1926, Copyright © Rose Macaulay 1926; 'Some Problems of a Woman's Life', *Good Housekeeping*, 1923, and 'Women as News', *Guardian*, 1925. Reprinted by permission of PFD (www.pfd.co.uk) on behalf of The Estate of Rose Macaulay.

Somerset Maugham, *The Constant Wife*, Methuen, 1927. Copyright © The Estate of Somerset Maugham. Reproduced by permission of Methuen and A.P. Watt Ltd on behalf of The Royal Literary Fund.

J.B. Priestley, *English Journey* (1934). Copyright © The Estate of J.B. Priestley, 1934. Reproduced by permission of PFD (www.pfd.co.uk) on behalf of The Estate of J.B. Priestley.

Winifred Watson, *Miss Pettigrew Lives for a Day*, Methuen, 1938. Reproduced with permission of Persephone Books Ltd.

Virginia Woolf, *Mrs Dalloway* (1925); *A Room of One's Own*, Hogarth Press, 1929. Reproduced by permission of The Society of Authors as the Literary Representative of the Estate of Virginia Woolf. *The Diary of Virginia Woolf*, Vol. 4., 1931–5, edited by Anne Olivier Bell, published by the Hogarth Press. Reprinted by permission of the Random House Group Ltd.

For permission to reproduce images in the text, the author and publishers would like to credit the following: Christie's Images, pp151, 179; Leonard Griffin, www.claricecliff.com, p119; Don Henshall, a past president of the

Potteries Postcard Society, p19; the *Sentinel,* Staffordshire Sentinel Newspapers Ltd, Etruria, Stoke-on-Trent, p46, Stoke-on-Trent City Archives, City Central Library, Hanley, pp51, 57, 100, 110, 115, 134, 135, 146, 160, 174, 175, 184, 189, 195, 197, 205, 206, 221, 225, 234, 236, 241; Charlotte Shorter and Ann and Martin Harris, pp74, 75; Lucas Swann, p231; *Tableware International,* p186; the late Dave Wallett for material from the Dave Wallett Collection, pp11, 68, 251; the Trustees of the Wedgwood Museum Trust, Barlaston, Staffordshire, pp32, 33, 42; Peter Wentworth-Sheilds and Kay Johnson, pp16, 63, 86; Alison Wright, pp14, 27, 28.

Christie's Images; Leonard Griffin, www.claricecliff.com; Stoke-on-Trent City Archives; Charlotte Shorter and Ann and Martin Harris; the V&A Picture Library and Maureen and Harold Woodworth supplied images for the plate section, where the images are credited individually. Archive photography is by Chris Rushton.

Every effort has been made to trace copyright holders in all copyright material in this book. The author and publisher regret any oversight and ask that the publisher be contacted in any such event.

INDEX